Psychoanalysis

£10.00

Soc Sci

10/23

pL

Psychoanalysis

A Critical Introduction

Ian Craib

Polity

First published in 2001 by Polity Press in association with Blackwell Publishers Ltd.

Reprinted 2007

Polity Press
65 Bridge Street
Cambridge CB2 1UR, UK

Polity Press
350 Main Street
Malden, MA 02148, USA

A catalogue record for this book is available from the British Library.

Library of Congress Cataloging-in-Publication Data

Craib, Ian, 1945–
    Psychoanalysis : a critical introduction / Ian Craib.
        p.   cm.
    Includes bibliographical references and index.
    ISBN: 978-0-7456-1979-8 (pb)
    ISBN: 978-0-7456-1978-1 (hb)

    1. Psychoanalysis.   2. Psychoanalytic counseling.   I. Title.
    BF 173 .C78 2001
    150.19′5—dc21   2001016367

Typeset in 10½ on 12 pt Sabon
by Best-set Typesetter Ltd, Hong Kong
Printed and bound in Great Britain by
Marston Book Services Limited, Oxford

This book is printed on acid-free paper.

For further information on Polity, visit our website: www.polity.co.uk

Contents

PART III THE NATURE OF THERAPY

Preface

In my internal world this book has had a tortured history. It developed from an idea that did not work but that, to my annoyance, continued and continues to seem worthwhile. Much of my academic life has been spent teaching the philosophy of social science and social theory to undergraduate students. This has given me an uncomfortable take on the theories connected with the other part of my life as a psychoanalytic group therapist. What I wanted to do was to try to set out psychoanalytic theory as I have at different times set out social theory: as structures of overlapping ideas and arguments that work at different levels in different ways trying to understand different things.

There seems to be something in psychoanalytic theory that resists this, perhaps because it involves a difficult process of acknowledging the limits of each approach – academics are more ready to criticize and argue with each other's theories. This book is the end point of several revisions in which I hope that I have maintained my original intention: to present psychoanalytic theory not as a historical story but as a body of ideas with multi-faceted relationships to each other and to the human psyche that is their object; and to do this in an intelligible way for students new to the field.

The second part of my intention involves the attempt to show that there are limits to theory. This is not news for the psychoanalytic world, but it is easily forgotten or denied in the academic world. The consulting room marks the end of theory as a coherent body of ideas, and the beginning of a creativity that does not depend upon theory. In terms of my own career I was an academic theorist before I was a group psychotherapist, and in that sense the book follows my own development. I want to combine a belief that it is a good thing to think rationally and rigorously and systematically about the world and a good thing to be open to the richness, complexity and unexpectedness of our experience of the world. It is too easy to let one get in the way of the other.

As ever, many people have helped me in the preparation of this book. I would like to thank in particular Dr John Walshe, Consultant Psychotherapist of the North East Essex Mental Health Service, for the time he spent reading and rereading various drafts; and in general the students who have argued with me and the patients who continue to teach me my job.

Ian Craib
University of Essex

Acknowledgements

Bion's grid (p. 100) is taken from Wilfred Bion, *Learning from Experience* (London: William Heinemann, 1962), and is reprinted by permission of Butterworth Heinemann, a division of Reed Educational and Professional Publishing Ltd. The poem 'My Sister and I finally arrive at the Hospital' (pp. 43–4) is taken from Selima Hill, *Violet* (Newcastle Upon Tyne: Bloodaxe Books, 1997), and is reprinted by permission of the publisher.

1

Introduction

psychoanalysis. 1. Originally a comprehensive dynamic theory proposed by Freud to account for human personality, motivation, dreams and mistakes, based on the assumption that motives are determined by the LIBIDO and that their expression is controlled by unconscious forces in which there is a conflict between libidinal urges and social training. . . .

2. A method of treating mental disorders . . . in which an attempt is made to give patients insights into the workings of their unconscious minds by interpreting their dreams, fantasies, free associations, mistakes and attitudes. It is unclear why such insights should overcome neurosis, and frequently they do not. Nowadays normal people often seek psychoanalysis in the hope that it will give them insight into themselves and help to resolve their personal problems.

psychoanalyst. A person who takes money from another on the pretence that it is for the other's good.

Sutherland (ed.), *The Macmillan Dictionary of Psychology*

These entries, from a contemporary student dictionary, capture well the ambivalent feelings about psychoanalysis held not only by psychologists but also by other professionals and academics. There is a degree of interest in Freud, not a great deal of knowledge about developments in psychoanalytic theory and practice since Freud, and a rather more than healthy scepticism about both theory and practice. Freud and psychoanalysis are equal only to Marx and Marxism in the ability to attract personal abuse and wholesale, often ranting, dismissals. I have suggested elsewhere (Craib 1998) that someone who receives such a barrage of criticism over a century or more, yet whose ideas still attract attention, cannot be entirely wrong, and remains very important.

In fact psychoanalysis embodies some of the most powerful ideas to emerge in the course of the twentieth century. Its popularity as a form of treatment ebbs and flows in different contexts, but it has spawned a range of sometimes rather strange therapies and counselling practices, the popularity of which grew steadily as the twentieth century neared its end. More than this, psychoanalytic ideas have been appropriated and used productively in the social sciences and the arts. Psychoanalytic ideas about the unconscious dimensions of the mind, about sexuality, and about the meaning of mistakes (the 'Freudian slip') have entered into popular culture. In some university bookshops there will be more books about psychoanalysis on the literature, sociology and history shelves than on the psychology shelves, doubtless much to the relief of many psychologists.

In Great Britain since the mid-1980s there has been an unprecedented growth of Centres for Psychoanalytic Studies in universities, cutting across conventional disciplinary boundaries. Many of these are establishing links with the private institutes that have dominated the training of psychoanalytic therapists. This book is a product of these developments and the intellectual and emotional conflicts to which they give rise.

What I want to do here has a more universal application than to Great Britain, but looking at the situation from which the book arises provides a useful starting point. Psychoanalysts and psychoanalytic therapists tend to see themselves as primarily concerned with people's internal and emotional lives. This is especially true in British psychoanalysis, where the development of object-relations theory has involved an increasingly subtle understanding of the unspoken and unconscious communications between analyst and patient. From the academic office the psychoanalytic world tends to seem like a strange ritual where nothing is clear, nothing is certain, but for which wild and unsubstantiated claims are made – at best a pseudo-science, at worst a form of witchcraft. From the psychoanalytic consulting room the academic world seems to be populated by 'brainboxes on sticks', people who use their intellectual abilities to avoid contact with the complexities and difficulties of their humanity.

I think that both sides are right, and it is not my intention to argue for some easy meld of the two ways of looking at the world. The dualism that most of us experience at some time between our thoughts and feelings, and of which this is an example, is a real one, and the two, thought and feeling, have a variable relationship with each other, as do psychoanalytic theory and practice. Sometimes the relationship might be unexpected: a central idea behind most of what I will be saying here, an idea that was a major force pushing me into writing this book, is that any worthwhile psychoanalytic psychotherapy is not only or even primarily about feeling. I will be suggesting that whilst those involved with psychoanalytic forms of therapy and counselling often see themselves as putting people in touch with their feelings, an important dimension of psychoanalytic therapy involves enabling people to contain their emotions in order to be able to think.

The gap is typified by two books, both of which I use in my academic teaching. On the one hand there is Neville Symington's *The Analytic Experience* (1986), a gentle and humane account of modern British psychoanalysis, with plenty of intelligible examples from his own practice, a book from which the trainee therapist can learn much, but one that would not hold its place on the normal academic reading list except as a text that might give a student the 'feel' of psychoanalytic therapy. On the other hand there is Anthony Elliott's *Psychoanalysis and Social Theory in Transition* (1999), which could be read without any realization that psychoanalysis is concerned with the easing of human suffering or that it has a huge body of clinical work at its disposal. Rather one would imagine that psychoanalysis is a general psychological theory developed as a building block in a totalizing social theory.

The tension between the academic and clinical is just one of several tensions that motivate this book, and throughout I will be concerned to keep both sides together. On the one hand I think we should maintain the importance of theory and theoretical argument against those therapists who think 'rationalization' whenever they hear an idea. On the other it is important to insist on the way in which human experience overflows the conceptual frameworks with which we try to understand it, an idea which seems to be beyond many concerned solely with psychoanalytic theory.

I have called this book a critical introduction because I will be presenting what is perhaps a very personal view of psychoanalysis, coming from my roles as an academic sociologist, concerned primarily with social theory, and as a practising psychotherapist. My psychotherapeutic work, however, is with groups, not with individuals, and that adds to the personal nature of my account, and generates another tension since I believe firmly that group work produces insights that are not available to work with individuals. One of my self-discoveries in the course of writing this book has been how far I have gone in becoming a partisan of group psychoanalytic therapy, since I believe that, unlike much individual psychotherapy, it challenges the more narrow, instrumental concerns and self-conceptions of our contemporary culture.

Another tension at work in what follows comes from within the psychoanalytic movement, between those who see it as a scientific enterprise and those who see it as a form of hermeneutics, a process of understanding and interpretation. Here I will be calling upon my work as a social theorist and philosopher of social science (Benton and Craib 2001) to suggest that the debate has been too narrowly conceived, often taking 'science' to refer only to one conception of the natural sciences that many argue is no longer appropriate. We can find philosophers talking about different *forms* of science, not just the contrast between the empirical and hermeneutic sciences that has traditionally framed the debate between the natural and social sciences, and there are wider conceptions that embrace a number of approaches. Modern critical realism, for example, cuts across the traditional divide (Collier 1981; Will 1980), and the German philosopher Jürgen Habermas talks about psychoanalysis as an *emancipatory* science that works at a number of levels. I will be suggesting that there are several, limited senses in which psychoanalysis may be regarded as scientific, but what really distinguishes it from other psychologies is that it offers a way of investigating and understanding the complex of individual meanings that form a person's life. Whatever the intellectual superstructure that surrounds psychoanalytic activity, its most original contribution is the understanding of an individual life, its meanings, its patterns, its possibilities and its specificity.

This leads on to an associated tension in the development of psychoanalysis of which Freud was aware, and that is often glossed: between psychoanalysis as a treatment, offering something like a 'cure' in medicine, and psychoanalysis as a way of establishing often unpopular knowledge of and insights into the human condition. I will be arguing throughout this book that the medical model is not a good one for psychoanalytic therapists to follow; it is associated with the most limiting of the available conceptions of science and draws attention away from the understanding of specific individuality. I am not saying that psychoanalytic therapy does not do any good. People change and in many ways might be said to change for the better, but in the words of the joke that the psychoanalyst R. D. Laing was reportedly fond of quoting, 'Life is a sexually transmitted disease for which there is no known cure.' However, I do think that some insight into the way in which we have made something out of what was given to us at the start of our lives, and a sense of our limitations and possibilities, can make life less difficult and limit the damage that we can do to others, as well as ourselves.

The psychoanalytic schools

The development of what I will for these purposes call the psychoanalytic movement is a complex one. My reason for calling it a 'movement' is that Freud himself was devoted to protecting his method and his theory against what he considered to be a hostile world, and he organized the original psychoanalytic societies to do just this; they were dominated by the centre and Freud defined a core set of beliefs just as one might expect a political leader to develop an ideology and a party. Ernest Becker (1973) suggests that this was Freud's way of ensuring his immortality, but whether or not this is true the effect was to leave psychoanalysis with some of the marks of a religious or political movement (see also Gellner 1985). One such mark is the tendency for disagreements to become schisms and for personality differences to generate factions. The overarching rationalizing values that (sometimes) mitigate these tendencies in academic disciplines and sciences seem to be weaker in psychoanalysis, but in a discipline which constantly questions the value of rationalization, perhaps this is appropriate. However, it does not make life easy for those more familiar with ideas that have developed within an academic context. In this book I will concentrate on those branches that can still be said to be attached, however tenuously, to the trunk.

The development of separate schools that remained largely within the Freudian tradition would have happened anyway if psychoanalysis was going to be more than a Viennese cult and develop into an international church, not to mention a respected intellectual discipline. We can see the beginning of the process in developments and arguments in the movement after the First World War, but the major developments came with the Diaspora that followed Hitler's rise to power. Freud himself moved to Britain, one crucial reason being a debate with American psychoanalysts about 'lay' analysts – the psychoanalytic training of analysts who have not undergone a prior medical training (Freud 1986). Freud thought that psychoanalysis would lose out if it did not draw on people with different intellectual backgrounds. In the United States the emphasis was on the recognition and professional status that prior medical training would bring.

One result of this insistence was that American psychoanalysis seemed to align itself with the political and social status quo. The school that acquired the label 'ego psychology' developed in the United States, although the starting point was Freud's daughter Anna's *The Ego and the Mechanisms of Defence* (1936). The main theorist of ego psychology, Heinz Hartmann, emigrated to the United States and worked there for the rest of his life. The central concern of ego psychology was adaptation – the ability of the individual to adjust to his or her social environment (Hartmann 1939). This gave American psychoanalysis a profoundly conservative colouring that a few decades later provoked a scathing reaction from the French psychoanalyst Jacques Lacan.

There is a sense in which American psychoanalysis has shared the values of its culture, an optimism about the future and about American society that implies that adaptation to such a society is a desirable achievement; this is followed through to the present day and the development of 'self psychology' in the work of Heinz Kohut (1971, 1977). He focuses on a conception of the self and revalues the concept of narcissism in a positive way, thus helping to provoke what I regard as one of the best works of social criticism in the Western world in the last three decades, *The Culture of Narcissism* by the social historian Christopher Lasch (1980). I will argue later that Kohut's self psychology represents one of the clearest ways in which psychoanalysis can come to reproduce the dominant values of the culture in which it develops.

It is almost a truism to compare the optimism of American culture with the pessimism of European culture that we can find reproduced at the heart of Freud's work. He introduced the notion of a death instinct into his theory as a response to the First World War. Paradoxically, this war led to a growing acceptance of psychoanalysis on both sides as it proved particularly effective in enabling shell-shocked troops to recover and return to the Front – and in that sense perhaps put itself at the service of the death instinct. Pat Barker's *The Regeneration Trilogy* (1991, 1993, 1995) deals with some of these issues in a fictional form. It was also in Europe that the notion of the death instinct was further developed by Melanie Klein, working first in Germany and Austria and then in Britain.

Whereas for Freud the notion of the death instinct was a theoretical category developed in response to historical events, rather than in the context of his clinical work, Melanie Klein gave it a clinical reference in her conception of envy: the attempt to destroy what is good. Klein in fact introduced a number of very important developments into psychoanalytic theory, beyond her conception of envy. She was interested in the very earliest stages of development, from birth onwards. Freud seems to have had little interest in babies and little contact with his own. He thought that the most important stages of development occurred around the ages of three to five, the oedipal stage. The crucial line of development was traced through looking at the development of our instinctual life. For Klein (1975a, 1975b, 1975c), the important events occurred in the earliest months, and as well as instinctual developments, they involved our relations to those around us, particularly the mother. This is the origin of object-relations theory, the theory of our relations to the 'objects' of our consciousness and emotions. Klein developed a technique of treating young children via play analysis and of treating long-term psychotic patients, both of which groups Freud thought would not be susceptible to psychoanalytic treatment.

Klein moved to Britain and developed her practice and ideas before the Freuds arrived, and she had built up considerable support in the British Institute of Psychoanalysis. Freud's daughter Anna was developing her own form of child analysis, which brought her into direct conflict with Klein, a conflict that split the Institute through the years of the Second World War. The arguments sometimes became bitter. One of Klein's foremost opponents was her own daughter, Melitta Schnideberg, and there was a series of debates – 'discussions on controversial issues' – that are still gripping and important for the contemporary generation of analysts (King and Steiner 1992). The end result was that the British Institute organized itself into three groups or streams that are still in existence today. There is a Kleinian group and a Freudian group and a third, independent group that has formed the basis of what is sometimes known as 'British psychoanalysis'; this group, which took from both Freud and Klein, is the soil in which object-relations theory has grown (Kohon 1986; Rayner 1990).

There is one further school of psychoanalysis that ought to be mentioned at this stage: that which came into being around the French psychoanalyst Jacques Lacan. The work of Lacan raises strong feelings amongst psychoanalysts. In French psychoanalysis there is a history of expulsions and splits, as well as a lot of anger (Turkle

1992). As befits a former surrealist, Lacan generated strong hostile reactions within and outside of the psychoanalytic community, yet his work has done more than anything else to bring psychoanalysis to the centre of modern European thought and to extend its influence into the academy, on the one hand, and into contemporary politics, via feminism, on the other. Lacan is not an easy writer; in fact I have heard it suggested that he did not intend his work to be understood, and it would be consistent with his theory that it should be very difficult, that it should make people think. Lacan's main claim is to return to Freud; and his emphasis, against ego psychology, is on the divisions within the psyche, the importance of the symbolic over and against what he calls the real, and the unavoidable imaginary dimension to our sense of our selves.

There is a useful contrast between the implications of much object-relations theory and Lacanian psychoanalysis. The former emphasizes personal growth and development whereas the latter emphasizes internal division and, often, conflict. This contrast will be one of the themes of this book, and there are many variations. I have already mentioned the difference between psychoanalysis as a means of defining and curing mental illness, on the one hand, and as a means of understanding one's life and investigating the human predicament, on the other. Some would see this as a conflict between psychoanalysis as a therapy and psychoanalysis as a science. I do not think that it is that simple: there are many forms of scientific activity, many forms of psychoanalytic theory and many forms of psychoanalytic therapy, and there is no simple relation between them. This makes it difficult to organize an introductory text.

The scope and organization of this book

When I first thought about this book I wanted to move away from the usual historical introductions, getting away from the idea that because one thinker follows on from another, the second thinker necessarily produces a development of the first. Historical succession is not necessarily the same as theoretical progress. I still think that is the case, but in the end it was easier to think in historical terms. I hope I have maintained the insights that I was trying to bring to bear in my first version, which have to do with the level of analysis and the level of reality at which a theory operates. I shall be arguing, for example, that some modern theories describe processes closer to the conscious surface than did Freud, and that some, not necessarily the same ones, are comparatively superficial.

Basically, my position is this: that psychoanalysis is a complex network of ideas and practices working in different ways and at different levels. I am concerned particularly with the following dimensions: psychoanalysis as a theory of underlying structures; psychoanalysis as a theory of human development and a hermeneutics; psychoanalysis as a cognitive psychology and an empirical science; and psychoanalysis as an understanding of human creativity.

Psychoanalysis as a theory of underlying structures

Psychoanalysis is a *depth psychology*. It offers, in the terms of modern critical realism (Bhaskar 1978, 1979), an analysis of underlying structures and mechanisms, not empirically available for observation, but none the less with effects that can be observed. We cannot see the unconscious, but we can see, hear and feel its effects.

Psychoanalysis as a theory of human development and a hermeneutics

One of the ways in which these underlying structures and mechanisms can be seen working is through the developmental processes as the infant becomes a child and the child an adolescent and the adolescent an adult. For Freud the nexus of this development is the oedipal stage, around the age of four or five, when the child's desires move (or not, as the case might be) to a heterosexual identity. Given the centrality of sexuality and gender in contemporary politics, it is not surprising that this part of Freud's theory has received a great deal of attention, especially from feminists, and it is perhaps one of the signs of the lasting value of Freud's thought that his ideas have stimulated much contemporary feminist theorizing in France, Britain and America (Bruhle 1998). It is in this area that Lacan's ideas have been particularly important.

I will be arguing that all too often these developments are seen in a rigid way, with one line of development being valued above others, whereas the psyche and the range of individual experiences that each of us go through are too complex to be grasped by a rigid developmental theory. There are as many ways through the oedipal stage as there are people to go through it.

I will also be tracing an apparently very different developmental theory from the work of Klein, but arguing that this shows a different aspect of the psyche to Freud's theory and adds to our understanding of its complexity. Modern work in this tradition has produced theories of symbolization, thinking, aesthetics and morality that I shall argue are especially important for understanding the goals of psychoanalytic therapy. I will be looking too at more recent ideas from the object-relations school, suggesting that these add to our understanding of the complexity of human psychological development without replacing the earlier insights.

These aspects of psychoanalytic theory provide us with a hermeneutics of human development and change. They are not causal theories in which one thing leads inevitably to another but more or less detailed maps along which we can plot the routes taken by human lives; they are ways of understanding our lives, not of explaining them. I will be suggesting that each of the developmental theories takes us to a different level of the psyche. As the notion of the self and the experience of the self begin to appear, replacing Freud's original structural model, we get nearer to the surface. The self and self-experience enable psychoanalysis to become a phenomenology, a description of the experiences of consciousness, and with some theorists the focus moves from the unconscious to the conscious. I will be arguing that these different levels add to our understanding of the psyche, but only if they remain connected to the deeper levels of analysis discussed in the earlier parts of the book. This is true especially of the next dimension of psychoanalysis.

Psychoanalysis as a cognitive psychology and an empirical science

I will also be concerned with the way in which this movement tends to lose the hermeneutic dimension of psychoanalysis and becomes a cognitive psychology of development generating empirical research into the relationship between early infant experience and later developments of the personality. I will suggest that this concern tends to limit both the theoretical understanding that we can have of psychoanalytic therapy and the hopes that we can place in it.

All these themes will be discussed in Parts I and II. I have divided the different thinkers and issues into those that belong to the first half of the twentieth century and those that belong to the second. Part I will deal with Freud himself, the work of Klein and Fairbairn and the development of object-relations theory. It is in the work of these writers that the basic depth theories of the psyche are developed. Part II deals with modern and contemporary developments, beginning with the work of Lacan, which adds to our understanding of the deeper structures and mechanisms of the psyche; the feminist developments of Freudian and Lacanian psychoanalysis; modern Kleinian concerns with symbolization, thinking and aesthetics; the modern object-relations concern with self-experience; and ending with attachment theory and self psychology. Throughout I will be asking questions about the nature of theory in psychoanalysis, what theory is intended to do, and the relationships of different theories to each other.

Psychoanalysis as an understanding of human creativity

Finally, in Part III, I will be trying to make sense of psychoanalytic therapy as a way of understanding what we add to or what we do with what we receive from our society and our family. I will maintain that there is something inexplicable here, and that psychoanalysis can identify this area but cannot and perhaps should not try to do any more than that. Here I will not only deal with the classical concepts of transference and counter-transference as a way of understanding psychoanalytic therapy, but I will also try to develop these ideas by looking at what goes on in psychotherapeutic groups.

It is here that psychoanalysis really comes into its own, as a way of enabling us to think and communicate about the meaning of our lives on an individual and a collective level, widening the space that we have for making sense of and carrying on our lives. The nearest I have come to a theory of *what* psychoanalysis does is Habermas's notion of an *emancipatory* science, enabling both an understanding of the physical limitations on our life and an understanding of the distorted communication that we enter into with others; but I think his approach manages to be at the same time too optimistic (too rational) and too limited, unable to understand what I shall call the creativity of everyday life.

One of my constant critical themes comes from the tension I have already mentioned between my work as a sociologist and my work as a psychoanalytic therapist. I will be arguing that psychoanalytic therapy can open up 'internal space' and that this can in some sense add to the quality of life and in another sense make it more difficult. At the same time there are powerful currents in contemporary society that work to close down 'internal space', to limit the capacity to think or understand. I will not be able to discuss these forces in this book, but I will be pointing out where some forms of psychoanalytic theory and practice contribute to such a closing down.

Part I

The Foundations

I am beginning with what I regard as the heart of psychoanalysis: the theory of internal psychological drives, structures, mechanisms and processes. In the following chapters I will be dealing with unobservables, things that we cannot see but the effects of which we experience. An understanding of these unobservables contributes to making sense of our experiences. Later on, I will be moving from the deepest level of psychic processes to those much closer to our awareness.

This way of setting out psychoanalytic theory is unusual. The convention is to start with Freud, his background and his life, and tell a story about the way in which he developed his theory. There are several excellent accounts available that follow this pattern (Gay 1988; Jones 1961; Roazen 1971), but my intention here is to present psychoanalysis as theoretical structure – an overview of the way Freud thought the psyche works rather than an account of the way he developed his theory.

The important historical period is from 1890 to 1939 (Freud was born in 1856), and for most of this time Freud lived in Vienna, emigrating to Britain after the Nazi occupation of Austria in 1938.

2

The Unconscious

I do not think that it is going too far to place Freud amongst the three most influential thinkers of the past 150 years. The other two are Marx and Darwin. All have had an influence way beyond their own limited discipline and all have entered into general awareness in the sense that, usually in distorted form, their ideas have become popularized throughout the world. All three have not only been subjected to systematic criticism, which is what we would expect, but have also been subjected to surprisingly vicious personal and intellectual attack. Darwin and Darwinism suffer at the hands of religious fundamentalists and Marx and Marxism at the hands of powerful political interests. Freud attracts a rather more varied selection of enemies.

In his way, Freud was as determined as Marx to change the world, not through political organization but through introducing what he saw as the truth of psychoanalysis into the modern consciousness in such a way that it would not be hijacked by other disciplines or professions, and it would not be watered down through compromising its more difficult and dangerous ideas. There are elements of the secret society in the way he organized his closest followers – for example his distribution of a ring to each member of his inner circle – and these elements can be seen in the modern organization of psychoanalytic societies, even in the (comparatively) liberal setting of the British Institute of Psychoanalysis (see Rustin 1991). Sadly, the psychoanalytic movement has sometimes displayed the worst features of political sectarianism – dogmatism, lack of tolerance and lack of human understanding – and there is a long history of splits and expulsions. A lot of this appears as a mirror image in the attacks on psychoanalysis, whether on Freud as a cocaine addict, as somebody who ran away from the reality of incest or child sexual abuse (Masson 1992), or as somebody responsible for the abuses resulting from the idea that traumatic memories can be lost and recovered (Crews 1997).

On the whole I think it best to adopt a critical attitude to both sides in these debates – they tend to develop into either/or, guilty/innocent arguments, and that is usually a sign that both sides have something to hide. Perhaps the model to take is the argument about Freud and feminism, or rather between Freud and feminism. The early classics of modern feminism (Beauvoir 1960; Firestone 1970; Friedan 1997; Greer, 1971; Millet 1970) raged against Freud as the arch-patriarch, the denigrator of women, a view that certainly has some truth in it; and the Freudian orthodoxy would stoutly defend his ideas. Slowly, however, there has been a separation of psychoanalytic ideas from the man who first thought of them and the social and cultural context in which they were produced. We shall see that since the early 1970s feminism has provoked some of the most interesting developments of psychoanalytic ideas; and psychoanalysis has contributed to some of the more stimulating ideas of modern feminism.

I shall try to set out Freud's theory as a model of the psyche, beginning first with the structures that he identified and the forces that bring them into existence.

Instincts and drives

Freud, in the popular consciousness, is known for having all sorts of possibly outrageous ideas about sexuality, and as the inventor of a rather disturbing and possibly nonsensical way of attributing hidden and unlikely meanings to people's actions; trained psychoanalysts seem to think that they know more about another person than that person does him- or herself.

Even in academic circles there is a common-sense knowledge of Freud that is far away from the truth of what he said. Amongst sociologists there is a sense that he is a biological determinist, attributing everything to a sexual instinct, the libido, which turns our anatomy into our destiny. This is certainly the view taken by the first modern feminists, whom I mentioned earlier.

In fact Freud is concerned with the difficult area between the physical and the mental, the point, one might say, where one becomes the other, the way in which physical impulses become mental representations. The term 'instinct' seems to come down on the physical side, but *drives* – a more accurate translation of Freud – are always also *psychic* entities. A useful way of thinking about drives is as a combination of physical energy and mental representation. It is in this way that the social begins to enter into our heads: if the energy comes from the inside, our mental representations, the ideas and objects which we associate with the energy, or to which we attach it, are taken from the outside. Juliet Mitchell (1974) suggests that Freud's achievement here was to transform the biological theory of instincts into the theory of human drives.

For Freud, the most important of these drives was sexuality, and from various more recent theories we can build up a sort of retrospective framework for this. Megary (1995) suggests that the human animal, in comparison with other animals, is born prematurely due to the nature of human evolution. Basically, we have developed increasingly large brains and our skulls are now so large that if we remained in the womb longer than we do, we could only be born at the expense of killing our mothers. This would not augur well for the future of the species. The result is that aspects of behaviour that might be genetically or hormonally programmed into other animals, such as heterosexuality, are not programmed into human beings. We have a sexual drive but this drive is not genetically directed towards any particular object – we can (and do) take almost anything as a sexual object. Horses do not wear designer jeans or short skirts to attract sexual partners. Human beings do. D. H. Lawrence thought he was speaking critically when he scorned 'sex in the head', but he was actually describing the human condition. Our sex is as much in our head as it is between our legs.

According to Freud, the development of the *libido*, sometimes referred to as sexuality or the life instinct, is what drives our psychological development. I think that it should be emphasized that the libido is not a generalized life force; it is our sexuality, and Mitchell (1974) is right to argue that one of Freud's achievements was to move away from vitalist ideas of a life force that were current in his time to a very precise concept of sexual drive and its organization and transformation. However, the 'life instinct' aspect of the libido becomes important when it is contrasted to Freud's later development of the theory of the death instinct, an opposition of Eros and Thanatos, the gods of love and death (Freud 1984b).

Whereas most of Freud's theory was developed from or eventually referred to his clinical work, his theory of the death instinct was drawn from his experience of the outside world, particularly of the First World War, from his difficulty in understanding how human beings could put themselves through so much misery without rebelling. He worked it into his metapsychology by arguing that both the life and death instincts come from the same root and have the same aim: a release of tension. However, they choose different ways to achieve that aim. The life instinct chooses a circuitous route through the formation of relationships with others, sexual activity and the production of children, the continuation of life. The death instinct chooses a more direct route: the release of tension for ever. However, it can be subordinated to the life instinct when it is directed against an external enemy, and Freud suggests that the two instincts are often closely entwined.

The usual criticism of the notion of a death instinct is that it was a flight into metaphysics, which in many ways it was, an element in a speculative system of thought. It was left to Melanie Klein to theorize it in a more down-to-earth way that had a clinical relevance (see below chapter 5). It is easier to think about it if we regard it as a natural destructive impulse, built into our physical movements and our ability to feel angry with the world around us. An infant or young child in a rage will often hit out blindly, and we can think of a psychological equivalent of this – not a blind but more of an unconsciously destructive process. It reaches its most conscious and explicit manifestation in times of war (see, for example, Bourke 1999; Browning 1999).

These two drives, sexuality and destructiveness, Eros and Thanatos, the life and death drives, can be seen as providing the energy for psychic life and the basis of the psychic structures. Most of Freud's work dealt with the handling of the libido, and it often seemed as if he were building an 'energy flow' model of the psyche where problems might be caused if safety valves were not working properly; energy would build up and would have to be released. Parts of *The Interpretation of Dreams* (Freud 1976a) seem to employ such a model, with dreaming enabling an important release as the barriers of consciousness are lowered in sleep. We can still find aspects of such an idea in modern forms of therapy that aim at the cathartic expression of emotion – some aspects of Gestalt therapy (Perls 1971), for example, or Janov's primal therapy (Janov 1973). The problem with cathartic release is that the energy builds up again so we get back to where we started from. Psychoanalytic therapy, in comparison, aims at changing the structures through which the energy is processed, the concept of psychic energy moving to the background as the theory develops. However, it is important to remember that our psychic energy is seen as dividing into two contradictory streams, the first of many contradictions that structure the human psyche.

The unconscious

If there is one idea at the centre of psychoanalysis, a touchstone by means of which one can distinguish those working or thinking within some sort of psychoanalytic framework, it is the idea of the unconscious. Even in the context of present-day arguments, the suggestion that people do not necessarily know what they are doing, that they are driven by forces beyond their consciousness or their control, that they can be mistaken about their own motives, is a scandalous idea. It is especially scandalous when it is suggested that *you* are the person who does not know what you are doing or that you are being driven by motives that you find dishonourable or perhaps even evil.

Sometimes Freud is placed in a long line of revolutionary thinkers who have transformed humanity's penchant for believing that we are at the centre of things. Galileo showed that the earth is not the centre of the universe, but simply one of a group of planets going around the sun; Darwin showed that human beings are not the centre of creation but the end product of a process of random selection; Marx showed that human beings were not the creators of society but rather the creatures of society; and Freud added, as it were, the final insult by showing that human beings are not even masters or mistresses of themselves.

In fact, the notion of the unconscious was not new, as Freud himself recognized. It was an idea which had been around in different forms in literature and philosophy for many years; Freud's innovation was to refine the idea and build it into the centre of a systematic psychological theory. One way in which he thought about the unconscious was as one of three levels or systems in the psyche. Our conscious mind, what we are aware of at any one time, is the tip of the iceberg. There is beneath our conscious mind a huge storehouse of memories and knowledge on which we can draw without too much difficulty. I can bring to mind sufficient knowledge of French to read a simple paragraph in a daily paper or, if asked, I can recall a conversation with a friend that took place about six months ago, and so on. I am not conscious of such memories all the time. Freud referred to this level as the preconscious. Some knowledge in this area is almost built into our bodies – I know where my left ear is and I can scratch it without consciously focusing on the ear or the act of scratching, and if I am absorbed in whatever I am doing, I might remain unaware that I carried out such an act at all.

The most important of the three levels, however, is the unconscious itself, and this contains the ideas attached to the most primitive drives. Some comparatively acceptable ideas or representations can also be attached to primitive drives and thus repressed. Thus some people cannot seem to experience anger for fear of what it might lead to – the idea of making a cutting remark becomes associated with cutting a throat. For whatever reason, ideas repressed into the unconscious are unacceptable to the individual and/or the culture and society in which that person is situated. For Freud these ideas were primarily sexual, while for Klein they were aggressive, envious ideas as well. We shall see later that ideas attached to other feelings can also be repressed. For the moment, however, I will stick with Freud (see Freud 1984a, 1984d, 1984g, 1984h).

The laws and dynamics of the unconscious

The unconscious is not in any absolute sense *un*conscious. We become aware of our own unconscious and that of others in all sorts of direct and indirect ways. There are *secondary* processes, the workings of the rational conscious mind and its preconscious materials, and there are *primary* processes, the dynamics of the unconscious, and they constantly interact.

To understand these dynamics it must be remembered that it is *ideas* that are repressed. They are separated from the energy or feeling to which they were originally attached. People often talk about unconscious feelings, but Wollheim (1971) points out that Freud calls such feelings 'a potential feeling which is prevented from developing'. It is rather as if a bud had been frozen but in the right situation it will come to flower. The unconscious ideas are not subjected to the laws to which our conscious ideas are subjected; they do not work themselves out rationally, and they do not take any notice of the restrictions of the outside world. They accept only the reality of the *internal world*. This explains one of the peculiar difficulties of psychoanalytic treatment, which is concerned primarily with the unconscious and the internal world. In a society which looks for causal, scientific explanations it is always tempting to look for external causes for psychological difficulties. In psychotherapy the truth of what is being talked about is not *necessarily* important – the fantasies, dreams and imaginings of the patient do matter, and they enable the growth of understanding.

Unconsciously, then, we live in our own world, and the unconscious refusal to accept the reality of the external world has to do with the unconscious demand for immediate satisfaction, the infantile demand that does not recognize any obstacle to its desires. It is as if we carry within us a demanding, screaming infant that will not rest until we feed it. Clearly if we acted in accordance with this demand life would become impossible; we repress it into the unconscious, where it works on us in all sorts of indirect ways, and most of us remain aware of the pain of recognizing that *something* we want very much cannot be had, that *something* is missing, even if we are not sure what it is.

Part of the primary process of the unconscious is the making of 'irrational' connections between ideas and images, through processes of condensation and displacement, which I will discuss shortly. One source of the 'irrationality' of unconscious processes is that the unconscious does not recognize the laws of contradiction that we hold to in our normal rational lives. It is very difficult to recognize that we can love and hate the same person – we might be able to feel it in an abstract intellectual way, but it is more difficult to conjure up hateful feelings for a loved one or loving feelings for someone for whom we feel hatred. The furthest most of us can get is to acknowledge that we can sometimes feel hatred for the person we love most. The unconscious has no such problems – love and hatred can be intimately entwined.

Here we find another problem for some critics of psychoanalysis – a problem that they express in terms of the ability of psychoanalysis to explain everything, including contradictory phenomena, in the same way. If I identify with my father and dress like him, and follow his profession, then it can be because I love him and want to be like him, or it can be because I fear and hate him and dare not break away. If, on the other hand, I try consciously to be unlike him (adolescents especially go through such swings), it can be because I hate him and reject him, or because I love him and need him to recognize my achievements as an independent person. And so on. I think the criticisms here only hold if we accept that human action and the meanings we give to the world *have* to be bound by the rules of formal logic, which quite clearly they are not. The meanings in which we live are multi-dimensional.

Finally, the unconscious is timeless. It does not develop or change; it does not mature, although if we are lucky the rest of our psychic apparatus does change, becoming more complex and handling the unconscious impulses in more creative ways. The internal demanding infant, however, is always a demanding infant. It is perhaps a sign of a narcissistic culture that some forms of contemporary psychotherapy urge the discovery of the 'inner child' and the satisfaction of its needs. The real problems of human life are set by coming to terms with the absence of satisfaction.

Everyday examples

One of the many 'logical' criticisms of psychoanalysis is that to talk of an unconscious is itself a nonsense: if something is unconscious, then how can we even know it exists? The psychoanalyst argues that the unconscious is knowable, even if we do not directly experience it, through the way in which we experience our conscious ideas and feelings. It forces itself through into our conscious lives in unexpected and often embarrassing ways, and beyond this we can have access to it along a 'royal road' – our dreams. I will look at the everyday appearances of the unconscious first.

The most evident irruption of the unconscious into everyday life has entered common parlance in the phrase 'Freudian slip' (Freud 1985d) – an occasion on which I don't say quite what I intend to say. When I reflect even momentarily on what I have said I realize that not only have I said something different to what I intended, but also I have said something acutely embarrassing, something that I certainly do not want others to know, and something that perhaps I have not actually allowed myself to realize at any conscious level at all. One of Freud's examples was of a man who announced of himself and wife: 'If one of us dies, I will go to live in Paris.' Such slips are not only slips of the tongue. Some years ago I was seriously ill and amongst cards wishing me well, I received a message from an ex-colleague with whom I had once had a serious argument, although we had managed to rebuild a working relationship. He offered me his sympathy on my demise. It is of course easier to use examples from other people; a real Freudian slip can cause agonies of embarrassment, or, in a therapeutic situation, reveal important aspects of a patient's feelings. I once listened to a patient talking about a suicide attempt some years previously; she said something to the effect that 'sadly' she had recovered. When I pointed this out, she was surprised but acknowledged that when she was depressed she was not always sure that her recovery was a good thing. Freudian slips are not necessarily written or verbal. Once when I was asked for a light for a cigarette, I thought I was gently tossing my lighter across the room, but it flew out of my hand and thudded into the wall behind my friend's head. In all these examples, unconscious aggressive, even murderous, desires, directed at another person or at the self, broke through the repressive apparatus into everyday consciousness.

All sorts of 'accidents' or casual actions can be seen in this way. If, for example, I leave a pen in a colleague's office, it might indicate a desire to return there for some important but as yet unknown reason. If I forget an appointment, or start tapping my foot in the middle of a conversation, or sit with my arms folded across my chest, all of these things may indicate something of which I am not necessarily aware. I think it is true to say that for psychoanalysis there is no such thing as a meaningless action (even though Freud said that sometimes a cigar is just a cigar), something that again often disturbs people when they first understand the full import of psychoanalytic theory. It strips us of what can be called our 'innocence': the illusion that our actions, statements and gestures cannot be 'seen through'. I think that there is a shock involved in recognizing that other people can try to interpret our actions in the same way that we try to interpret theirs. Understanding other people is often more preferable to being understood by other people, or even understanding oneself, and psychoanalysts are (not always correctly) seen as having special powers of interpretation.

In *The Psychopathology of Everyday Life* (1985d) Freud suggests a range of origins for such slips. Most of my examples have been of cases where an urge has been insufficiently repressed, but they can also occur when an urge is released without repression (the cigarette lighter example) or when there is what one might call an 'over-repression' and I cannot act at all. For example, if I find somebody very sexually attractive, I might not be able to have any contact with this person at all for fear of what it might lead to (perhaps a familiar experience in adolescence). I will not be aware of avoiding this person but others might very well be aware of what is happening.

Jokes (Freud 1976b) are also ways of expressing unconscious desires and hiding them at the same time; 'It was only a joke' is a common way of trying to defend oneself when a desire that one does not want recognized or does not want to recognize in oneself has come to the surface. The pleasure of what Freud calls 'tendentious' jokes, jokes that risk offence (and in our society would probably be about race or sex), is that they express a desire that, if expressed openly, would meet strong opposition, not only from other people but also from oneself. As a good liberal I cannot really approve of my sexism and racism. If I hear what I (secretly) think is a good racist or sexist joke, it first of all removes the seriousness of the impulse, which is one source of pleasure, but also enables the expression of the impulse, another source of pleasure. On the one hand I can gain secret pleasure; on the other I can condemn the person who tells the joke and gain some satisfaction for my self-righteousness. The trouble with the unconscious is that it makes us all hypocrites; the joke, according to Freud, shows a 'duplicity in speech'.

Dreams and dream work

Dreams were at the centre of Freud's work (Freud 1976a), not just his theory of the unconscious but also central developments in his therapeutic method. They were, in the oft-quoted phrase, *the royal road to the unconscious*. This discovery – or perhaps it would be better called an understanding – seems to have developed as much as anything from Freud listening to his patients talk. They would often, as people do, talk about their dreams, and as they talked so the dreams seemed to make sense in terms of their lives and their treatments.

When Freud tried to theorize this experience in *The Interpretation of Dreams* (1976a), he makes an interesting transition. He starts with a hydraulic, energy-flow model but ends with an interpretive hermeneutic model. Here, more clearly I think than anywhere else, he crossed the bridge from the physical to the mental, and here we find what might be called the two halves of psychoanalysis hinged together: psychoanalysis as a causal explanation of psychological processes and psychoanalysis as a way of understanding our individual experiences and the meanings we give to them. The energy-flow explanation is in terms of energy building up within the psychic system. When it does not find an outlet in action, when it is turned back by the censor, it finds an outlet, as it were, within the psyche itself, through an 'internal' acting out. Hence the central proposition of Freud's argument: that all dreams are wish fulfilments. They are not necessarily obvious wish fulfilments: even though the censoring mechanism is relaxed during sleep, it would still be too dangerous for the dreamer to dream the straightforward fulfilment of the wish or he or she would wake up. In this sense the function of the dream is to protect sleep.

Here there is a causal explanation in terms of an energy flow within the psyche, a disguised acting out of the wish that protects sleep and thus enables the dreamer to function during the day. It sets up a sort of detective story: we know the wish did it, but we do not know which wish. It is easy to think that when we find the guilty wish (the wish that produced the dream and that dare not speak its name openly), then that is the end. In fact there is much more to it than that.

The dream does not express the wish directly – that would be too disturbing and would awaken the sleeper. We can see the dream (like practically everything else in our psychological life) as a product of a conflict between the unconscious desire and the internal censor. The latter is weakened by sleep and a compromise develops that allows more through than in our waking life but it is still in a disguised form. The disguise is achieved through a series of movements. I will first of all discuss these processes, which Freud refers to as the 'dream work', the processes by which the dream is encoded; I will then talk about the nature of dream interpretation, make the link with the therapeutic technique developed by Freud, and then finally look at the significance of all this for unconscious processes in everyday life.

First, then, the processes of dream work. During the day (and not only the day of the dream) unconscious impulses will attach themselves to real objects and events that enter the dreamer's life. They will distort the objects and events, which will then appear in a 'strange' way in the dream. The desire itself will appear in these distortions in a disguised form. Freud refers to four types of dream work, all of which are going on in any one dream: condensation, displacement, symbolization and secondary revision.

Condensation   This is a process by which a number of different ideas are condensed into one dream symbol. In one of my own dreams I found I was walking along a city road under a railway bridge. I was looking up and blood splashed on my face. The immediate associations led in three different directions: the first led to a place where I lived with my first wife when we first met, and an argument we had there; the second led to a surrealist painting (René Magritte's *La Mémoire*) that included a bleeding statue, and thence to a different aspect of my relationship to my first wife; the third led to a physical fight that I witnessed between my mother and my grandmother when I was an infant. Each of these associations led elsewhere to others and they were connected to unconscious ideas about sex and violence, but all condensed into that one dream scene.

Freud referred to this process of condensation as one of 'overdetermination', whereby a number of causes could combine in one effect. Some seventy years later, the French Marxist philosopher Louis Althusser (1969) used the concept to describe social processes, finding the same idea in Lenin's analysis of the Russian Revolution, and it is an idea that should be held on to by everyone concerned with the human sciences. There are no simple cause–effect processes to be found.

Displacement   This is a matter of metaphor, the description of one thing as if it were another in order to shed new light on or add new dimensions to what one is really talking about. 'My love is like a red, red rose' does not mean that she has petals and thorns but is a comment that tries to convey her beauty. Displacement in the dream work, however, has the opposite end in view, not to throw new light on but to hide what is being dreamt about. It does not simply invert the metaphor – the dream does not say the red, red rose is like my love; rather it hides my love and makes me an expert on roses.

Displacement sometimes works through a process of similarity between objects, the hackneyed train/tunnel representation of sexual intercourse for example, but there could be a quite contingent association where the meaningful connections are harder to trace. I replaced, in one dream, a penis with a tampon, which is easy to understand when the two are connected in the context of a discussion of Freud but less easy when one is just presented with it. The same is true of the dream of a colleague who felt that he had a particularly suffocating mother – he dreamt he was being chased by two large Christmas puddings. Dreaming of a cat was more difficult to understand until it was realized that the connection was this time with the female genitalia via the word 'pussy'. Any one symbol will be at the nexus of any number of associative chains – another dimension to overdetermination. Each chain of associations will be peculiar to each dreamer – it is not a matter of simply decoding universal symbols.

Symbolization   This is sometimes referred to as 'representation' or even 'dramatization'. The cat example was as much an example of symbolization as it was of displacement, but there are more dramatic examples, involving the translation of ideas into pictures. A colleague told me of a patient who dreamt that she was laying a table with knives and forks without handles, and realized that it was a dream about something she felt she couldn't handle. A member of one of my experiential groups dreamt that the whole group was in a house without a roof, and she was trying to chase other group members out. If a group can allow itself to work with a dream like this, then all sorts of interesting connections appear. In the course of the discussion, somebody mentioned the word 'roofless' with respect to the house, and the connection was immediately made with 'ruthless' and the ruthlessness of the group itself and of the dreamer.

Secondary revision   Freud was ambivalent about whether secondary revision should be included in the dream work itself. The revision is the story into which we sort our dream images as we wake in order to make them into an intelligible whole. This is likely to be as much a further masking of the dream as part of it, and the real dream material consists of the images and symbols.

The interpretation of dreams

Those who have not experienced psychoanalytic psychotherapy often imagine that the patient recounts the dream and the therapist provides the meaning. What in fact happens is that the therapist asks the patient to free associate around the dream symbols, to talk about the connections he or she makes to each symbol. Ideally the patient will do most of the work, but between them they will construct an interpretation that will be relevant to what is going on in the analysis. It is important to emphasize, as should be apparent from my discussion of condensation and displacement, that there is no 'right' or 'correct' interpretation of a dream. An analysis can refer back to the same dream any number of times and find different meanings there; at the best of times meaning is never straightforward and a dream is more like a poem than an instruction booklet. There is a sense in which it is unconscious poetry, and we can return to it again and again, just as we might do to our favourite poets or authors, and find something new there. In this sense the unconscious is an intriguing source of creativity that is at work within us without our awareness.

Freud's development of his theory of dreams was of greater moment than simply a theory of dreams. From it he developed an understanding of *free association*, the method of psychoanalysis. The patient is instructed to – as far as possible – empty his or her head of everyday concerns and allow the mind to focus on the dream and talk about whatever comes into his or her head in connection with it. If it works, the patient will trace back the connections of the dream work and come closer to, if not actually arrive at, some of the unconscious material.

This has become generalized in the process of psychoanalysis; from the start the patient is asked to free associate and there is a sense in which everything anybody says has unconscious roots, but the roots can be more, or less, close to the surface. In a therapy group, for example, when free association does not take place in quite the same way, a collectively constructed conversation can enact the unconscious concerns of some if not all of the members. Talk about an employer at work for example, or a doctor, is often a disguised discussion of feelings about the therapist, and talk of emotional relationships outside the group will always carry some disguised reference to emotional relationships within the group.

Another way of putting this is that Freud's description of dream work is in fact a discussion of the working of the unconscious itself, a process that goes on all the time whether we are awake or asleep, although it all becomes more obvious when we are asleep and dreaming. When we are awake, the censor is at its strongest. Our waking concerns are with our inner, conscious life and the outside world, including other people, but these concerns are linked to our unconscious concerns. There is a sense in which our waking life consists of 'rationalized dreams'. This leads us again to the 'peculiarity' of psychoanalysis and psychotherapy when people first come across them. Thoughts and statements about the outside world are heard by the therapist as thoughts and statements about an internal world of which the person concerned is only aware in distorted form. The fact is that our thoughts and feelings always point in at least two directions at the same time: at the world around us and the people who populate it and at an inner life, a large part of which is unconscious. For much of our lives the former takes priority; in psychoanalytic therapy, the latter becomes the most important. One of the attendant difficulties is that we can use the external world to escape from things that we find difficult in our internal lives. Sometimes, for example, a group, when faced with the apparently intractable misery of a member, will resort to practical advice, which of course makes no difference to anything.

Conclusion

The dynamics I have just described are very basic, and I will be looking at other developments and ways of thinking about the unconscious, especially when I discuss the work of Melanie Klein and Jacques Lacan. Freud's account of dream work has been modified since he wrote – for example, I think most psychoanalysts would now take the story of the dream as significant. However, what the reader should hold on to at this stage is the idea of an unconscious dimension to lives, which works in various non-rational and impulsive ways and which can be accessed through different forms of waking behaviour as well as our dreams. The processes of condensation, displacement and symbolization are not 'caused' by anything but are free creative acts of the imagination – this is where we move from biology to a hermeneutic psychology. It is also important to remember that our words themselves are multi-dimensional, that they carry meanings of which we are not necessarily aware. We always say more than we think we are saying.

3

Freud

Psychic Structures, Internal Agencies and the Defences

Unconscious processes are timeless, do not obey the laws of formal logic, and involve processes of constant re-symbolization. To live in the world only with an unconscious would be impossible – we would be gabbling wrecks taking no account of other people except insofar as they could satisfy our needs. You might think that you know people like this, but they are very mild versions of what somebody who really acted entirely according to impulse would be like. The impulses have to be tamed, and the existence of the unconscious and repression is already a step towards that; it implies the development of other levels of, and a split in, the psyche. It must be remembered that as far as psychoanalysis is concerned, we are not simple agents, but constantly divided in (and against) ourselves.

Wollheim (1971) points out that Freud was not content with assuming that there is a simple division between the conscious and unconscious levels of the mind; that view does not enable us to grasp the dynamic processes of repression and of the way the repressed can reappear in consciousness. The division I discussed earlier between unconscious, preconscious and conscious levels was insufficient to describe the complexity of the processes that Freud was trying to describe, and it was in response to these complexities that he revised his earlier conceptualization (Freud 1984c). Wollheim points out that in his paper on 'The Ego and the Id' (1984c) Freud generalizes beyond his evidence in an inspired way. I think that what he is doing here is the real theoretical work – the rational conceptualization of underlying structures. When he worked with the notions of conscious, preconscious and unconscious, there was no way of understanding how ideas were transformed when they moved from one level to the next. The developing understanding of the laws of the unconscious that I described in the previous chapter, which does show how that transformation takes place, was part of a reorganization of the conception of the psyche into three levels: the now well-known id, ego and super-ego. For the time being I will refer to these as 'structures' but they might also be referred to as 'internal agencies', since they are involved in dynamic relationships with each other. I will return to a discussion of how we can best conceive of them at the end of the chapter.

The id

Freud did not himself use the Latin terms when he was developing his theory; they were introduced by his translator in the hope that using them would bring psychoanalysis greater respectability in the medical profession (Bettelheim 1983). The German words translate as 'it', 'I' and 'over-I', and these do in fact convey a better common-sense understanding of what Freud was on about. These are concepts that refer to underlying structures that have experiential, or at least experienceable, effects. They have both conscious and unconscious dimensions.

What we get from the 'it' rather than 'id' is the sense of something inside that can push in one direction or another against our will, something that is beyond our control and that can reassert itself against all attempts to control or divert it. In Christopher Badcock's words: 'The id [is] an impersonal, chaotic inferno of primitive drives and dynamically repressed material which constantly [agitates] for expression. It [goads] the ego with pain and [seduces] it with pleasure' (Badcock 1988: 111).

I can experience my id in a number of ways, through feelings the origin of which I do not understand and that I often try to avoid by trying to find some reason for them in the outside world: if I am angry, then it is because something or somebody makes me so. My physical reactions, the tension, the need to keep moving, jumping up from my chair and pacing the room, these are responses to messages from the id that demand some satisfaction, some release, and sometimes the release is as irrational as the source of the feeling: punching a wall or kicking the cat. For some it might be a matter of cutting or killing themselves, the impulse is so unbearable. The id is basically but not wholly unconscious: I am not aware of what goes on there but I am aware of the effects of what goes on there. I am aware of having a particular drive; I suspect there are few if any people who are not aware of being sexual animals, of having a sexual energy, but we are by no means aware of what we might want to do with it. Sometimes the discovery of our desires can be frightening.

The id, then, is a sort of chaotic power-house of the personality, pushing energy through the system towards the outside world, and demanding immediate satisfaction. The difficulty is that immediate satisfaction is not available, even on a simple economic level. We live in a world of comparative scarcity: if we are hungry, we do not have access to an inexhaustible supply of food – we have to find it, or work for it, or for the money to buy it; and if we sought immediate satis-faction for all our sexual desires, the species would disappear very quickly. The Marxist philosopher Herbert Marcuse (1969) con-structed a sort of speculative utopia where we could allow our sexual instinct far more free-ranging satisfactions than we do at present, and it is interesting that a major criticism is that there would be no place in such a world for the sacrifices involved in raising children (Chodorow 1985).

The ego

We are then caught between inner demands for immediate satisfac-tion, and the demands of the outer world, which threatens us as much as does the inner world. The ego is what develops in the attempt to maintain a balance between the two. The most effective way in which it can deal with the internal pressures of the id is repression, and it was the problem of this aspect of the ego's work that contributed to Freud's development of his structural model of the psyche. If it were going to work effectively, the repressing mechanism could not enter consciousness (if I know I am trying to repress something, then by definition I am not repressing it); and if repression is part of the work of the ego, then the ego cannot be assigned simply to the conscious or the preconscious. Like the id, it has both conscious and unconscious aspects.

The ego or the 'I' grows out of the struggle between the demands of the internal drives and the demands of the outside world, in order to mediate between them. It originates in identifications with objects that were 'cathected' by the id, and then lost. Another way of putting this is that the ego is formed by loss of intensely loved objects (the womb, the breast perhaps), and by identifying with and taking in the lost object as part of oneself. We shall see that the theory of loss and mourning plays an important part in psychoanalysis, and we might say at this stage that a central part of the self and my sense of self is built upon an early and primitive mourning process.

The conscious element of the 'I' is that sense of personhood that we have when we use the pronoun, the sense of a reasonably coherent agency that can result for periods when we have the conflicting internal and external demands in an approximate balance. I would emphasize that this only occurs for periods: the psyche is a combination of dynamic processes and an absolute, stable balance or integration is never achieved. One of my criticisms of some contemporary psychoanalytic theories is that the 'self' comes to be identified only with the conscious part of the ego, and the attempt to produce a strong or stable self involves encouraging an omnipotent attitude towards the external world.

The unconscious part of the ego, made up of internalized objects that were once vital for the infant's survival, is the repressing and defending mechanism and what one might call the internal negotiator between the outside and the inside; this can be seen as setting the framework for conscious deliberations on what to do in the world. But as Juliet Mitchell (1974) points out in no uncertain terms, the ego is the originating point for all anxiety. One might say that anxiety is the price we pay for possessing a self. Perhaps the most straightforward anxieties are those that belong to dealing with the outside world itself, but these are complemented by internal pressures and the difficulties of somehow reconciling the two; and all this has to be achieved in the context of the conflict between the libido and the death instinct. Moreover, as we shall see shortly, the super-ego becomes another important force in generating anxiety through its function of reinforcing the ego.

The super-ego

The colloquial term that Freud used for the super-ego is, as we have noted, the 'over-I', an internal agency that, as it were, lays down the law for the rest of the personality, often providing a critical commentary on a person's actions. It is tempting to see it as a conscience, which, through the internalization of the parents', particularly, for Freud, the father's, prohibitions, takes in wider social prohibitions. In fact I think Freud was trying to get at a much deeper process. Certainly our conscious experiences of judging ourselves and giving ourselves ideals, and of guilt when we feel we have done something wrong, are connected with the super-ego. But they also have important unconscious dimensions that make 'super-ego' much more than another term for a simple process of socialization (Freud 1973a, 1984c, 1984e, 1985c).

The super-ego is formed from the same sort of psychic material as is the ego and in order to reinforce the latter in its task of managing the drives. However, there is what on the surface is an unexpected connection between the id and the super-ego, because the latter is formed, according to Freud, from the introjection of objects in which the id has invested most energy. The principle seems to be that the more powerful the desire for the object, the greater the force needed to repress that desire, and that force is attached to the introjected object and turned against the id. It is important to think of this as an internal, psychological process rather than something that occurs primarily as a response to outside forces. The strength of and force behind a person's self-critical and self-controlling functions is not necessarily related directly to the strength and force of parental prohibition. Some believe that, if anything, the opposite is true – if parental prohibition is weak, the internal control has to be that much stronger for the ego to cope with the world.

Freud believed the super-ego appears around the age of four, at the end of the oedipal stage. We shall see later that this is when the authority of the father is paramount, and for Freud it is probably true to say that the major component of the super-ego is paternal; it is the father who forces the child (of both sexes) to give up its desire for the mother. It is apparent, however, that we can find severe self-criticism and a powerful sense of guilt in much younger children, and the understanding of how this happens marks one of the major theoretical divisions between Freud and Melanie Klein.

The ego-ideal

Freud talks about the ego-ideal sometimes as if it were part of the super-ego, sometimes as if it were the super-ego, and sometimes as if it were a separate agency within the psyche (Freud 1973b, 1984c; Laplanche and Pontalis 1988). It is most usefully understood as that part of the super-ego or that agency which is 'over-I', but not necessarily in a punitive way. Rather it is an ideal to which the ego *wishes* to conform, not under threat but through an admiration of and desire for certain qualities. It should not be confused with the 'ideal-ego' (Freud 1984f), which is more a matter of self-idealization from which one emerges as the developing ego identifies with the parents and then with the wider rules and qualities which they represent.

The place where Freud talks most interestingly about the ego-ideal is in 'Group Psychology and the Analysis of the Ego' (1985b). The basis of group relations, according to Freud, is the transformation of instinctual drives – a form of sublimation which can bind us together with our fellows. A further important part of the group bond, however, comes through the internalization of the group leader as an ego-ideal. The internalized figure here is not a punitive figure whose ideals we feel persecuted into following, but an admirable figure whom we would like to resemble, whose ideals we would like to follow. The fact that the group members share the same ego-ideal provides a powerful bond. We can find in Freud's discussion of the ego-ideal a view of the individual not just as involving an underlying complex psychic structure but also as having multiple identifications with external groups:

> Each individual is a component part of numerous groups, he or she is bound by ties of identification in many directions, and has built up an ego ideal upon the most various models. Each individual therefore has a share in numerous group minds – those of his race, of his class, of his creed, of his nationality, etc. – and he can also raise himself above them by the extent of having a scrap of independence. (Freud 1985b: 161)

It is clear from this account that the ego-ideal is closer to consciousness and the outside world than is the super-ego, which takes much of its strength from the id. We also arrive at the possibility of numerous internal objects, although in the above quote Freud seems to be talking about something closer to cognitive internalization than introjection.

The defences

To protect itself, the ego develops a number of defences or defence mechanisms with which to deal with the internal and the external world and keep a manageable balance within the psyche. There are various mechanisms dealt with in the literature, although the major source is Anna Freud (1936). It is important to say at the outset of this discussion that defences are necessary; we all deploy them all the time, and they are what makes something like normal life possible. In everyday life, calling somebody defensive is usually a criticism; in psychoanalytic treatment the analysis of defences is considered vital since it can open up paths of communication and levels of under-standing within the psyche. But defences cannot be 'cured'; they are problematic only when one dominates over the others or they are too rigid. Most of the time for most of us, it is a matter of deploying a range of defences as and when appropriate.

Repression and sublimation

The most successful or 'healthy' way in which the ego defends itself is through repression or sublimation. It is important to distinguish between repression, which is an unconscious act that keeps the threat-ening idea out of consciousness, and suppression, which is the attempt that people often make 'not to think about it', to turn their attention elsewhere. Suppression means the threat is already con-scious; repression keeps it out of consciousness, although it is con-stantly trying to climb back in again and will try various routes. A 'successful' repression involves a sublimation. The idea is repressed and the energy to which it was attached is transferred to some other idea or object – in one of Freud's classic examples Michelangelo's homosexuality was sublimated into his artistic work; more generally, homosexuality is sublimated into same-sex friendships (Freud 1990). Our desire to watch our parents engage in sexual intercourse, or at least to find out what goes on when they are alone together, is sublimated into a disinterested pursuit of knowledge; my desire to expose my genitals to all and sundry is sublimated into my desire to wear fashionable clothes.

Here again I suspect the reader might sense the peculiarity of the psychoanalytic way of looking at the world, connecting everyday activities with sexual desires unknown to the actor. This is often difficult to accept and leads to rather pointless 'Yes it is'–'No it isn't' arguments that lead nowhere. The proof of the pudding here is in the coherence of the theory and the scope of understanding that it offers. For an excellent example of the power of this sort of understanding I would refer the reader to Gitta Sereny's discussion of Albert Speer's relationship to Hitler (Sereny 1996); she is not a psychoanalyst but she brings out well how a person can both know and not know things at the same time, and how a power of unknown (homo-erotic) motives can overcome rational and moral assessments of the situation.

There are three implications of this that can be followed up immediately. The first is that the process of repression and sublimation inevitably involves the same features as the normal workings of the unconscious. This is what leads to psychoanalysis becoming a constant affront to our desires for simplicity and wholeness, for clarity and certainty about ourselves. I think that this feature of psychoanalysis is often more disturbing than its concern with sexual motivations.

The second implication is the similarity between the structure of 'normal' sublimation and the structure of a neurosis – here too the original idea is repressed and the energy is attached to another object, and one of the crucial differences is not in this internal process but in whether the new object inhibits the neurotic's performance in his or her everyday life and whether the new object is socially approved or acceptable. In other words it is possible that a neurosis may be defined primarily not by some sort of deformed psychological process, but by personal and social moral judgements. If this were true across the board, it would put mental health professionals in an interesting position.

Third, if the only way in which a manageable life becomes possible is through sublimation, it follows that a manageable life must involve a renunciation of satisfaction – we have to give up the first objects of our desires and replace them with something else, less satisfying but more acceptable to those around us and more likely to enable us to survive in a dangerous world. The more developed, complex and organized our lives become, the more we have to give up. This is the basis of a Freudian framework for understanding society and history, and it is a pessimistic one. The more civilized we become, the more miserable we become: civilization and misery go together; and the more we give up instinctual satisfaction, the stronger our destructive instincts (Freud 1985a). Whilst this is far too simple to explain the complexities of modern societies and modern social conflict, it is a useful warning of the dangers of social utopianism and of ignoring the contradictory nature of human being.

There is one further point I want to make about the process of repression and sublimation. Sometimes it seems that any new object could not possibly match the pleasure promised by the object that has been renounced. It is as if the unconscious says what many people say fully consciously in the first flush of disappointment: 'If I can't have all of what I want, then I will have none of it, no substitute, and it is too painful even to remember what I want.' The original idea is repressed but the energy is left as free-floating anxiety in the psyche, attaching itself to whatever the world offers. Again there is a sense in which anxiety is helpful – it makes sure we look both ways before we cross the road, and it makes sure that we think about things before they happen so that we can take precautions; and we all possess a degree of free-floating anxiety (especially perhaps when we wake up in the early hours with nothing else to do but feel anxious). Whether such anxiety can be labelled neurotic is again a matter of possibly unfoundable judgement.

Introjection and projection

In terms of making sense of the defences, I think introjection and projection should be considered basic. Introjection is a much stronger term than the 'internalization' that we come across in the social and human sciences and that usually means taking in an idea or a view of the world. Introjection is by comparison more like swallowing something; it is as if in unconscious phantasy* I take the thing that is outside of me inside in order to be able to keep and control it. It is one of the ways in which we try to hold on to what we might lose,

---

* I will be following the practice developed by Kleinian psychoanalysts of referring to unconscious thoughts as *ph*antasies and conscious day-dreaming or conscious assumptions for which there is no evidence as *f*antasies.

and, as we saw above, it is at the basis of the development of the ego and super-ego.

In adult life, it is possible to think of introjection as lying behind some of the stranger things that go on between couples, for example where one partner will buy drink for an alcoholic mate, or try to control a partner's supply of lovers. By taking in a threatening situation and treating it as if it belongs to me and I can control it, I ease the anxiety that it raises in me. A parent who tells a child 'I know you better than you know yourself' is doing the same thing. Psychotherapists are, of course, particularly vulnerable to such an illusion, one that offers protection against anxieties about, amongst other things, professional competence and the limits of one's understanding.

Projection is the opposite of introjection, it is a matter of putting something that is actually within oneself outside, on to some other person (or object). It is one, if not the, basis of communication, a matter of seeing some part of ourselves in another person. Projection defends the ego in a number of ways. First it is a way of protecting against external dangers by investing another person with the qualities we feel we don't have ourselves. As children, we do this all the time, not just as projection, but as a necessary and accurate perception of reality – we expect our parents to protect us. As children, we are likely to welcome and resent such a situation, and as adults we still struggle with it.

The more familiar form of projection is that of a threatening or anxiety-provoking desire or internal object on to the outside world, where it can be more easily dealt with. Although they might have other causes in the wider society, projection is the principal psychological mechanism involved in such phenomena as racism and homophobia, and the hatred of the opposite sex; these are good liberal examples, but projection is also involved in the hatred of paedophiles, murderers and criminals. The hatred, condemnation and even persecution of evil is a popular past-time, much facilitated if the evil can be located in others. Psychoanalysis tells us that although it might be in others, it is also in ourselves, and this is another psychoanalytic idea that people find difficult.

Splitting

Projection is part of a number of defences, and it is certainly central to splitting. As the ego experiences increasing pressure, it tries to deal with its anxiety by splitting the threat, or the world in general, into two, on a sort of divide-and-rule basis.

In everyday terms there are more practical forms of splitting. If a patient in therapy feels threatened by what he or she is discovering, he or she might look for a 'supplementary' therapist using different techniques so that psychic material that could be threatening if it came together is divided between two people and two locations. Alternatively one therapist becomes 'bad' and the other 'good'. This is often the reproduction of a splitting of parents into good and bad, which at the appropriate age is quite useful for the child. We also engage in an internal splitting, fearing that our good parts or experiences might become contaminated by the bad. Some people, for example, find it difficult to admit that life is going well, because they fear that the acknowledgement will be cancelled out by their bad parts or experiences – a sense of internal conflict that is often described as superstition.

At one end of a continuum we can think of splitting as the putting of part of one's personality into another person or object and keeping part to oneself, and at the other end splitting is behind the breaking down of problems into manageable proportions, and at the basis of analytic and scientific thought. There are a range of possibilities in-between. For example, if I fear I am becoming too close to a partner, and I fear that I will be swallowed up by her and lose my independence, then I might make sure that I have another partner to protect me from such a fate; or I might divide myself up between different groups of friends, different types of friends. One personal piece of splitting is my pursuit of my career as an academic, on the one hand, and as a psychotherapist, on the other. There are times when they seem to feed each other in creative ways but also times when I am aware of escaping from problems in one by concentrating on the other.

Denial

The notion of denial, or of being 'in denial', seems to have entered popular consciousness over recent years, often connected with the sort of counselling that concentrates on alcoholism or child sexual abuse. There is often a tendency to think of denial as a conscious process, a sort of deliberate misleading. I am prowling around my house feeling angry and muttering to myself; my wife asks me why I am so angry and I say that I am not angry. That is not denial; it is lying. If I walk into the house, utter a few grunts and sit down in front of the television, my wife feels similar responses to when I am prowling around the house. This time I say that I am not angry, just tired. I do not feel angry, I am conscious only of being tired. This is denial proper – when the feeling and the ideas attached to the feeling are not available to my conscious awareness but can be 'read' or picked up by those around me. Denial often goes with projection:

'What's wrong with you today?'
'Nothing's wrong with me – what are you on about?'
'You're sitting there looking as miserable as sin; what's up?'
'Nothing's up; for God's sake, get off my back and leave me alone.'
'Don't you talk to me like that.'

Here a number of different defences are run together.

There are some people who will deny not just particularly threatening ideas, but the whole possibility of possessing an inner life; it is as if they live entirely outside of themselves in the world. Christopher Bollas (1987) has coined the term 'normopath' or 'normotic' for such characters.

It is not only the inner world that can be denied. Dangerous aspects of the outer world can go without being observed, or they can be explained away in some more or less rational manner that lessens the threat that is unconsciously experienced. I am constantly surprised, both in my practice as a psychotherapist and in my everyday life, by the human propensity not to see things in the outside world that are disturbing or frightening. Husbands and wives do not see the signs of their partner's affairs, or their growing disillusionment with the relationship. We do not notice the signs of illness in someone we love; we are surprised by what in retrospect we could have seen coming. In therapy groups there are 'slips of sight' or 'slips of hearing' as much as there are slips of the tongue. The person sitting in tears is not noticed; the expression of desperation or fear, or even suicidal intent, does not seem to be heard.

People's reactions to the bereaved or the seriously ill are frequently denials. There is a wonderful rendering of denial in Selima Hill's poem 'My Sister and I finally arrive at the Hospital':

She sweeps onto the ward like a bride
with armfuls of white nighties and fresh flowers
that beam *Come on*. My sister beams *Get back*.

You mustn't touch. You mustn't speak to her.
Or even look as if you're able to.
You have to stand where I can see you, Darling,
but not too close. And never say a word.
But, very quickly, once, I risk a whisper.
My mother whispers back. We both agree
it won't be long before she dies. However
my sister must be humoured till she does.

(Hill 1997: 19)

In cases like this the denied idea is often very close to the surface and the tension of the poem captures the force of the denying impulse. There is, I think, a narrow line between such a denial and a rather shifty avoidance where the feared idea is more or less conscious but cannot be owned.

Reaction formation

This can be understood as one step beyond denial – where the feared impulse is so strong that it can only be fought by consciously embracing its opposite with all the strength at one's disposal. During my early adolescence I became a very serious and very enthusiastic pacifist. One might say that I embraced pacifism with a violent passion. It was only from the vantage point of several decades that I began to understand that this was my way of keeping at bay a violent rage against my parents that came with puberty. I think it is the failure of this particular defence that is the mechanism behind sudden, radical conversions to the other side, like St Paul's on the road to Damascus. It is as if the strength of the repressed wish is so great for the ego that it breaks through to consciousness and the only course left for the ego is to embrace it with as much energy as it once suppressed it. I recently noticed that the name of one of my 'hardest' comrades on the Trotskyist left of my student days had reappeared as a political adviser to one of the far right London local authorities.

The general message of psychoanalysis here is to beware of passions that are felt to the exclusion of all else; they have a reverse side, and I think the way to identify such passions is that they do not allow too much reflection. The cause is all.

Rationalization

Rationalization is a rather slippery word. It is, to begin with, a very normal activity: when I am giving a reason for my action, when I am explaining something that happened to me or happened in the world and affected me, I am rationalizing. Since we are, at least in part, rational beings, I am doing no more than might be expected from my species. Yet rationalization has connotations of dishonesty, of not giving the *real* reason behind an action.

As a therapist, I have never found it useful to suggest to somebody that he or she is rationalizing; it is too much like an accusation. It is, however, often helpful to point out to somebody that what he or she is saying is OK on a rational level, implying that there are other levels at which we operate, which people are usually able to recognize. On the whole, a truly rational account of an action or a situation will recognize that there are non- or a- or ir-rational features involved in everything we do, and everything that happens to us. I think that a rational account can be called defensive when it does not recognize a troubling affect (and/or the idea attached to it) or when it masks the speaker's agency; when it is given as a causal account of an action, with the implication that the speaker had no choice. One of the clearest examples of rationalization in both these senses occurs within the confines of our own heads, when we think that we have done something 'wrong' and are open to criticism. We launch into all sorts of imaginary explanations and justifications.

Like denial, rationalization can defend against threatening aspects of the outside world as well as internal impulses that one does not want to acknowledge. Some years ago I denied the symptoms of a serious illness for some weeks before consulting a doctor, putting them down to 'stress'. Yet the symptoms were dramatic and in retrospect I am horrified at my denial; and I suspect that if the symptoms had been described to me prior to the event, I would then have been horrified at the idea of waiting several weeks before seeing the doctor. My rationalizations not only protected me from a very unpleasant reality but also left me in charge of my difficulties. I managed to imagine that they were symptoms that I was creating for myself, even if unconsciously. I shall return to rationalization later when I discuss omnipotence, and I wonder if this defence is not an occupational hazard for psychoanalysts and psychotherapists. I think that what I was denying most actively in this case is that there is often no reason behind the threats that come to us from the outside. Matters of life and death are often matters of chance, not purpose or reason or even of our unconscious, and that can be very frightening.

Conclusion

This brings us to the end of the foundations of psychoanalytic thought laid down by Freud, and we will be referring back to these ideas regularly in what follows. A number of points should be kept in mind: first, the complexity of the psyche as Freud outlined it: human beings are not simple creatures, and are not only divided against each other but also divided within themselves, having to live with their internal conflicts; second, the fact that we are not driven by our biology, but that we transform impulses, instincts, into drives, unconsciously selecting ideas, representations of objects to which the drives are attached, these representations being related to others through our language once this occurs; third, the existence of the unconscious itself as the constant unwanted guest at the party, and the ways we try to keep out the threatening desires or ideas that it pushes forward. Not only is there no 'real' self, but the self is divided and internally contradictory; what we think and say about ourselves is always open to question and to interpretation, revealing things about us that we would like not to know.

4

The Development of the Psyche
Freud and Oedipus

Introduction

In chapters 2 and 3, I presented Freud's conception of the psyche as involving conflicts and obscure processes, obscure both to the experiencing and acting individual and to those witnessing that experience and action. Freud's analysis of the development of the psyche adds new dimensions of conflict and ambiguity. I will argue throughout this chapter that Freud is not presenting a determined process that everybody goes through in the same way. Our psychological development can best be seen as finding a path through a possibly dangerous forest, but one with lots of animal tracks that we can follow. We all have to go through the forest, but each of us has to find his or her own way and that will be different from everybody else's. So our development will be different depending on our culture, our social class and our family history; it will also vary with the internal conscious and unconscious metaphors and interpretations by means of which we try to make sense of our experience.

One way of understanding Freud's theory of development is that he is suggesting that the basis of all metaphors can be found in our experience of our bodies before, during and after our arrival as a separate human being in the world. For Freud this takes us to the infantile libido and transformations through which it must go as we mature, and this leads us to the issue of sexuality, and, in particular, infantile sexuality.

Infantile sexuality

I have already talked about the way in which the human infant is born prematurely in comparison with other animals and is dependent for longer on adult members of the species. A result of this is that we are born before heterosexuality is genetically programmed into us and it has to be passed on to us in some way or another by our society. Freud's account offers a theory of how this happens. The account that I am going to embark on here is like unravelling a knotted ball of string to find that there are several separate strands. When Freud discussed infantile sexuality, he said, I think with some justification, that he was only talking about what every nursemaid knew. Indeed the most elementary empirical observation would confirm that babies gain some sort of pleasure from manipulating their genitals from the moment that they are able to do so. Yet the notion of childhood sexuality is still socially problematic, and it still seems socially important to maintain an idea of the 'innocence' of children. In Britain and America in recent years the context for discussion of childhood sexuality has been that of child sexual abuse and incest, and any suggestion that children possess sexual desires or feelings can be taken as an attempt to justify adults embarking on sexual relations because it is 'what the child wants'. This, however, does not follow. The fact that as children we do have sexual desires, and therefore sexual phantasies, even in the best regulated conditions, leaves us with all sorts of difficulties to negotiate in later life (Gittins 1997), and it does not mean that adults, from their position of power, should exploit a child's sexuality.

These issues are all the more difficult because Freud's 'discovery' of childhood sexuality is associated with his attitude to his patients' claims of incest or sexual abuse. He believed that there could not possibly be as much incest or abuse as his patients claimed, and eventually he came to understand some of these claims as the recall of early phantasies rather then early realities. Modern critics such as Masson (1992) accuse Freud of dishonesty and cowardice, but the paradox is that the theory of infantile and unconscious sexuality that he developed has brought him more attacks than any other part of his work.

Freud begins his discussion of infantile sexuality (Freud 1977e, 1977h) by attributing the neglect of infantile sexuality to infantile amnesia – the fact that most people cannot remember much from their earlier years. There is a degree of truth in this: it is certainly more difficult to remember things from the period before we could speak, but these things can be recalled through physical sensations. In any case there is more to it than Freud suggests: it is not just that we cannot remember our own experience, we cannot always see or understand what children around us are doing. There are certain things that perhaps we don't want to know. Freud also suggests that there is a period of latency between the age of round about five years and the onset of puberty, during which the earlier sexual ideas and fantasies undergo a massive repression. I am less than convinced by this, as I am less than convinced by any attempt to take his stages of development as clear-cut and separate. They are all there all the time, although perhaps at different times one is more dominant than the others, and they return in different disguises throughout life.

One way of thinking about these stages is suggested by Erik Erikson (1977), an American ego psychologist, who was interested in the social framework in which development takes place. He suggested that each of Freud's stages can be seen as involving the acquisition of or failure to acquire certain fundamental characteristics. I will refer to Erikson's work at the same time as I discuss Freud. This is not because I think it is an improvement on Freud's work – Erikson, like most ego psychologists, tends to lose sight of the power of the unconscious and the presence of internal conflict – but he does add a useful dimension of intelligibility to Freud.

The oral stage

Freud portrays himself as giving an account of an organic development – the libido becomes primarily focused on different organs as the child matures – but it is plain from his first example of infantile sexuality – thumb sucking – that he is talking about the construction of metaphors, first of all physical metaphors: the thumb as a displacement of the nipple. The erotic satisfaction aimed at by the libido is first attached to the act of sucking at the breast (or the bottle), but the act of thumb sucking shows that the satisfaction has become detached from the need for food, which, as the child is weaned, is no longer taken in by sucking. Here we come across auto-eroticism for the first time:

> The child does not make use of an extraneous body for his sucking, but prefers a part of his own skin because it is more convenient, because it makes him independent of the external world, which he is not yet able to control, and because in that way he provides himself, as it were, with a second erotogenic zone, although of an inferior kind. The inferiority of this second region is among the reasons why at a later date, he seeks the corresponding part – the lips – of another person. (Freud 1977h: 98)

In the next paragraph Freud produces an argument that for some would be a conclusive proof that he was a biological determinist. Not all babies suck their thumbs, but in some there is a 'constitutional intensification' of this particular zone, and as they mature such people might become experts in kissing, or might be strongly attracted to smoking or eating, or might talk a lot. This is Freud at his worst, a sort of determinism that can undermine the value of his theory. I want to suggest another set of links, other than the causal, that relates our adult behaviour to this infantile stage.

The form of the connection is universal. We cannot avoid our childhood and we have to make something of what we experience during this period. The most important experience is loss. There can never be any such thing as perfect satisfaction of a desire, and one of the first losses in infantile life is the loss of the ideal of perfect satisfaction. This is so not least because we have to give up the breast, and so we make do initially with the thumb, or a bit of sheet, or whatever it is that we have available as a substitute. We all then make a constant series of displacements, seeking the original oral satisfaction in symbolic form. It might be that oral deprivation or overstimulation in infancy intensifies this search, or inhibits it. This is one of the infuriating things about psychoanalysis: it can appear to offer causal explanations that turn out not to be explanations at all. What actually happens is that we all have to deal with variations of the same general problems and we all create our own personal metaphors, somatic and later linguistic, in our attempt to deal with the loss, to fill the emptiness at the root of our being. There is a very general organic basis – we outgrow the breast – and in that sense an organic 'cause', but we create the effects of the cause from a potentially infinite range of possibilities.

Erikson talks about this stage in terms of the development of a basic trust in the world, or alternatively of a basic mistrust if the infant's needs are not met or are met erratically. He gives the impression that these are either/or possibilities, but there can be no such thing as perfect satisfaction, nor would it be a good thing if we developed a perfect trust in the world – that would be a recipe for disaster because the world is not trustworthy. The two are not alternatives but end points on a continuum, and perhaps the optimal point is somewhere around the middle, allowing the infant to develop with the experience of both trust and mistrust and, one hopes, as he or she gets older, an ability to make judgements about when each is appropriate.

What should be apparent in the comparison of Freud and Erikson is that the former is describing processes at a more fundamental or deeper level and the latter processes closer to the surface, a more conscious level. It is easy to fall into the trap of imagining an either/or achievement if one stays at the surface level; the analysis of the unconscious reveals the impossibility of an either/or solution and the beginning of a chain of displacements, none of which are quite as satisfying as the original object.

The anal stage

It is not just oral satisfaction that provides the basis for physical and then linguistic metaphors. The mouth is just one of several 'erotogenic zones' of the body. In fact the whole body, or any of its parts, can be an erotogenic zone, but there are three significant zones that Freud suggests are 'predestined' erotogenic areas. Each is an area of skin, or mucous membrane, that is subject to a pleasurable excitement through a rhythmic manipulation. What is noticeable about all three of them – the mouth, the anus and the genitals – is that they are all regions on the borderline of the inner and the outer, the places where we take things in from the outside or expel them from the inside.

The zone that follows on from the mouth is the anus:

We learn with some astonishment from psychoanalysis of the transmutations normally undergone by the sexual excitations normally arising from this zone and of the frequency with which it retains a considerable amount of susceptibility to genital stimulation throughout life. (Freud 1977h: 102)

Like the mouth, the anus can play an important part in adult sexuality, and it too provides material for physical and symbolic metaphors – these connections become particularly important in the development of female sexuality, as we shall see later. In another essay Freud (1977a) talks about the pleasure gained from defecation, especially when it has been stored up, and children who refrain from defecating in order to gain such pleasure. Most adults are aware of such pleasure – even if they do not deliberately set out to gain it – from those occasions when they do not have access to a toilet until it is almost too late. Freud suggests that as the child gets older this pleasure is repressed through a process of reaction formation – this is true for all forms of infantile sexuality but especially, Freud thought, in his contemporary society, anal sexuality. He rather tentatively suggests that people who are primarily anal erotic in their infancy develop an adult character dominated by orderliness, cleanliness, parsimony and obstinacy:

> The intrinsic necessity for such a connection is not clear, of course, even to myself. But I can make some suggestions which may help towards an understanding of it. Cleanliness, orderliness and trust-worthiness give exactly the impression of a reaction-formation against an interest in what is unclean and disturbing and should not be part of the body. (Freud 1977h: 212–13)

As a sign of obstinacy, Freud talks about the way in which a young child might withhold his or her stool, something with which many parents will be familiar; the opposite is also true – the infant can decide to defecate in various inconvenient places, an equally obstinate reaction. On a more general level we can see again opposite ways of dealing with anal eroticism – the defence of the reaction formation that Freud talks about or the enjoyment of mess and dirtiness. The latter can of course become a source of adult sexual enjoyment.

At this stage Erikson talks about the development of autonomy and shame, and he would see the environment as being most important: the more rigid and controlling the form of toilet training, the more likely the child is to become ashamed of his or her ability to act in an autonomous way. It is not a new insight but it is worth pointing out the irony in the idea that the individual autonomy upon which modern capitalist society places so much emphasis first manifests itself through our freedom to shit where we wish.

The phallic stage

The phallic stage or phase was a notion developed by Freud later on in his work, and it takes us into the central and, for many contemporary students, the most problematic aspect of his theory (Freud 1977b, 1977e, 1977g). The phallic phase is the precursor of adult genital sexuality. The various component instincts, which in the earlier stages have been separated, come together for the first time, under the command, as it were, of the genitals, which become the major source of excitement and release.

From the point of view of my approach in this book, the most important point to be made about this stage is that, like the two stages that precede it, there is no essential difference between little boys and little girls. The lack of difference is perhaps easier to grasp for the oral and anal stages: boys and girls, men and women, all eat and defecate through similar orifices. When it comes to genitalia, however, there are usually clear differences. Freud suggests, however, that even at this stage, there is no fundamental differences between the sexes. The little girl's experience of the pleasure she gains from her clitoris is similar to that which the little boy gains from his penis. A bisexuality remains until the age of four to five years.

At this stage, the manipulation of the genitals – masturbation – becomes a major way of gaining pleasure. Erikson talks about this stage as involving the development of initiative and guilt. Whereas shame, attached to the anal stage, is a directly social emotion, our most acute feelings of shame having to do with direct exposure to the gaze of others, guilt involves internal psychological processes. It is still of course a social emotion, involving some act that is or is thought to be socially forbidden. However, the forbidding agency of which we have the most experience is an internal agency, suggesting the more primitive aspects of the super-ego. It is because the pleasure that we can gain from our genitals is so strong that we need to call on powerful persecutory forces to control ourselves.

In contemporary Western societies guilt seems to be experienced as a difficult emotion to bear. Of course, it *is* a difficult emotion to bear, and it would be more accurate to say that in our society people have become increasingly reluctant to feel guilt, and a common way of dealing with it is to blame someone else for *making* one feel guilty. Perhaps this too is a sign of an increasingly narcissistic culture. Whereas many people have a tendency to persecute themselves with guilt, most, if not all of us, will occasionally act in a way about which we *should* feel guilty.

It is important to emphasize that the sources of pleasure discussed here are sources of pleasure from birth, or even from before birth (Piontelli 1992); what changes is their significance as the body grows. It is not very helpful to see them as clear-cut stages or as somehow 'causing' certain character traits or neuroses in later life. Rather the activities involved (sucking, eating and drinking, defecating, urinating and masturbation) provide us with the raw materials for the first metaphors with which we attempt to make sense of our existence in the world. If we see these stages in the light of the social directing of the sexual drives towards a degree of heterosexual genitality to ensure reproduction, then we have got as far as the focusing of pleasure on to the genitals. The big, and difficult, step is from here to heterosexuality.

Freud and Oedipus

The notion of the oedipal complex or the oedipal stage is at the centre of a series of problems for Freud and psychoanalysis generally – problems about attitudes to women; about the universal applicability of the theory, or what we would now call ethnocentrism; about attitudes to homosexuals; and about straightforward credibility.

I will begin with the last issue first. When Freud (1977b, 1977e) discusses the movement through the oedipal stage, he does it in a deceptively simple way, talking about what happens when the little girl and the little boy become consciously aware of each other's genitals. This becomes most important around the age of four or five, and it poses problems for both sexes in their understanding of the world. The first question that my undergraduate students ask is: what happens if a child doesn't see the genitals of the other sex? When Freud was writing a century ago, of course, families were much larger and one might surmise that children of all classes would have noticed the difference; with families of one or two children, this might be more difficult, and students certainly revert to personal experience. 'I never knew. . . .'

There is a problem here; one dimension of it has to do with the assumption that what cannot be remembered was not known. Most babies come into contact with parents of the opposite sex and are likely to become aware of the difference, which is a central issue from an early age, and we know that babies are very efficient learners from the moment of birth.

To my mind there are more interesting possible responses to this question, and I find it difficult to believe that the whole process depends on direct experience, given that the unconscious is so powerful. It is an interesting fact that we all begin life as females and the male appendages are exactly that, appearing at a later stage of development. And of course the existence of something raises the possibility of its loss, or its growth. Since I have arms, I can imagine being without them, and one could imagine that the more pleasurable the protuberance the greater the awareness I will have of its possible loss. Similarly a small organ – the clitoris – that provides much pleasure could perhaps arouse the desire for it to be larger. I am suggesting here that it is quite possible to have the idea of having a penis (for the girl) or not having one (for the boy) without actually having seen the genitals of the opposite sex.

The next problem is the universality of the oedipal complex. Freud is often accused of basing his theories on Western European families, if not just nineteenth-century families selected from the Viennese bourgeoisie. If we go back to the conceptions of theory I have been arguing for in this book, this criticism presupposes a fairly simple conception of theory: that there is a close, almost one-to-one relationship between a theoretical concept and a particular empirical reality. I shall argue shortly that Freud's account of the oedipal complex is an account of an underlying structure, the empirical manifestations of which can vary from society to society, or, indeed, family to family, but it is worth pointing out here that there is some evidence that this stage can be identified in very different sorts of society (Kline 1977). The theory is like a town map with lots of back alleys, side streets and culs-de-sac. There can be different towns in different societies and many individual routes from one side of the town to the other – but nobody can avoid going through a town.

Finally there are the problems of homosexuality and of women. Both of these raise issues at the level of theory as well as the difficult task of sorting out the cognitive content of a theory from the prejudices of the theorist. In the case of homosexuality Freud seems to have been fairly liberal in his attitudes, but his theory emphasizes the possibility of different routes to heterosexuality and the bisexuality with which we all start. In the case of women it is a little more complicated and there is a clear case to be made that Freud shared the more unpleasant patriarchal attitudes of his time – there are occasions when he writes as if he believes that women really are inferior because they do not possess a penis (see, for example, Chodorow 1978). The question here is whether the theory depends upon the prejudices or whether the prejudices can be peeled away to leave a more rigorous theory. My assumption here is that the coherence of a theory and its usefulness are dependent upon the rationality and rigour with which its ideas are connected to each other; this rigour may be reinforced or undermined by the personal and social circumstances and prejudices of the author, but it is possible to attempt to unravel these influences. This does not occur in a once and for all way, but is a constant process.

The most sensible approach seems to me that of Juliet Mitchell (1974) when she argues that Freud was describing the structure and reproduction of a patriarchal system, not *necessarily* supporting such a system. Later I shall argue that in various ways Freud's theory actually undermines both the traditional ways of thinking about the differences between men and women and more contemporary ways of thinking that draw on one version or another of psychoanalytic theory.

The oedipal stage: sociological background

I have talked about the oedipal stage in terms of the necessity for a society to ensure that enough of its members are heterosexual for enough of the time to reproduce the population, since this is not guaranteed at the biological level. There are, however, other sociological reasons for, or more accurately functions of, this stage. These become apparent in Lévi-Strauss's structuralist theory of kinship. Lévi-Strauss (1969) suggests that in settled societies we can find very elaborate rules of kinship, which govern who shall marry whom for generations to come. There are all sorts of modifications to these rules in practice, but that is less important than the pattern that is embodied in these rules. The outstanding feature is that they involve the exchange of women between different kinship groups, whether the tribe is exogamous or endogamous. Over a long period each group will receive as many women from the wider society as it circulates into the wider society.

One achievement of these rules is to regulate population growth or decline, which depends on the number of women of child-bearing age that a population contains, a very important concern for societies that might only just be self-sufficient. The rules of exchange ensure that if there is a surplus of women of child-bearing age, then they are not paired with men, and the society does not produce more children than it can feed; and if there is a shortage, then all available women are paired and the population does not enter into radical decline.

A necessary precondition of the oedipal stage is the incest taboo – in one sense it is what necessitates the oedipal stage. It seems that the incest taboo is the nearest we have to a universal feature of human societies. All marriage rules prohibit taking certain partners from the individual's immediate family, although the positions occupied by the forbidden partners may vary from society to society. The importance of this taboo, which ensures the circulation of women, is that it also provides a form of social cohesion. If incest were permitted, then the danger would be that the society would split into small, inward-looking groups with no need of each other. With the incest taboo, it is as if each group invests its women in the wider society and is guaranteed a return that over the years is equal to the original investment.

The oedipal stage, then, brings together a number of important, even vital, issues: the social establishment of what might be called a 'socially sufficient' degree of heterosexuality; a high level of social cohesion; and the means for population control. Juliet Mitchell, amongst others, sees all this as the basis of patriarchal society (see also Rubin 1975).

It is useful to think of this social framework as an underlying structure; returning to Lévi-Strauss, he suggests that the basic unit of kinship is not, as one might expect, the nuclear grouping of mother, father and children but it also involves the maternal uncle. In many societies there is a complementarity in the roles adopted by the father and maternal uncle in relation to the children: if one is the disciplinarian, the other will be playful, companionable and supportive, and vice versa. The maternal uncle is the man who 'gives' his sister to her husband. In modern societies the two roles tend to come together in the father, but what is important is that all these roles exist as structured positions independently of the real people who fill them. If there is no father in a contemporary family, then the child will fill that position with an imagined kindly figure and an imagined hostile figure; if there is a father, the child will still have such internal figures.

The main difference is that for the latter, the phantasies will be brought into relation and perhaps modified by the reality.

The oedipal stage for boys

It should be remembered that for Freud both sexes come up to the oedipal stage having shared the same development. The simplistic version of what happens at this stage, found in some psychology text-books, is that the little boy falls in love with his mother and desires to kill his father, and the little girl falls in love with her father and desires to kill her mother. The former is often called the oedipal complex and the latter the Electra complex, this despite the fact that the only significant mention of the Electra complex that I have found in Freud's work disowns the concept (Freud 1977c: 375). However, the process is much more complex.

The starting point is that the emotional preconditions of incest are there in every family unit, and the unconscious phantasy of incest is always there. Paradoxically these preconditions and phantasies and the way we deal with them do not threaten civilization but provide its foundation. Little boys have a painful but comparatively straightforward journey through the oedipal stage. The little boy's desire for his mother brings him into conflict with his father, possibly the real father, certainly the phantasy father. On a conscious level most parents are aware of the jealousies between parents and children, which are often the surface manifestation of such desires. Winnicott is reported to have described the little boy at this stage, when, remember, desires are organized under the phallus, as all dressed up with nowhere to go. The conflict with the father is experienced as a threat to the most sensitive and pleasurable area of his body, the area that is directed towards gaining pleasure with his mother. He experiences the jealousy and the resultant conflict as a threat to his penis, the threat of castration. This will be experienced in phantasy and perhaps reinforced by warnings about masturbation (especially of the 'I'll cut it off' variety). Under this threat, the little boy agrees to a compromise: he gives up his desire for his mother in return for a promise of a woman of his own when he is old enough. The threat of castration is reinforced by his realization, conscious or unconscious, that there are 'castrated' beings in the world – women.

As part of this compromise, the little boy takes in the father's prohibition as an essential part of his super-ego. It involves the realization that at this stage he cannot win. Theorists of patriarchy might say that this is the point where patriarchy is reproduced, when the little boy submits to the power of the father. Lacan puns on this as '*Le nom (non) du père*'. The function of the father is to turn the little boy away from his mother and towards the world, to prevent the development of the closed, inward-looking incestuous unit. It could be suggested that at this point the little boy takes on the weight of the whole culture.

Now this introjection of the prohibitive father in contemporary society arguably complements social processes that have been operating since the industrial revolution, when work was moved out of the home and into the factory. Fathers have become increasingly absent from the child-rearing process, and this means that the close identification with a real person lessens in favour of identification with a strict and punitive phantasy father, which in turn increases the chances of a narcissistic personality continuing into adulthood. This reinforces the negative image of the father on a cultural level: fathers seem to gain publicity because they sexually abuse children, subject them to physical violence, and rat on their financial and emotional responsibilities. There is comparatively little cultural emphasis on a loving father who can modify the internal prohibitive father.

In Freudian terms, this perhaps reduces the scope for the formation of what Freud calls 'the negative oedipal complex', the boy's sexual attraction to the father, the place where bisexuality comes to the centre of his theory. The little boy can form erotic attachments to and identifications with the father that can modify the more punitive internal object. Blos (1993) suggests that the negative oedipal complex is responsible for the structural development of the ego-ideal.

The oedipal stage for girls

Whereas the little boy simply postpones his desire for his mother until he can get a woman of his own, the little girl has to achieve a more radical outcome. Both go into the oedipal stage with the same love object: the mother, a woman. The boy emerges still desiring a woman.

The little girl emerges desiring a man. She has to change her love object, and give up the mother. This brings into play two of Freud's most controversial concepts – the female castration complex and penis envy.

Juliet Mitchell begins her feminist defence of the notion of the castration complex and penis envy in women with the statement that, '[p]aradoxically, that most egalitarian of notions – bisexuality – spelt death for the oedipal equivalence of the sexes, to which Freud had clung so pertinaciously' (Mitchell 1974: 74). The castration complex, she suggests, marks the psychological distinction between the sexes. Whereas the little boy surrenders his desire under a threat, there is no such threat for the little girl. The little girl goes through the experience of already being castrated, of already having been punished for her desire. The little girl's experience in the phallic stage is as powerful as the little boy's. She too is 'all dressed up with nowhere to go', but she must realize that she is not, after all, dressed up at all: she has already lost the organ that brings the little boy such a terrible threat. She cannot possess her mother and has to give up her desire, accept her inferiority in this respect. The desire is displaced through a series of stages, which, as Juliet Mitchell notes, often gives greatest offence to Freud's feminist critics, suggesting that these feminists are opposed to the idea of an unconscious *per se*. Freud argues that one significant chain of connections for little girls is the connection between faeces and the baby, stemming from a childhood speculation (or belief) that babies are born anally (where else could they come from?). Mitchell describes this connection carefully, and it is worth quoting at length:

> Children believe that babies are born anally, like faeces: the straining, the release, the production of something new out of oneself is a prototype of birth. The faeces produced for the mother, or whoever cares for the child, are offered as a gift; from here one train of 'thought' leads to an equation with money, but another to a reconfirmation of the production of a baby which is also always 'given', a gift ('he's *given* her a child', 'she's *given* him a son'). At the same time the faeces, a column that stimulates the membranes of the bowel, is – in psychic terms – a forerunner of the penis –, unfortunately, like the faeces, the penis is also thought to be a part of the body that can be lost, given up, renounced (castration). (The penis also inherits the feelings the infant had for the mother's nipple.) (Mitchell 1974: 102–3)

This unconscious chain of associations is facilitated by the little girl's sense of inferiority and her desire to make up for it by possessing a penis. Freud suggests that the desire for the penis is first of all for the father's penis and then for that of a man of her own, a husband or lover, and then finally for a boy child, which, Freud seems to imply at one point, is the only thing that can bring real satisfaction to a woman. As part of this process, there is a transfer of the source of the little girl's pleasure from the clitoris to the vagina.

The result of the girl's oedipal complex is different from that of the boy's not only in its course but also in its results. Again Mitchell describes this well, and again I will quote at length:

> The overcoming of the Oedipus complex of both [little boy and girl] is a sign to start identifying finally with the parent of the same sex – so that society can go on accordingly. The *confirmation* of his first love object for the boy *which is his Oedipus complex* is renounced till he grows up like his father, whom he meanwhile internalizes as his super-ego by means of identification. The *contradiction* of her first love object for the girl, *which is her Oedipus complex*, never really need be renounced, for that is her feminine destiny. She may feel some rivalry with the mother for the father, but its strength will not be commensurate with the boy's rivalry with his father for the mother, because in a sense, the father is only second best anyway, and furthermore, how much point is there in competing with another one of the same 'castrated' sex? Identifying with and thus to some degree internalizing the mother does not provide for the formation of a strong superego for it is not she who, in a patriarchal culture, ever has the final word. (Mitchell 1974: 111–12)

As Mitchell points out, the little boy must build on his desire for his first love object, the little girl on her identification with her first love object. Another way of putting all this is that the little girl must undergo a repression of her active aims (to possess the mother) and the little boy a repression of his passive aims (to be possessed by the father).

This leads on to what Mitchell calls marks of womanhood, the first of which is part and parcel of the dominance given to the little girl's passive aims – women are masochistic (and, of course, passive as well). Part of the problem of this discussion comes from a consideration of the notion of active and passive *aims*. The very notion of an aim implies an active intention, and one can be actively passive (sulking, for example) or passively active (the psychoanalyst's silence as his or her patients free associate perhaps). The woman is also vain – as a result of penis envy and her lack of a penis she unconsciously desires to turn her whole body into a penis by beautifying it, by, perhaps, making it 'stand out'. It is also worth pointing out the bi-sexuality of all this: men also beautify their bodies, and not only in contemporary cultures. There are no such things as 'innocent' ways of adorning or not adorning the body – anything we do to our body has both social and sexual meaning. Finally, women have weaker social interests, not having to internalize the father and the rule of the father in the super-ego.

Mitchell goes on to follow Freud in delineating three paths that the adult woman can follow out of the oedipal development. The path to 'true womanhood' involves the little girl identifying with her mother as she gives up the oedipal desire for her father. As ever, this identifi-cation will possess a degree of ambivalence: she will have been angry with the mother about both her mother's and her own 'castration'. But her identification with her mother will enable her to attract the oedipal male's love for his mother. There are a range of deep psychological and existential factors behind our choice of partners with whom to fall or refrain from falling in love, but one important influence has to do with reworking, or trying to rework, the oedipal and other problems we had with our own parents. Often we look for the solution that we failed to achieve during the oedipal stage: the perfect, uninterrupted love of a woman, on one side, or a man who can grant all wishes and satisfy all desires, on the other. It is only when the bitter disappoint-ment of not finding such a partner is lived through that the real work of adult relationships can begin.

The second course open to a woman is to retain the original love object, the mother, which of course every woman does to some degree, but if the first object is held on to in a determined way, the result is likely to be lesbianism. The other alternative is what Mitchell calls an 'unrestrained' penis envy, the following of male pursuits, the 'masculine woman'.

The outcome of the oedipal stage

There are two ways of thinking about the outcome of the oedipal stage that are still debated within psychoanalysis. The first is that this stage and its resolution produce a new psychic organization very different to what has gone before, and the second is that what goes before mediates progress through the oedipal stage – previous experiences of love, for example, modifying the experiences of hatred appropriate to this stage. The advantage of the first view, as far as I am concerned, is that it emphasizes the power and violence of this stage (Castoriadis 1991); on the other hand it does not take place in a vacuum, and must be affected by previous stages even as it changes their meaning.

There is a tendency, which is shared by Mitchell, to see the identity which emerges from the oedipal stage as fixed and heterosexual, but there are also good reasons to suggest that the psychological bisexuality remains even if it is subordinated to heterosexuality. The main point of all this is 'only' that enough of us end up heterosexual enough of the time to enable the reproduction of the population, not that we all fit into rigid gender stereotypes. In the psychoanalysis of individuals it is apparent that bisexuality remains in all sorts of cross-identifications (Elshtein 1984). The basis for this is there in the negative oedipal complex for the boy and in the suggestion that the little girl can never completely give up her first love object (Chodorow 1978).

However, we are still left with penis envy and the experienced inferiority of little girls, which often seems to be carried into adult life and which Mitchell clearly thinks of as resulting in patriarchy. I would agree in the more limited sense that it reinforces patriarchal relations, but it seems to me that what Freud has to say about penis envy is probably right, and that it is wrong to try to explain it away as simply the result of the little girl's perceptions of the power relationships between mother and father. However, looking forward to the next chapter, if we can think of envy as a normal feature of the psychological life of both sexes, the notion becomes one amongst a number of forms of envy: the little boy will also be envious of the little girl and her potential ability to produce babies; the little girl will be powerful and creative in a way that he is not. My son dealt with this for a while, round about the age of three or four, by insisting that he would have a baby when he grew up. Karen Horney (1993), a second-generation psychoanalyst, suggested a number of modifications to Freud's ideas that, interestingly, have not often been taken up by later analysts, arguing that penis envy was a secondary rather than a primary construct. I tend to think it as more convincing to suggest that Freud did not fully realize the force of envy as a universal human emotion and was therefore unable to identify its importance for the development of both love and hatred for the other sex in both men and women.

5

Klein

Envy, Phantasy and the Development of the Infant

Introduction

The work of Melanie Klein and her followers, which has been influential well beyond the limits of their own grouping, involves modifications and developments of Freud's ideas, but falls firmly within the main psychoanalytic tradition. In the first part of the chapter I will be concerned with Klein's development of Freud's drive theory and in particular her theories of envy and of unconscious phantasy. I will then look at her developmental theory, which involves the notion of positions rather than stages, and some further modifications of Freud's theory, particularly around the concept of the super-ego and the defence mechanisms, and I will discuss some reactions to her ideas. Finally I will look at her concept of internal objects and object-relations as the basis of the development of British psychoanalysis, comparing her work to that of Fairbairn, one of her contemporaries, not only in terms of content but also as an illustration of different ways of theorizing.

Throughout this chapter I will be concerned with the nature of theory in psychoanalysis. I will try to show how Klein developed some Freudian ideas and changed the emphasis of others, adding a complexity to the understanding of the unconscious and in some ways moving the locus of analysis closer to the surface. I do not think that it is helpful to take sides in a Freud vs Klein debate: each understands something important about the psyche.

The death instinct and unconscious phantasy

As I mentioned earlier, Klein (1975b) gave a clinical grounding to the notion of a death instinct. She developed the idea of a 'constitutional' destructive drive, which she saw as being of fundamental importance, referring to it as envy. She defined it in relation to jealousy and greed. If I am greedy, I recognize that what I want is good, and I want to get as much as possible; any harm that it does to others is unintentional – I finish the chocolate for my pleasure not to deprive my partner. If I am jealous, then I again recognize that something is good and I want it for myself – the fact that I might deprive my wife's lover of his pleasure is secondary to my securing an exclusive sexual relationship with her. Envy is different in that it destroys what is good; it is as if I were saying: 'I can never imagine possessing something so good, so I cannot recognize that it is good; my inability to have it would be too painful, therefore I must find some way of devaluing it, spoiling it.'

The classic example of envy is the 'sour grapes' story – the fox jumps up to take a bunch of succulent grapes from the vine, but cannot reach them, so he goes off muttering that, anyway, they were sour. The envious attack can be violent in the extreme – envy is involved in torture and murders that involve mutilation, especially of sexual organs, but it is also involved in everyday comments of the 'It's all right for you' variety, comments that subtly or not so subtly undermine somebody's achievement or something good that has happened to him or her. If my friend tells me he's off to Switzerland for a skiing holiday, my unthinking response is a half-joking 'It's all right for you, some of us have to stay here and keep this organization going', perhaps half-hoping that I might spoil his fun by sending him off feeling guilty. Although it is easy to discuss envy in a sophisticated and humorous way, and often easy to spot it in other people, it is very difficult to recognize and acknowledge in oneself. Its recognition, whether by oneself or another person, can bring the same sort of acute embarrassment as the Freudian slip.

If we stay with Freud, we tend to concentrate on the unconscious as concerning drives and impulses. Klein offers us a way of thinking about basic unconscious processes as related to our bodies in a rather different way (see Isaacs 1952; Klein 1975a, 1975c). The impulses and repression are still there, but the repressed ideas take the form of unconscious phantasies – the spelling distinguishing them from conscious *f*antasies, such as day-dreams. These phantasies use basic bodily processes – eating, defecating, sexual excitement, and so on – as metaphors for our relationships to the outside world and other people. They mark the borderline between the inside and outside world and they also mark the borderline between the body and our unconscious symbolization of its meaning.

We use such metaphors in our everyday language. We might say somebody looks good enough to eat or feel that we are being eaten up by some relationship. People and organizations metaphorically shit on us, and words describing sexual activities are put to use to describe other types of relationships on a regular basis. In the unconscious phantasy there is no awareness of metaphor – the unconscious thinks, feels and fears that these things are really happening. Our emotional reactions can be as much reactions to these phantasies as they are to events in the real world, and a failure to be able to symbolize these phantasies in an adequate, though not necessarily direct, way can be immobilizing. As we shall see in chapter 6, Hanna Segal (1981) talks, for example, of a violinist who could not play in public because of the unconscious identification of performing and masturbating and the unconscious fear of envious attacks that would result.

One of the differences between Klein and Freud is that Klein thought it was possible to treat psychosis – the more dramatic range of mental 'illnesses' – through psychoanalysis, and in the development of Kleinian theory the process of symbolization in this treatment becomes more and more important. The common sense of the psychotherapeutic world seems to concentrate on putting people in touch with their feelings, and conceptual thought is often seen as an avoidance of feeling, an 'intellectualization' or even 'rationalization'. We will see that the work of Wilfred Bion, one of the most creative of the Kleinian thinkers, pays a great deal of attention to the difficulty of thinking, the way in which people often do all they can to avoid serious thought, and will use feelings as a defence against ideas. Part of psychoanalysis is the attempt to shift from the direct expression of emotion to the understanding of emotion, from hitting you because I am angry to telling you – angrily – that I am angry and why.

Klein on early life: narcissism

Another of the differences between Freud and Klein is that whereas Freud talks about developmental stages, Klein talks about positions that emerge during the infant's development but are available through-out life. This is close to the way in which I suggested Freud's stages might be conceived, and in this way we avoid the deterministic picture of development and can see a life in terms of complex interpretations of experience.

Freud sees the early development of sexuality as involving auto-eroticism, the infant seeking satisfaction through its own body (as in thumb sucking), then taking itself as a primary love object. This is a narcissistic stage of development, but for Laplanche and Pontalis (1988) it becomes a structure, rather than or as well as a stage, a structure in which the ego invests more energy in itself than it does in its object. Freud accepted the idea of Karl Abraham, a first-generation German psychoanalyst, that this is what happens in psychosis – in lay-person's terms, when somebody loses touch with what is generally recognized as external reality.

The issue from Freud's position is whether or not narcissism depends upon identification with another or precedes it. This is resolved by distinguishing between what Freud calls '*primary* narcissism', which involves no relationship to the outside world (so intra-uterine existence becomes the archetype for this state), and secondary narcissism, which involves object identification. Laplanche and Pontalis describe the dangers of this view clearly:

> If we pursue this line of thought to the letter, we incur two risks. First, there is the danger of running counter to experience by asserting that the newborn baby is without any perceptual outlet to the outside world. Secondly, we may find ourselves re-opening the door – and in the naivest way – to a version of the idealist fallacy made all the more flagrant by being expressed in 'biological language': just how are we supposed to picture the transition from a monad shut in upon itself to a progressive discovery of the object? (Laplanche and Pontalis 1988: 257)

We can also add to primary and secondary narcissism a 'narcissistic object choice', perhaps a homosexual choice of an object because it resembles oneself. It seems to me that perhaps this type of object choice plays a part in all love relationships.

Evidence from what has become known as pre-natal psychology (Chamberlain 1987) indicates that there is an elementary ego and an elementary object-relating at birth, and if this is the case it leaves the newborn infant with two available positions: absorption into its own internal world and object-relating, with the mother or some part of the mother. As we mature, it becomes a matter of balance. If too much energy is invested in the external world, there is the danger of what Bollas (1987) calls a 'normotic' pathology, whereas investing too much energy in the ego or self runs the risk of narcissistic problems. This is close to Klein's position. She argues that narcissism and object-relations coexist (Klein et al. 1952); this may be regarded as part of her critique of the notion of clear-cut stages of development. She seems to be suggesting that we can find traces of all stages at all times – so indications of an oedipal stage can be identified very early on. I think this fits better with everyday experience and with clinical evidence than the idea that we develop through clear-cut stages. As Hinshelwood (1991) points out, Klein substitutes the notion of narcissistic stages with that of narcissistic states, although, once again, if we think of stages of development as providing layers of the personality that we can deploy or return to at any stage in our lives, the two ways of seeing narcissism are not mutually exclusive. Heimann (in Klein et al. 1952) suggests that for the child the object is always seen as part of oneself, whereas the adult can see the object as having an independent existence, but I think that this is too simple. We shall see that one of the much-needed lessons that Lacan brings to psychoanalysis is that this sort of 'easy' distinction is never satisfactory. However 'mature' we become, the object is always at the same time part of oneself and part of the outside world.

When dealing with children, it is fairly easy to see how the child sees the parent as part of him- or herself and, often, vice versa. When my son was young, I seemed to be at times a portable climbing frame. Sometimes he goes back to using me as a climbing frame, walking into my study, coming up behind my chair and putting his arms round my neck and trying to swing on me. He was at first genuinely surprised that I do not have the same reaction to his fifteen-year-old self (he is now taller than me) doing this as I did to his five- or ten-year-old self. He is treating me as if my external reality were exactly the same as his internal object, which, of course, can still cope with such activity. It is much more difficult for me to see how I treat him or my wife or my friends or my students in the same way. Part of a difficult life experience is to learn that our objects, whether they be people or things, do have a recalcitrant external reality, and we never finally abandon the idea that our objects are part of us; presumably if that were possible we would then lose all connection with the object.

Hanna Segal, probably the best-known contemporary commentator on Klein's work (see Segal 1964, 1979, 1983), points out the connection between narcissism and envy. The contrast is again with Freud, who sees hatred as arising when the infant emerges from primary narcissism to discover the external object on which it might become dependent for its satisfaction. Segal describes Klein's position as making envy and narcissism two sides of the same coin: envy and hatred arise on discovering that the source of goodness and life is outside oneself, and narcissism, the attempt to find satisfaction within oneself, is a defence against both. I think the difference here disappears in the light of my earlier comment that we can be seen as beginning life with an elementary ego and elementary object relationships. For both Freud and Klein the source of envy is the discovery of dependence on the outside object and the existence of a destructive drive, and for both there is a period of fairly intense narcissism, which for Klein defends against hatred. This leads us into Klein's developmental theory.

It is, in Hinshelwood's terms, a theory of developmental stages and of states (Hinshelwood 1991). They are stages in the sense that they are necessary steps by means of which the infant builds its ego, and they are states in that we can, and indeed do, re-enter and move between them in adult life.

Envy and aggression

One of the ways in which it is customary to distinguish between Freud and Klein is to suggest that whereas for Freud sexuality was the 'driving' instinct, for Klein it was aggression – the aggression or hatred against which narcissism defends. For the infant the aggression is directed against the object on which it is dependent for its life, and the development takes place in the attempts to deal with this. Once again it is not an either/or situation – both drives are at work, both leading to their own lines of development that are structured together within the psyche. In practice, the question of which is dominant at any one time can be seen as an empirical matter. It is, however, important to be aware of Klein's conception of aggression to understand her theory of development.

It must be remembered that Klein worked with very young children, and it is arguable that unconscious phantasies are closer to the surface at that stage. I suspect that in many – but by no means all – circles, childhood sexuality is a more readily acceptable

idea than early infantile aggression, and indeed Klein acknowledged that the aggressive phantasies that she attributed to the
young child are difficult to accept. The following passage, which
Hinshelwood also quotes, gives a flavour of the aggressive phantasies that Klein suggests the baby experiences within its first year
of life:

> The child expects to find within the mother (a) the father's penis, (b)
> excrement and (c) children and these things it equates with edible sub-
> stances. According to the child's earliest phantasies (or sexual theories)
> of parental coitus, the father's penis (or his whole body) becomes incor-
> porated in the mother during the act. Thus the child's sadistic attacks
> have for their object both father and mother, who are in phantasy
> bitten, torn, cut or stamped to bits. The attacks give rise to anxiety
> lest the subject should be punished by the united parents, and this
> anxiety also becomes internalized in consequence of the oral-sadistic
> introjection of objects and thus is already directed towards the early
> superego. (Klein 1975c: 219, quoted in Hinshelwood 1991: 50)

Here we have the bodily metaphors and displacements that I discussed earlier, but this time they are put to the use of aggression,
although they are *also* sexual metaphors. The two drives are not
separate but intimately bound together. It is this aggressiveness that
Klein develops into the notion of the death instinct, which she sees
as at its strongest during the first year of life, and which lies at
the root of sadism.

There has been some discussion about how this modifies Freud's
notion of the unconscious. Juliet Mitchell (1986) suggests that by
the time of her later work Klein saw the unconscious as a container
full of contents from which everything emerges, rather than a system
of thought with its own laws. This is a much less precise concept
than Freud's, and whilst it serves Klein's purposes well, we end up
with a less profound theory of psychic depth. If, however, we think
of psychoanalysis as a depth psychology that leads us through more
subtle shadings of levels than unconscious, preconscious and conscious, we can place phantasy at a level between unconscious and
preconscious. Its contents are the product of the unconscious system
– rather like a deeper level of dreaming – but not yet preconscious in
the way that some earlier commentators on Klein suggested. I shall
suggest in the conclusion to this chapter that there are other ways in
which Klein's work lays the foundation for moving even closer to
consciousness.

The paranoid-schizoid position

This brings us to the first developmental position: the paranoid-schizoid position. The infant has both good and bad experiences, and both types of experience come from the inside and the outside world. Hinshelwood (1991), in his excellent commentary on these ideas, points out that for Klein the ego was not just the controller or organizer of instinctual gratification but also developed through this function an experience of itself, of what might now be called its reflexivity. Later object-relations theorists often seem to talk about this process as conscious or near conscious, but I think that Klein is talking about a profoundly unconscious process. Insofar as the infant is aware of what is happening, it is an object not a subject of the experiences.

The basic anxiety of the nascent ego is of being fragmented (as an adult I would talk about feeling that I was falling apart or going to pieces). The fragmentation would come as a result of persecution either from an internal or from an external source. As the infant's destructiveness is projected into the outside world, it is experienced in turn as a threat from the outside world. We enter a vicious circle: the more I attempt to expel the threat from my self, the more threatening the outside world becomes. The paranoid-schizoid position is so called because I split my experience into good and bad and expel or project the bad into the outside world (the schizoid element) and then experience the outside world as persecuting me (the paranoid element). The ego develops not only in handling the instinctual drive, as Freud thought, but also in handling these persecutory anxieties, of which the fear of fragmentation is the most basic.

It is appropriate here to talk briefly about the notion of *projective identification*, a Kleinian modification of the notion of projection: it is not just that I locate some part of myself in the other person, but I call out that particular feeling in the other person. An adult example would be when a patient (while still coming to sessions) insists that the treatment is useless and the analyst does not know what he or she is talking about; the analyst begins to experience the feeling of desperation and uselessness – or the sense of falling apart or of persecution that the patient him- or herself is experiencing. Anybody who has looked after a screaming baby and been aware of his or her own feelings might recognize this; it is a primitive form of communication, pre-linguistic in origin and very basic.

The developing ego alternates between achieving a degree of integration and experiencing a process of fragmentation. Its success in achieving a reasonable degree of integration depends, for Klein, not only on the sort of care the baby receives but also on its constitutional strength. Kleinians sometimes talk about the 'good' breast and the 'bad' breast, as part of the splitting; sometimes a real baby will favour only one breast, but Klein was talking about the phantasy breast. Bion (1962) elaborates on this in a helpful way: the bad breast is actually the emptiness, the pain of not being fed or being fed badly – it is experienced as a positive internal pain and persecutory threat and must be ejected from the body. However, once this happens, of course, it becomes an external persecutory threat.

The basis of persecution is always the infant's own destructive drives projected into the outside world, and thus experienced as being directed against it. The life instinct must struggle against this in order to achieve integration. Kleinian thought has many subtleties, but here I am primarily concerned to get across the general framework. In terms of development at this stage problems arise because objects are not reintegrated back into the ego (a task that often faces the individual in later life during psychoanalysis); integration in the infant can result in feelings of omnipotence – the ego cannot distinguish itself from its objects.

I think there is a sense in which we all, to a greater or lesser degree, maintain the fluctuations of the paranoid-schizoid stage throughout our lives, although if we are lucky it is never quite as dramatic as it is for the young infant, and we never experience persecution in quite the same way. There is a sense in which what we might call madness (a term I prefer to mental illness) lies at the basis of our personalities and we have recourse to some later modification of the position in our everyday lives. People go through something like this experience when a close relationship breaks up – we might experience an ex-partner as both responsible for the break-up (it was his/her fault) and as persecuting us (chasing us through the law courts, trying to deny us access to possessions or to children). The more I am caught up in this position, the less able I am to re-establish communication and separate some grasp of external reality from my paranoid-schizoid perceptions. It is important to remember that such a separation can never be complete. There is truth in the old joke that just because you're paranoid, it doesn't mean that they're not after you. And there is truth in its converse – just because they're after you, it doesn't mean that you're not paranoid.

An even more serious point that is worth thinking about at this stage is our fascination with those who act out the more brutal aggressive phantasies that Klein attributes to the human unconscious: the serial murderers, those who mutilate the sexual organs of their victims, and those who torture. If we accept Klein's view of what we repress into the unconscious, it is perhaps less of a surprise when people who might be recognizably like ourselves, honest upright citizens, become, in the right circumstances, torturers, concentration camp guards or ethnic cleansers. What is going on here is the attempt to deal with one's intense persecutory anxieties by trying to destroy those in whom one has lodged them.

One of the differences between Freud and Klein is not only that she sees signs of the oedipal stage at a much earlier age but that she also sees the super-ego as developing earlier; the early super-ego is powerful and irrational, a result of the death instinct being turned in against the self. We develop phantasies of idealized parents and of purely evil parents and both images can be persecutory, the idealized image because we can never live up to it and the evil image because of the murderous intents that are directed towards us. These phantasies are introjected into our psyche at a very early stage; one is attached to the libido and the other to the death instinct. In this case it easier than it is in the Freudian framework to see why the super-ego should also threaten as well as protect and help the ego in its task.

Klein (1975a, 1975c) went on to suggest that as these primitive images were compared with what one hopes will be a more benign parental reality, the destructive strength of the super-ego might be modified, but it is important to understand that the irrational figures remain more or less strong in all of us, however good or bad the behaviour of our real parents.

The depressive position

Returning to these positions as stages rather than states, Klein's argument is that as the ego gains in strength through the fluctuations of the paranoid-schizoid position, through the strength of the infant's constitution and through the effects of good, or at least non-damaging, parenting, so it is able to reintegrate more and more of its projections, or, more accurately, its projective identifications, into itself. Crudely: instead of trying to make my mother feel awful, I begin to allow myself to feel awful. The depressive position develops as the child becomes able to relate to the *whole* object not just a part: the mother and not the breast. Later object-relations theorists sometimes talk as if a complete integration is possible, but there are very good reasons why this is not the case, and these will be discussed later.

In the depressive position the split between the good object and the bad object is lessened. Much of Klein's earlier work is concerned with aggression and what happens to bad internal objects, but when she develops the theory of the depressive position she begins to think about the good internal object and how that is experienced. The implication of the paranoid-schizoid position is that there is a split between the good and bad objects and in phantasy the bad objects are expelled from the psyche and fragmented. In the depressive position the ego is strong enough to bring the bits back together and reintegrate them into a whole object that is both good and bad. While the split is there, there is a constant movement between the idealization of the good object (oneself – a narcissistic state) and a hatred of the absolutely bad object. It is possible to see these things in adult life and in the movement of the culture, the regular transformation of heroes and villains.

The depressive position, then, involves recognizing the whole object, which has both good and valuable qualities, and also bad, possibly even persecutory, qualities. I also recognize the same ambivalence in myself: I am no longer the omnipotent and perfect object of my own love; I can recognize some of my own destructiveness, the dangers of my own envy. As we shall see, this is a significant developmental position, and it is also a position that we move into regularly in adult life: when, for example, I cannot help but acknowledge that a particular failure was my own fault, or when I realize that my rage or anger has led me needlessly to hurt somebody I love, or simply when I realize that I am an ordinary person.

As a developmental stage, the depressive position develops a new capacity for or ability to love; concern for the other person becomes less a matter of one's own gratification – although that is still present – and more a concern for the whole person and his or her interests. I can love the other person despite his or her faults or failings (especially failure to satisfy my needs), or even, in some cases, because of them, and this enables a comparative psychological stability.

This moves the child towards a third internal struggle: after learning about its drives and its destructiveness, it has to devote energy towards maintaining the internal good object, which is perhaps always threatened by rage and envy. If I have a furious row with somebody I love, and I say all sorts of cruel and destructive things, it might very well leave that person feeling hurt and desolate, but it can also leave me feeling hurt and desolate, not necessarily because of what the other person said (because as I calm down I can begin to understand that part of it), but because I have damaged or even wrecked my own sense of internal goodness. It can sometimes take days, if not longer, to repair this sense.

There are two developments that come with achieving the depressive position. The first arises from what Klein calls the 'depressive anxieties', which are fears of the death instinct, of the rage. If the rage is projected outwards, I suffer a persecutory anxiety, the fear that others are out to destroy me; the depressive anxiety proper is my fear of my ability to destroy the loved object, which perhaps we experience most often as guilt. We can retreat from this position into the paranoid position or develop manic or obsessional defences.

These defences protect one against the recognition both of one's own inadequacy and of one's own destructiveness. They are defences against entering into the depressive position. I find it difficult not to think of the manic defences as purely negative, in the sense that they always inhibit growth, but it should be remembered that, like all defences, they inhibit growth in order to protect what is there to grow. All defences serve a useful purpose as well as an inhibiting purpose.

Klein (1985) suggested that the manic defences grew out of the obsessive defences, although Hinshelwood (1991) questions this link. What is common to both is a sense of omnipotent control of the world: the manic defence carries the feeling of 'I can do anything'. I think of the obsessive defences as magical attempts to control the world through repetitive actions: washing one's hands every few minutes, for example. At their worst, these defences, like most of the others, can make everyday life impossible. I generally feel that I am in control of the world if my newly clean shirts are hung at the left end of the row of shirts in the wardrobe, but I am pleased to say that I am only momentarily upset if they are hung at the other end. If when I found them out of order I had to rewash every one, then it would be time to worry.

Where manic defences are concerned, I think it is true to say that the sense of control is closer to consciousness and very strong. Klein seems to regard this as the main feature of a manic defence, and perhaps that implies that the threat is all the greater. A truly manic person can be very persuasive, and it is easy to get drawn into his or her fantasies. Several decades ago I was almost persuaded by a manic friend that it would be a good idea for the two of us to break into a local army base, steal a tank and drive it through the streets of South London in support of peace and nuclear disarmament. In phenomenological terms the manic person seems to experience a speeding up of the mind, a racing, and the fear is of running out of control. Hence the need to assert a phantasized control. The attempt to control is important and involves disparagement and/or contempt as a central element – I know everything about what is happening and you are an ignorant pig. If I am omnipotent, I cannot allow myself to be dependent on anything. The good things in the outside world or in the internal world threaten to make me dependent upon them and so I subject them to an envious attack: they are not as good as they seem, the grapes are sour. And I can do anything, I can find much sweeter grapes.

Paradoxically as well as disparagement and contempt there is also an idealization. Idealization protects the very object that the disparagement threatens, and the envious attack arouses feelings of guilt or concern. It becomes important to protect some absolutely wonderful object. The anxiety of entering an educational institution, which always carries the possibility of failure, can be handled by an idealization of a teacher; similarly entry into therapy might be accompanied by the idealization of the therapist. Such idealizations are always subject to radical and sudden inversions. In my clinical experience the use of manic defences is important and understandable. The invitation that the therapist offers the patient is to suffer in a way that he or she has been avoiding, possibly for decades.

If the depressive anxieties can be managed, the infant develops the ability to make reparation; it is, if you like, a 'healthy' way of dealing with the anxiety. Reparation, as I understand it, is *primarily* an internal act. What I do over the period in which I recover from a major row with somebody I love is to restore the internal good object – this makes it sound intentional but I do not think it is that conscious. If there is a sufficient period of quiet, if neither of us resurrects the argument, then there comes a point when I feel ready to apologize, and this is independent of whether I think I was right or wrong. There comes a point when I want to make things better, but before I can try to do it in the outer world, I have to do it in the inner world. Some goodness needs to remain, and that can be developed. Guilt is the motivation of reparation, but I think that it should be distinguished from the action that tries to dispel guilt or the need to feel guilt. Reparation involves the recognition of guilt.

I could, for example, try to remove my guilt by trying to deny my rage – by claiming that I didn't mean what I said, when in fact when I said it I meant it, or by denying that I meant to hurt, when that was the very reason I said it. Or I might try to blame my rage on some external factor – stress at work – or some physical condition – I had a headache, or I was tired – when there can be no causal relation or necessary connection between a physical state and the words that came out of my mouth. None of this is reparation; that involves acknowledging my own destructiveness – yes I meant to hurt when I said that and I meant what I said when I said it, but I now regret behaving like that. Reparation attempts to repair, not to deny. I think it is the acknowledgement that is important; the paradox is that trying to deny one's destructiveness is, in my personal and clinical experience, more likely to increase its dangers.

There is another important development involved in the depressive position, and this connects with some earlier themes. The depressive position is a matter of loss, and especially loss of the idealized good object of the earlier narcissistic stage. It involves a process of mourning; the lost idealized internal object has to be replaced by a more realistic and therefore stronger internal object. This involved Klein in a major development in the theory of mourning. In *Mourning and Melancholia* (1984c) Freud presented a sort of energy-flow model of mourning. Energy that has been invested in another person who then dies is withdrawn into the self and leads to a period of withdrawal from the world. There is to begin with a constant testing and retesting of reality until the ego has to accept that the loved one has really gone, and then slowly it becomes possible to re-cathect to another object. The 'pathological' form of mourning is melancholia, where the psyche attempts to keep the loved one alive inside and therefore cannot reconnect to the outside world and form other relationships.

Abraham (1927) suggested that this internalization of the lost object was normal and not pathological, and what made the difference was the ability to internalize the lost person as a good object. The critical issue here is ambivalence and the degree of hostility to the lost loved one, and this theory slips easily into Klein's work (Klein

1986). The depressive position, although it is a very significant developmental step, is not necessarily a happy position. Like mourning, it involves the recognition of loss, and, at least to some degree, its acceptance. The first reactions against loss are the manic defences – instead of accepting my powerlessness I insist that I am all-powerful. In developmental terms I retreat to the primitive splitting of the paranoid-schizoid position, defending against the external persecution by imagining my absolute power. The acceptance is a slow and complex psychological process that is perhaps never achieved. Even those of us who have had 'good enough' childhoods will find ourselves feeling mysterious resentments about the way our parents treated us or let us down.

This model of mourning, involving a battle to restore the good object, can become a model for life itself, which from the moment of birth is a process of separation and loss and the struggles to internalize some reasonably good object from this loss. Perhaps one way of looking at the process of ageing is that it is a matter of leaving things behind in the outside world but carrying them on with us in the internal world, and in the later stages of ageing the internal world expands as those areas of the external world that are significant to us become fewer and fewer. The first real act of mourning is the loss of the ideal object. Or perhaps it should be 'ideal objects' – the ideal self and the ideal mother and the real object as they are replaced by an internal symbolization.

As a developmental stage, the depressive position opens the way to understanding the self and the outside world, of experiencing concern and love for others and a willingness to engage with others in the world. Care, the desire to make reparation, balances the strength of the punitive super-ego, but, contra Hinshelwood (1991), does not replace it.

It is an important dimension since it raises the possibility of moral choice and moral argument, a degree of freedom in the way we behave. The capacity for concern and for reparation refers to internal processes that might have external as well as internal consequences. It is conceivable, for example, that following the row with my partner, I might be able to restore the inner good object, and the lesson that I then learn from the argument is that I can take avoiding action, deal with my rage in a different way. This widens my choice, or perhaps rather it inserts a narrow degree of choice where before I was overwhelmed with rage. It means that the more I am able to restore the good object, the more choice I have about letting my rage run its course. And this choice is a moral one – there can be circumstances where I decide it is right to let myself rage against my partner and circumstances where it is wrong, and there will still be occasions where I seem to have no control or choice about my rage.

It does mean, however, that there is an important internal process that can intervene between the treatment one receives from the outside world and the way one reacts to that treatment. People can be subjected to the most appalling treatment yet still maintain a generosity of heart against all the odds. As I write this, I am by coincidence reading a book called *The Boys: Triumph over Adversity* by Martin Gilbert, a history of a group of Jewish children who survived the ghettos, concentration camps, labour camps and forced marches of the Second World War. The following story is particularly relevant:

> Jack Rubinfeld was sixteen when the Americans reached Ludwigslust, where he had been taken during an eight-day rail journey from a slave labour camp near Berlin. 'They just dropped us there like living dead,' he recalled. 'No food. Lice eating us alive. Some Russian prisoners started eating dead human corpses. Prisoners were dropping like flies. I could hardly walk any more. We were just lying on a dirt floor and dying slowly. One morning after a week or more, we realised that the Americans had arrived. A jeep with two soldiers entered the camp and we realised we were free.
>
> A few days later, walking down a road near the camp, Jack Rubinfeld picked up two loaves of bread from an abandoned railway freight car. 'A German woman with two small children approached me asking for food. She said they had not eaten for a day. I looked around, ashamed to let my friends see. I broke off half a loaf and gave it to them.' This was, he reflected fifty years later, 'a decisive moment, showing my inability to seek vengeance'. (Gilbert 1996: 244)

There are several such stories. The language of psychoanalysis would only offer an inadequate translation of these occurrences, but I hope my point is clear.

In defence of Klein

Melanie Klein's work comes in for more criticism from other psychoanalysts than one might expect. It seems to bring out a particular sharpness that is not there in people's attitudes to the Jungians or other groups whose origins lay in more dramatic splits with Freud. It might be that some of this reaction comes from the bitterness of the debates between the Freudians and the Kleinians in the 1940s – this is what happens when human beings gather around important ideas to which they are intellectually and emotionally committed. The division and conflict are also part of normal institutional dynamics as people compete for position and resources. Yet I think that there is another dimension since these battles are now long past in what seems to be a lasting organizational compromise. I would suggest that it is because Klein, like Freud before her, is telling us things that we don't want to hear, the things that we dislike most about our possibilities. Like Freud, she attacks our desire for innocence; we are not just sexual but violent and cruel beings who cannot compensate for our hatred with a fairytale world where everything is possible and where we hurt no one, and we ourselves are not hurt.

Neville Symington suggests that perhaps we should think of a third position that follows on the depressive position, and that he calls the 'tragic position'. He describes the development of a particular patient:

> A deep realization came that the deficiency in her early caring could not be attributed to her mother or father's fault alone and that she was not responsible for it altogether either. There had been other factors beyond the control of mother or father: an economic crisis in the country they lived in meant that her father had to go abroad for employment. This caused many of the difficulties suffered by the father, mother, and all the family, including my patient. It was this realization that brought my patient in touch with the tragic: an integral part of *la condition humaine* and extremely difficult to bear. I believe that the depressive and paranoid-schizoid positions are a defence against this deeper abyss of non-meaning. (Symington 1986: 276)

I have spent some time thinking about this because my gut reaction is both sympathetic and critical. I have a different understanding of the term 'tragic'. My first problem with the idea is that it can be easily read as an avoidance of the conflicts and pain that Klein talks about. Many patients start therapy with at least an intellectual recognition that not much could have been done to change their family situation although they still have a long way to go before that can be recognized on an emotional level. A premature resort to this position can enable the avoidance of a range of contradictory feelings and ideas that we attach to our parents and it is important to allow ourselves to recognize these contradictions and their emotional difficulties if we are to change. But even the emotional recognition of this does not seem to me to carry dangers of slipping into an abyss of non-meaning – the patient's story is saturated with human meaning.

I think that Symington's implication is that the tragic is something we can do nothing about, but there is another sense of the term conveyed in Lucien Goldmann's book on Pascal and Racine, *The Hidden God* (1970). Tragedy in this study is to be caught between two conflicting forces both stronger than oneself and neither of which can be renounced. If God retreats from sight in the world yet I cannot give up my belief, how do I live such an impossible situation? If I was born into the wrong period of history, or to the wrong parents, if my life is wrong, how do I live it? To a greater or lesser degree all our lives are wrong: the human condition is an impossible condition; that is the tragedy, which is not a depth of un-meaning but the beginning of meaning, and what Symington described is a transformation of the way in which this patient produces meaning, the way in which we live an impossible situation internally and externally, and forge meanings from it, simply because it is impossible. Behind this there must always be a backcloth of meaninglessness, but the human condition is to be condemned to produce meaning in a meaningless world.

Symington also makes a point about Melanie Klein's style, which I would like to take up because I think it raises a difficult but important point about the nature of theory and its relationship to practice in psychoanalysis. He argues that 'the quality of the object is not considered sufficiently'. I will quote his argument in full, and I will include his quotation from Klein – which he does not reference:

> . . . I want to start by drawing your attention to the quality of Klein's language:
>
> > If the undisturbed enjoyment of being fed is frequently experienced, the introjection of the good breast comes about with relative security.
>
> Cast in that language this sentence does not have emotional meaning for me but in the following form it does:

> If the undisturbed enjoyment in being fed is frequently experienced, the child takes in the mother's love for him, and he feels secure in his possession of it. (Symington 1986: 274)

I would agree that there is a significant difference between the two sentences, but it is a difference between a theoretical statement and a statement that is closer to a descriptive comment that can be used in a clinical situation. It is important, if we are thinking theoretically, to distinguish between a conceptual language and a descriptive language. A concept might be difficult but it is not jargon; it brings together a number of different elements into a relationship within the one word. A description, on the other hand, simply says what something is like. It does not add to our observational knowledge of our object.

Now in the quotation from Klein there is what might be called a conceptual statement about the introjection of the good breast, which Symington translates as 'taking in the mother's love'. I think that there is a world of difference between the two formulations. Introjection is a much stronger idea than 'taking in'. I 'take things in' all the time: I take in what I read, what people say to me, and so on. 'Taking in' is a phrase used to denote 'understand', not something which is absorbed as a part of myself that I can experience inside me, which is the meaning of introjection. And it is not love, a feeling, that I am introjecting: all one can do with a feeling is feel it. It is the very source of life itself that I take in as something inside myself, and that I can draw on to enable me to experience the love I am given. The good breast is not the love itself, it is what makes it possible to experience love. Most important of all, in Klein's conceptual framework, the introjection of the good breast implies a relationship to the bad breast, something that is completely absent from Symington's translation. He manages to lose the most important primary metaphorical link by means of which we begin to be able to think about the world.

A theory is an account of structures and mechanisms (Symington doesn't like Klein's emphasis on mechanisms) as opposed to the qualities of objects. Qualities, however, are specific to specific objects, not something that can be described in advance by a theory. Face to face with the patient, I am concerned with the quality and specificity of that patient, and with saying something that the patient can understand in everyday language. When I am theorizing, I use a conceptual framework that enables me to make links that go beyond the specific experience of one patient and lead towards an elaborated general theory of the psyche.

Internal objects

People often question the psychoanalytic use of the term 'objects', particularly since most of the time it seems to refer to people (see, for example, Dworkin 1981); when Freud talks about 'object choice' in his theory of sexuality, he is usually talking about the person, or at least the sort of person, to whom we direct our sexual desires. The argument is that the use of 'objects' in this context objectifies people, takes away their personhood or free will.

It is certainly the case that there is a creditable moral rule that we should not treat people as objects, and we should by and large try not to do so in our conscious life; but even at this level of analysis, people are objects of our consciousness, and we are subjects of our consciousness. When I look at you, I am the subject and you are the object of my gaze. The notion of other people being our objects is inherent in language (we are the subjects and objects of verbs) and in actions including looking (we are subjects and objects of deeds). We cannot avoid being objects in this sense, and that would be sufficient to justify the psychoanalytic use of the term; but there are stronger senses in which we take each other as objects.

The first stronger sense is that we take people as the objects of our desire, and since the unconscious dimensions of that desire demand immediate satisfaction, there is a dimension to any relationship that takes the other person purely and simply as a means to satisfaction. Part of any relationship in which we have an emotional involvement is an internal struggle to modify that desire. During infancy in particular, but throughout our lives, we need these objects, and when we lose them, when, for example, we lose the breast when we are being weaned, or, even earlier, when we lose the security of the mother's womb, or later we lose the security of the mother's uninterrupted presence during our waking hours, we introject the object, take it (in phantasy) inside us where we can have permanent recourse to it. We have seen that this is what Freud saw as the 'stuff' of the ego and, later, the super-ego.

The second stronger sense has to do with the notion of internal objects, which becomes more complex in Klein's work. While Klein herself is rather more than an object-relations theorist, her work contributed significantly towards that theory's development. I think Hinshelwood (1991) is wrong when he says that for Freud the object was simply the object of an instinct – it is, already, after introjection, part of the mental representation of the drive, and this is Klein's starting point. For Klein, internal objects are the constituents of our unconscious phantasies and our relationships to them are motivated by the drives: by love, envy, the desire for reparation, and so on.

Hinshelwood (1991) points out that these internal objects are perceived by the infant as the causes of physical pain and pleasure. Initially, because of the undeveloped perceptual abilities of the infant, they are part objects – a breast, for example. Abraham (1927) talked about a patient who had fantasies of biting off parts of the people he loved (clearly they looked good enough to eat), and I used to play a game with my own infant son of eating parts of each other's body, then regurgitating them and restoring them to their rightful owner. Whole objects develop, all being well, with the physical maturation of the infant. Internal objects for Klein are good or bad. We will each carry good parental objects and bad parental objects within ourselves, and although they might be modified by our experience in the external world, they remain more or less good and more or less bad. Sometimes we can overcome the splitting involved here, which I think is certainly connected with the life and death instincts, and grasp the whole object that is both good and bad. As we have seen, this plays an important part in Klein's theory of development.

Our internal objects charge our perception of external objects – I can, if I am lucky, differentiate between the feelings generated by my mother as an internal object, which are frequently a matter of fear and anger at being dominated by a large powerful woman, and feelings generated by my mother as a little old lady standing in front of me and arousing a combination of tenderness and irritation. Sometimes I find myself reacting to her in one way and sometimes I find myself reacting to her in the other, each of which produces difficulties of either guilt or frustration, and sometimes I can manage to understand both perceptions, which does not so much avoid the difficult feelings as make them more bearable.

Object-relations

One of the results of the debates around Melanie Klein's work was the emergence within the British Psychoanalytic Society of a group that became known as the 'Independent Group' or the 'British

School', whose approach has been marked by a more or less complete break from instinct theory (Greenberg and Mitchell 1983; Guntrip 1961; Kohon 1986). In this quotation from Guntrip – a major post-Second World War object-relations theorist – we see psychoanalysis portrayed as almost a simple socialization theory; the internal psychodynamic processes described up to this point become simply a 'complication':

> The inner and outer worlds have a two-way causal and reciprocal influence. The kind of relationships parents set up with the child, complicated by the child's own reactions to the situation, are internalised by the growing psychic structure and later on will be compulsively externalised again and reimposed on situations in the outer social world, or else they will be rediscovered in outer situations which correspond in some way to inner ones. (Guntrip 1961: 360)

This will become an important line of criticism in Part II. I have argued elsewhere (Craib 1989) that it is possible, indeed it makes very good sense, to combine both drive and object-relations theory. This is for two reasons: first, drives can help us understand why we invest such emotional energy in and introject objects or part-objects; second, one of the achievements of Freud's thought was to open up the relation between the biological and the psychological, whereas object-relations theory tends to leave the biological behind.

As with other theoretical disputes, I think it is a matter of the level of analysis. We move with object-relations theorists from the deepest of the underlying psychic structures, which are constituted by the most powerfully cathected, introjected objects of the drives, through to objects introjected at levels closer to consciousness; we move towards a phenomenology of the self. Another of the originators of object-relations theory, Ronald Fairbairn (1952), based his ideas on drive theory and provides a useful bridge here.

Fairbairn's most important work was carried out in the 1930s and 1940s, mostly in isolation. He lived and worked in Edinburgh, which even then was not a sufficient reason to be isolated, but in Britain the psychoanalytic establishment has always been firmly London-based, and those living outside of London seem to be regarded rather as poor relations. Rayner (1990) describes him as the most systematic thinker to influence British psychoanalysis since Freud.

Fairbairn suggests that, to begin with, everything is subordinated to the infant's libidinal satisfaction with its mother. This is not basically different from Freud, but tends to be taken for granted (as it does in the work of a number of object-relations theorists), and in that sense to lose its import. It also loses its import in that Fairbairn began to look for other sources of satisfaction. He suggests that everybody has a number of egos, and the basic units of psychic structures are ego–object relations, which have an emotional charge. He seems to have abandoned the id as a source of energy and fragmented the ego, suggesting that a separate ego is attached to every drive in an intricate feedback system. We see in Fairbairn the beginning of the movement that later object-relations theorists took much further. The most important feature of psychic life became relationships with others; to begin with, the infant with the mother. Rayner puts this well, distinguishing Fairbairn's position from Klein's:

> Neither psychological nor physiological drives took precedence. In both cases the primary process reigned supreme at unconscious levels. For Fairbairn the experience of intimacy with the mother was paramount; feeding satisfaction from her breast was, at times, secondary to this. His view was the reverse of Klein's. She saw greed for the maternal breast as primary. For [Fairbairn] this greed could often largely be a consequence of loss of intimacy with the mother. (Rayner 1990: 147)

Some considerations on theory

I do not want to pursue these differences too far. Like many theoretical differences between academics and scientists of all sorts, such debates too easily become invested with a personal energy and a concern to be 'correct' rather than to understand whatever part of the world is being considered; psychoanalysts are no less immune to these human fallibilities than anyone else. As in so many other cases, it seems to me more a matter of deciding what level of analysis and what stage of development we are looking at. There is a tension in psychoanalytic work, which I have already noted in my discussion of Klein and Symington, between theoretical levels of analysis, the understanding of individual patients, and the way of working preferred by individual analysts. The tension is between the generalization of theory and the specificity of individual meanings and psychodynamic processes between individuals. One of the accusations levelled at psychoanalysis by upholders of the more traditional understanding of science is that it is not possible to make wide theoretical generalizations from individual case studies. They are of course quite right, but many psychoanalysts continue to write as if it were possible, as if psychoanalytic theory provides causal explanations of individual phenomena.

I am trying to argue throughout this book that psychoanalytic theory provides tools of understanding rather than tools of explanation. The adequacy of the theory then depends, on the one hand, on its own internal coherence and economy and, on the other, on whether it offers us tools that are sufficiently subtle and flexible to make some sense of what is going on between two people, or perhaps eight or nine people, as they sit together in a room. In this sense a theory is like a relief map, and the more detailed the map, the smaller the area through which we can find our way with its help. Now it seems to me that if we look at the work of Klein and Freud and a number of later theorists, they are struggling to develop the overall general map. The danger at this end of the enterprise is dogmatism and the rejection of innovative and useful ideas. On the other hand, many object-relation theorists are writing as if they are trying to map in detail a small hamlet on the wider map – that is, the events between one patient and one analyst. To use this level of theory to map another hamlet requires adapting the details of the first map to suit a new and different therapist/patient relationship. Thus, for example, on those all too rare moments when I am sufficiently open and sensitive to what is going on in the consulting room, I find myself drawing on and using in my own way some comment I had come across in, say, Winnicott's work. Winnicott would probably not recognize himself in my use of his insight, and my use might never be relevant to another occasion. The danger at this end of the continuum is that of fragmentation and a negative incoherence.

Conclusion: Object-relations and drive theory

I mentioned earlier that Freud had comparatively little to say about the development of object-relations and it was left to Klein, and later to the British object-relations school, to develop this side of psychoanalysis. I also suggested that object-relations and drive theories are not mutually exclusive, that we can only understand what happens to the drives if we understand the object-relations in which they are implicated; and we can only understand object-relations if they are seen in the context of id impulses. As we shall see over the following chapters, the development of object-relations theory adds many new dimensions to psychoanalysis but perhaps distracts attention from some of its more fundamental ideas. This is less true of the Kleinian tradition than it is of some of the later object-relations theories.

Part II

Divergent Paths

If one were to pay attention even to some of the informed public debates about psychoanalysis, one would imagine that the whole business began and ended with Freud. I hope that Part I was sufficient to indicate that Freud was only the beginning, and that even before his death, significant developments had taken place. Since the end of the Second World War the developments have proceeded apace. I suspect that it is not possible, at least in the space of one small volume, to do justice to the full range of psychoanalytic theories and practices that are now around, so I am concentrating instead on the main blocs, which coincide, almost but not quite, with national boundaries and the intellectual traditions into which psychoanalysis developed after Hitler's rise to power. These very different traditions provided the soil in which very different forms of psychoanalysis could grow.

I will employ as an organizing principle the critical apparatus that I tried to construct in Part I; and I will develop another, which I only mentioned in passing in the introduction. The first apparatus is the depth of the analysis – whether the approach works at the same deeper levels of Freud and Klein, or it moves towards the surface of the experience, to the conscious and preconscious, perhaps losing touch with the deeper levels of the unconscious. The second apparatus is the extent to which each contributes, in its implications, to restricting our conception of internal space. There is one example of this near the end of chapter 5, in the quote from Guntrip describing an object-relations view of the relationship between the internal and the external world, where the role of the internal world is marginalized.

In chapter 6 I will follow through the development of Kleinian psychoanalysis. There are a number of important theorists who have worked at the same depth as Klein and opened up interesting possibilities, not least in our understating of symbolization, thinking and aesthetics, not to mention group processes. In chapter 7 I will look at the development of object-relations theory, particularly in relation to infancy, and I will argue that it moves closer to a surface phenomenology of the self and in some cases offers a view of human development that can underplay the place of internal space. In chapter 8 I will look at what has become known as attachment theory in Britain, developed in part against Kleinian psychoanalysis, and self psychology in the United States; the latter has clear similarities to ego psychology. These approaches move closer to the surface and tend explicitly to limit the importance of internal space. In chapter 9 I will discuss Lacanian psychoanalysis – possibly the most original of the modern variants – which paradoxically takes us back to Freud and the importance of internal conflicts and the centrality of internal space.

Finally, in chapter 10 I will look at the way in which feminists have taken up the ideas from the different psychoanalytic schools: the more orthodox Freudian, the object-relations school and Lacanian psychoanalysis. This is important because of the significance that feminist interpretations of Freud have had in spreading psychoanalytic ideas way beyond the boundaries of professional psychoanalysis and for the light they throw on the differences between the schools.

6

The Later Kleinians
Symbol Formation, Thinking and Organizations

In this chapter I want to follow through the development of Kleinian ideas in the second half of the twentieth century. There are two
significant lines of development: most of the chapter will focus on the
development of the theory of symbolization, and in particular the
work of Wilfred Bion; the second line of development, the psychoanalytic understanding of groups and organizations, also draws on
Bion's work but will take up less space here, although it has possibly
had more influence in the outside world.

Behind most of what I have to say here lurks the central
motivating idea that I mentioned in the introduction: psychoanalysis, and any worthwhile psychotherapy, is not only or even
primarily about feelings. In my clinical practice I find people coming
for psychotherapy when they are well defended against their
feelings, and my sense is that my first task is to try to find some
way of enabling them to get in touch with their emotional life. This
is easier said than done. Sometimes I feel that such people would
be better off with a Gestalt therapist, at least to begin with, but
once again I am privileged to be working with groups; there
will usually be people in the group who can help in this task
more effectively than I can. At this stage, in this sort of case, the
focus is on feelings, and often on the highly sophisticated ways
in which such a person might use his or her intellectual powers
to avoid recognizing underlying feelings, to maintain what
Bollas calls a 'normotic state'. However, if such a person succeeds

in getting in touch with some underlying feelings, the main task is only just beginning.

Another person might seek therapy precisely because he is in touch with his feelings and as a consequence he thinks that there is something wrong with him. People can seek medical or psychiatric help because they are experiencing all the symptoms of grief or depression, having lost a close relation, or because they experience anger or depression when those feelings are intelligible responses to a situation, or part of the routine ebb and flow of emotional life. In many cases the worry that 'these feelings are abnormal' translates into the tentative question 'Am I strong enough to bear these feelings?' coupled with 'Will I be punished for having them?' Clearly there is a different task here, also focused on feeling. But in this case the raw material is already available to the patient.

There is a third example, that of somebody who is not only fully in touch with her feelings but often feels completely swamped by them, finding it difficult or sometimes impossible to control rage or desire or sadness, often finding that feelings knock her off the course of her everyday routines. Once again the therapy is 'about' feelings and the raw material is there in no uncertain terms. That is also the case with the person who fits into none of the above categories, but is absorbed with and in her own feelings and takes endless delight in exploring and expressing them.

Whichever of these directions one comes from, emotions seem to be there at the centre, but it is what *happens* to the feelings that matters. The prime aim of therapy is not to get rid of the bad feelings and start feeling good about oneself, nor is it a matter of receiving a reparative love from the therapist, learning to express one's feelings, discover and express one's needs, become more or less assertive, discover the inner child, or learning to control one's feelings, although all these things and more might describe what happens in the course of therapy.

I would suggest that one way to embrace all these things and to take them further is to talk about self-knowledge and self-understanding. Our feelings might abate or intensify as we become aware of the world in different ways, but the most important change will be in the way we relate to our feelings, the ways in which we do or do not take them into account in our daily activities. But to be able to achieve anything in psychotherapy, one needs to be able to learn, to become open to new knowledge and to be able to think.

Freud and the *fort/da* game

There are two ways in which we can approach these issues in the context of Freud's work: the first is from what Freud has to say about symbolization, and the second is from his positing of an 'epistemophilic' instinct, an 'instinctive' desire for knowledge. Both of these ideas have been developed by Kleinians in the context of their work with psychotic, particularly schizophrenic, patients.

I will begin with symbolization. Freud tells a story in 'Beyond the Pleasure Principle' (1984b) about an infant playing a game with a cotton reel on a string. He would throw the cotton reel away, saying 'there' (*'da'*), then pull it back, saying 'here' (*'fort'*). This is a fairly simple example of symbolization: the game as a whole or even the cotton reel stands in for something that is lost and at the same time provides a means of mastering the loss – in this case the comings and goings of the mother. Some years later the British psychoanalyst Ernest Jones (1948) argued that a true psychoanalytic symbol is of something that is hidden and the process is not reversible. In Rayner's (1990) graphic example a church spire may symbolize a penis but a penis will never symbolize a church spire. What is symbolized is the body, its parts and its functions. Jones also plays a particularly nasty version of the psychoanalytic trick of saying that if you disagree with me it means I'm right. It is, he seems to suggest, a defining feature of a psycho-analytic symbol that its interpretation will be met by disbelief and ridicule. The symbol proper stands in for the original object: my cigarette stands in for the breast that I still unconsciously crave. Now this is very close to the idea of sublimation: the original unconscious desire is displaced onto some other, more socially acceptable object that we can now call a symbol. I find this a rather unsatisfactory way of thinking about both sublimation and symbols. It seems to me that sublimation usually carries the notion of a possibly destructive impulse being turned to a socially useful activity: for example, my sadism is turned into my work as a brain surgeon. I don't think that, strictly speaking, it would be wrong to call my skills at brain surgery symbolic of my sadism, but I don't think either that it would be very helpful. Symbols are different from sublimations.

Klein on symbolization

For Klein, symbolization was less a matter of substituting a symbol for an object that has to be renounced than a way of escaping in phantasy from conflicts and feelings of persecution in relation to the mother's body; the symbol is sought as a conflict-free object, but pushes the psyche into the familiar constant process of displacement.

Hinshelwood (1991) argues that while Klein herself did not develop a theory of symbolization, there is an embryonic theory in her work:

> Symbols are a *primary resource* of the ego in expressing, both internally and externally, the unconscious phantasy activity at any given moment. Externalizations of these phantasies in symbolic play and personifications were driven by the need to put internal states of persecution away at a distance. Thus Klein was showing that symbols, as substitutes, are a defensive strategy, and an analysis of the process of symbolization is an analysis of defences. (Hinshelwood 1991: 446)

Klein introduced into psychoanalysis work with very young children when the orthodoxy was that they did not have a sufficiently strong ego to be able to cope. Her major innovation in technique was play therapy – giving the child toys and allowing him or her to play games which are then interpreted as an adult patient's free associations might be. Her work suggests that there is a pre-linguistic period where the organs and functions of the human body provide what I would see as a basic vocabulary and grammar. In these early phantasies, and perhaps later ones as well, experiences are understood as relationships with objects. We can see this continued in adult life when we look for an object that causes us to feel the way we do – a cause for our depression or anxiety or our general state of elation. Sometimes a description of the state is regarded as its cause. My tense state is caused by stress and I need to learn to relax; this is not unlike saying that I have measles and need to get rid of the spots.

In infancy we deal with these difficult feelings through phantasies and phantasy objects, and we tend to do the same in adulthood when we imagine an explanation for somebody else's actions or behaviour. We tend to think, or like to believe, that we are being intuitive or engaging in well-informed speculation or using our common sense, when in fact we are constructing little internal dramas with their roots in our own unconscious as much as in the activities and comments of other people. Within a group analytic situation where such phantasies can be articulated as fantasies and tested against reality, the underlying phantasy world can at least be revealed, if not understood.

So, there is a process of creative symbolization going on all the time, beginning with body parts and functions and then moving further and further away from this basis. And of course there can be problems arising on the way. Klein opened up the psychoanalytic study of psychoses in a way that had not been considered before. In fact the received wisdom was that psychoses could not be treated by psychoanalytic methods. Her basic idea was that the psychotic patient suffered from an inhibited process of symbol formation, a difficulty in moving from one object to another along the chain of displacement. This difficulty generally limits learning capacity (Klein 1930).

Hanna Segal (1981) makes an intriguing and clear distinction between a severely inhibited form of symbolization and a normal form. Instead of the symbol standing in for the object (the normal process), the symbol *becomes* the object, with all the meanings and conflicts attached to the original object. The difference is between symbolic representation and symbolic equation. Segal offers the example of two violinists. In both cases the original displacement is from the penis and masturbation. In one case, where symbolization has been achieved, the violinist is able to trace the process back by means of free association after a dream in which he was playing a duet with a girl. In the other, the violinist was unable to perform at all and experienced the act directly as masturbating in public. If we continue using Kleinian terms, we can think of this as a projective identification into an object. In the depressive position we become able to grasp the symbol as both standing for something else and having properties of its own; amongst other things this fact should remove the danger of the analyst falling into reductionist interpretations. There is a sense in which a violin represents a penis, but there is another sense in which it opens us up to the whole of Western music.

Segal (1981) began to try to think through artistic creation and aesthetic judgement in terms of reparation from the depressive position. The aesthetically pleasing work of art is a result of pining for the damaged object and the struggle to re-create it. Klein also talked about manic reparation – the attempt to 'make better' that is also an attempt to deny that anything was ever destroyed. In the work of art that is a form of manic reparation, the emotional depth that is present in the aesthetically pleasing object is missing: the aim is a pretty or attractive object that does not disturb or challenge in any way at all.

My own view is that this does get us some way towards understanding aesthetic judgement, but if we stop there we are in danger of a reductionist understanding. Just as the symbol perceived from the depressive position can be seen to possess its own qualities, so the work of art should be seen as more than the result of the unconscious reparative phantasies of the artist – it is something that has a much wider cultural and historical significance as well.

Bion and later Kleinian work on thinking

Bion develops the notion of the desire for knowledge and talks about it as a process of making links to objects and other people through projective identification. This process can go wrong in a number of ways. I think that Bion manages to encapsulate what is best and worst in psychoanalysis at the same time: a clinical brilliance combined with a stilted and naïve theoretical basis. The difficulty of his work and his originality are together summed up in his exhortation to the analyst to approach the session without memory or desire. On one level this is clearly impossible, unless of course the therapist is dead, but in that case there will not be much benefit for the patient. On the other hand I can understand the exhortation if it is concerned with cultivating a particular sort of attentiveness and openness to the world, not unlike the state at which a religious mystic might aim. If he meant something as simple and straightforward as taking what would now be called an 'objective attitude', which (simply because it *is* an attitude) is subjective, then I don't think we can get very far. If he is suggesting something closer to a mystical state, then, paradoxically, I think we are on firmer ground, and I will return to this idea when I discuss the process of psychotherapy.

For the moment I want to concentrate on Bion's account of how we build up knowledge in the psychoanalytic session. Joan and Neville Symington (1996) begin by situating Bion in the terrain of object-relations theory, describing him as concerned with the phenomenology of the psychoanalytic session, whereas I think it would be more accurate to describe him as an epistemologist of the psychoanalytic session. Epistemology is the theory of knowledge, and we shall see that Bion is more concerned with knowledge than with perception and experience.

The Symingtons also point out that Bion sheds much of Freud's theory – notions of the libido and internal structures slowly disappear from his work. They portray him as a sort of purely original thinker, or at least as a purely original clinician, and they reveal a common suspicion of theory, praising him for showing the way in which theory can get in the way of experience.

I want to contest this way of thinking about Bion. It is certainly true that a theory that is used rigidly and thoughtlessly *can* get in the way of experience, but a theory used with sensitivity can not only enable the understanding of experience but also deepen it. And although Bion does not seem to use many of the conventional Freudian concepts in his writings it is clear that his work is built on the classical theory and implies it.

The best way into Bion's work is his grid (see over), which seems to appear like a personal coat of arms in all his books (see especially Bion 1962, 1963, 1965, 1967). The grid has multiple functions, and there is no point in pretending that it, or Bion generally, is easy to understand.

We can see the vertical axis as describing a process of working similar to what many people regard as the activity of the natural scientist: a process of observation of the world and the development of a theory out of that observation, a process of induction, and indeed Bion seems to be seeking regularities that in the natural sciences would be regarded as possible laws that could then be tested.

The vertical axis is the description of the growth of thought. The material in row A is the raw material of experience; the only way in which I can understand this is in the same sense that it is found in phenomenological philosophy (see, for example, Schütz 1972): raw data as they impinge on the senses, the chaotic flow of experience, which Bion refers to as the beta elements. The second row, B, represents what Bion calls the 'alpha' elements, which the Symingtons (1996) call the 'primitive' elements of thought, derived from the 'basic data' of the mind. Bion sees these as hypothetical entities whereas what follows is real. Row C is the next stage up, including materials of the sort that a patient will often present in a session, dream material and its associations produced from the operation of the alpha elements on the beta elements. Row D consists of pre-conceptions, which actually enable mental growth. A pre-conception is waiting for some material to which it can be attached, and when this happens we experience it as understanding the meaning of

	Defini-tory Hypo-theses	ψ	Nota-tion	Atten-tion	Inquiry	Action	
	1	**2**	**3**	**4**	**5**	**6**	**...n.**
A β-elements	A1	A2				A6	
B α-elements	B1	B2	B3	B4	B5	B6	...Bn
C Dream Thoughts Dreams, Myths	C1	C2	C3	C4	C5	C6	...Cn
D Pre-conception	D1	D2	D3	D4	D5	D6	...Dn
E Conception	E1	E2	E3	E4	E5	E6	...En
F Concept	F1	F2	F3	F4	F5	F6	...Fn
G Scientific Deductive System		G2					
H Algebraic Calculus							

Source: Bion 1962

something in the patient's material. In this way the pre-conception becomes a conception (row E).

From then on there is a process of generalization and purification; from conception we move to the concept (row F), which involves losing whatever might mask the truth – the Symingtons suggest as an example the analyst's excitement at having reached a conception. Once we reach the level of concepts, they can be organized in a more abstract hierarchical form involving the observed regularities from which hypotheses can be derived (row G) and the abstract formulations of algebraic calculus (row H).

The horizontal axis has to do with the different uses to which thoughts can be put. First, there is a tentative hypothesis about what might be going on between the patient and the analyst. The second column is relevant when the analyst makes a comment to reassure him- or herself that he or she knows what is going on; I find this is a particular danger in groups, where levels of anxiety can sometimes grow rapidly and it is very difficult to sit and wait for the material to emerge. My comment about what's going on is for my benefit, not anybody else's, and it cuts out whatever might have emerged from the silence. The third column, *notation*, as I understand it, refers to the noting of something that is happening in a session: if the group move from talking about their emotional reactions to the members of the opposite sex in the group to making general statements about the nature of men and women, I might simply note that fact out loud. The next stage involves drawing the patient's attention to the analyst's hypothesis. The inquiry and action columns and beyond, up to *n*, contain what I would regard as ever more positive or definite interpretations, column 5 pursuing the inquiry further and column 6 involving confronting the patient with what the Symingtons call an 'irrefutable fact' about him- or herself.

Now what are we to make of the grid? I am comparatively happy with the columns if we take them simply as a list of interventions rather than as the psychoanalytic personification of the scientific method, although I do not think there is any place in the psychoanalytic enterprise for 'irrefutable facts'. There can be no naïve perusal of the psychoanalytic session or of the material offered by the patient – we are constantly using cultural, common-sense and more elaborate psychoanalytic theories, and comments or interpretations within the session cannot easily be placed in one box at one level of abstraction or another, as Bion seems to think. Even if we take my 'noting' comment that 'the group has started talking about the outside world', it already carries more than a notation. For a sophisticated group it is an interpretation and a confrontation and a hypothesis at the same time, and different members will take it in different ways. The logical classifications along both axes make an odd supposition for a psychoanalyst – that clear logical divisions and levels are possible and that meaning is univocal. The increasingly abstract and general categories on the vertical axis presuppose a possible clarity of meaning that is in fact an emptying of meaning – when we get to algebraic calculus, meaning disappears altogether.

If we return to the impossibility of a neutral observation language, it becomes apparent that theory can appear at any of Bion's levels above the basic raw material, the beta elements. The construction of dream symbols draws on language which must be at work in the alpha elements. And we need a theory that tells us what a regularity is before we can spot one, and so on. 'Pre-conceptions' too sound suspiciously like unconscious ideas waiting to be expressed. This part of Bion's work seems to be based on a now rather discredited conception of the scientific enterprise (see Benton and Craib 2001; Kuhn 1970). However, it is possible to disregard the scientism in Bion's schema and look at it as involving a significant valorization of thinking and of knowledge, for me the prime value of Bion's work. He understands as well that thinking is an increasingly abstract process. However, I would suggest that it is less a matter of absorbing everything in a formal logical system than a matter of being able to develop an ability to engage in dialectical argument with others and oneself. This possibility emerges from other parts of Bion's work, and this is where he becomes exciting and also where his Kleinian background becomes most evident.

The Symingtons point out that Bion's model of thought involves the fluctuation between the paranoid-schizoid and the depressive position. The starting point is absence, the absence of the breast, and this is what comprises the beta elements. Thinking is the attempt to make up for that absence by symbolization, but the absence is felt as persecution and the first thoughts are paranoid; or, perhaps more accurately, the first thoughts are attempts to transform these persecutory feelings.

It is difficult to disentangle Bion's theory from the specificity of his clinical practice with schizophrenic patients, but the way in which I interpret his argument is that the schizophrenic cannot bear to think certain things – if you like, he or she cannot bear to think the experience of absence; the absences are experienced as bad objects that have to be expelled. Thinking involves bringing things into relation with each other, bringing, for example, my sense of the outside world, my knowledge of the world, into relation with my feelings about the world; it is a matter of linking together different aspects of my experience, of my feelings, and of my knowledge. In a famous paper, 'Attacks on Linking', Bion (1967) shows how the schizophrenic finds it difficult to allow connections to be made. The origin of such difficulty is seen as the lack of success in forming a link with the care-taker in infancy – the failure of the baby's projective identification or the caretaker's failure to understand the projection and eventually feed it back in manageable form.

Thinking is a steady development of connections, and there is another way of working with Bion's insights that doesn't take us towards the formal logic at the most abstract level of the grid. As I have suggested, there is a sense in which formal logic brings every-thing under its umbrella; it links everything together, but it does so by emptying thought of its content, of its meaning. The difficult work of linking, and of thinking, lies in holding together ideas of disparate and even conflicting meaning and allowing oneself to reach the level of abstract thought where this is possible. To do this one must be able to invest thought with an emotional power – one has to feel strongly about thinking, and to be able to think as clearly as pos-sible about feeling. This is where I think Bion has most to offer, particularly through what he has to say about the alpha function.

At the level of the beta elements there is no distinction between experiences that belong to the external world and experiences that belong to the internal world; they have to be subjected to the alpha function. This is the means by which I gain subjectivity and make experience my own. Experience becomes transformed into dream images and starts the journey towards conception. The Symingtons (1996) head their chapter on the alpha function with a quote from Dostoevsky to the effect that it is better to talk nonsense in your own words than sense in somebody else's; they comment that it is pos-sible to know the external world but not oneself if the alpha func-tion is not working: 'A philosopher . . . may be able to abstract from sense data but be unable to achieve self-knowledge' (Symington and Symington 1996: 63).

Again I am by no means sure that this is the way to understand what Bion is talking about, and it reproduces an easy and rather com-forting way of thinking of the relationship between thought and feeling. If we are to make sense of this aspect of Bion's theory, then the alpha function has to be present for knowledge of the outside *and* the inside world. Concepts such as external and internal are depen-dent upon each other; one can only be aware of knowing the outside world if one has some conception of knowing oneself, and vice versa. The Symingtons' philosopher could not exist and thought and feeling are intimately bound together, but not always in ways that we might find desirable. The denial of thought can be as strong as the denial of feeling, and it is important to hold on to Freud's insight that it is the denial of an *idea* attached to a feeling that is important. And if the idea is denied, connections cannot be made. I will return to this at the end of the chapter, but first I want to elaborate my criticism of Bion by looking at another psychoanalyst who uses symbolic logic.

I. Matte-Blanco (1959, 1975, 1976 1988) is generally regarded as a member of the British object-relations school. He suggests that there *is* a logic to unconscious processes but that this is not the logic of conscious thought. In conscious thought we do not think of relationships as reversible. In conscious thought a possible causal relationship involves the notion that one thing follows another – that, for example, if my parents divorce I will be upset; in unconscious thought that relationship can be reversed – my parents divorce because I am upset. I am thus the cause of the difficulty. Matte-Blanco calls this process 'symmetrization', and different psychic processes can be understood as different combinations of 'normal' asymmetrical logic with symmetrization.

Matte-Blanco goes on to to introduce notions from mathematical logic into psychoanalytic theory, which I will not follow through here, partly because I am not sure that I understand them, but more importantly because, insofar as I do understand them, they seem to offer only a redescription of what is going on, not any new or further understanding. If we take symmetrization as an example, it provides a logical redescription of my sense of being responsible for my parents' divorce, but like Bion's more abstract categories it lacks the understanding of motivational and relational content that comes with talking about defences and omnipotence and anxiety. Also, as with Bion's categories, we lose the sense of internal psychic structures and mechanisms – we are left only with an understanding of abstract cognition.

Symbols, thinking and creativity

By way of bringing this discussion to a close, I want to try to draw together some of the main themes and elaborate on some psychoanalytic theories of creativity, as well as insist again on the importance of thinking in the psychoanalytic process.

It is apparent from the work of Freud, Klein, Bion (and, as we shall see later, Lacan) that the ability to symbolize involves entry into the world as a more or less capable human being, and the implication is that the greater our ability to move through the world of symbols, the more human we are. One way of conceptualizing these issues is to think of them as taking place at different psychic levels – and in this respect Bion is helpful. The most basic level of symbolization is that of dreaming, the basic level of our subjectivity. I'm not sure that it is true that our dream symbols become preconceptions or conceptions; I think it is often the other way around. But our dreams and our primary processes, our unconscious phantasies, are the areas where we make the world our own through the processes of displacement. It is through the oedipal stage that we begin to do this in a more disciplined and conscious way: there is a sense in which the law of the father is also the law of grammar and of formal logic. We have to subordinate ourselves to these laws in order to be able to use them to work effectively in the world with others. If my feelings push me out of the range of these laws – if I am so angry that I simply splutter and cannot speak coherently – then I am lost. Similarly if my desires overpower my reason, so that, for example, I believe that a woman is in love with me, although there is no evidence for this and despite the fact that everything she says denies it, then I am lost. Psychoanalysis must concern itself with the ability to think in more or less rational and coherent ways.

This is one way up from the dream and out towards reality. There is another form of symbolizing activity that perhaps stays closer to primitive symbolization: the deployment of the alpha function. Nevertheless, like rational thought, this involves the acceptance, deployment and questioning of rules and conventions. This way involves activity across the range of what we refer to as the arts. Segal's work on symbolism suggests that the ability to create and the ability to symbolize freely – to think – are closely related.

This notion is elaborated in the work of Marion Milner (1950, 1955, 1958, 1969), herself an artist as well as a psychoanalyst. More rigid developmental accounts of psychoanalysis tend to see certain earlier stages or processes as regressive and therefore 'bad'; although these states are permissible in dreams, they are perhaps not to be encouraged in waking life except in certain very limited areas such as sexual intercourse. Milner argues that the experience or illusion of fusion, of identity with another – a return to a pre-linguistic, pre-oedipal stage – and then a separation is the source of artistic creation. I wonder as well if sometimes rational creativity, the development of ideas and arguments, also entails a return to such states, or at least a loosening of the barriers between conscious and unconscious processes, perhaps a lot of which goes on without our realizing it.

More recently a contemporary Kleinian, Donald Meltzer, has suggested that there is an aesthetic instinct based on the baby's aesthetic appreciation of the beauty of the breast as it re-establishes the link to the womb (Meltzer and Williams 1988). Whereas Bion sees envy in terms of an attack on linking, Meltzer sees it as an attack on beauty; both involve an identification with the destructive parts of the personality. Meg Harris Williams (1999) has suggested that psychoanalysis is a combination of science and art in which a scientific model allows us to see those aspects of experience that lie outside its scope and it is revised by what she and Meltzer call an artistic method. They suggest that psychoanalysis combines a spiral of science and art in its production of new knowledge. This is closer to the dialectic process that I mentioned earlier – thinking is an inter- and intra-personal process that involves all levels of the psyche; a matter not only of formal logic but also of dialectical logic – the logic of contradictions, of aesthetic judgements, unthought intuitions, and so on. It is an ongoing process, not one that ends in a logical system.

The psychoanalysis of organizations

The move from discussing theories of symbolization and thinking to the psychoanalysis of group processes and organizations might seem obscure, but Bion is a key figure in both fields, and it should become apparent that what he has to say about group processes is closely related to the ability to think in groups. Although psychoanalysis is often accused of being concerned only with individual psychology, it should be clear by now that through the importance placed on early relationships and, in Freud's work, the centrality of the oedipal stage, it is also a social psychology, intimately involved with the wider society.

One of the ways in which we defend ourselves from both internal and external threats is by entering into relationships with other people. Within groups it is possible to see all the defences I discussed earlier and 'defences' that are specific to groups. I use the scare quotes because it is not usual to think of what follows in terms of defences, but they are collective ways, outlined by Bion (1961), in which groups avoid the tasks they are set, and, by extension, avoid thinking. It seems to me that in the context of therapy and experiential groups, these can be seen as defences against the forms of learning about oneself that can bring the individual face to face with internal threats.

Bion describes three forms of what he calls 'basic assumption groups', forms of unconscious relationship between group members that defend against both intellectual and emotional learning. In any one face-to-face grouping, all three will be present to varying degrees, together with what Bion calls 'the work group', which engages in the main task of the group. The relationship between them will vary from time to time – it is as if there is a kaleidoscope of unconscious relations jockeying for dominance.

The first basic assumption group is *dependency*, which occurs when the members of the group rely on the group leader to control and organize what they do. In other words they expect the leader to carry out their work, and if the leader complied they would be relieved from what they find threatening in the task. The leader is expected to think for the group. Paradoxically the dependency group often appears in the situation where it is least appropriate: in the university seminar or class. This should be a place where everybody engages in thinking, but there is often a long struggle in which the teacher refuses to acquiesce to the explicit or implicit demands that he or she fill the space.

The second basic assumption group also rescues the members – or most of them – from this threat. Bion calls it a *pairing* group – where there arises a relationship between two members of the group that seems to relieve other members of the group from the responsibility of participating. In my experience pairing can be of either same- or opposite-sex members, but I think Bion's argument still applies: the unconscious phantasy is that the couple will produce a messiah – in the form of a new idea – who will rescue the group from all its problems. I have noticed that if a group member becomes pregnant in the course of a group, then similar expectations seem to be placed on her future child. Often this particular phantasy seems to remain a long way from consciousness, but there can be a feeling of what I think is best described as passive excitement about the pairing.

In teaching situations involving younger students and mature students, two mature students will often pair, dominating the discussion and frequently arguing with each other. Once again the effect is to locate the thinking process in one or two people rather than allowing it to pervade the whole group.

The third basic assumption group is *fight–flight*. This is the group form of defensive projection. The group will find an external enemy or an internal scapegoat, and the criticism of and attacks on the enemy will enable an internal cohesion and feeling of identity within the group, or, if the scapegoat is a group member, within the rest of the group. The enemy carries the blame for failures in the achievement or management of the group's task, or simply carries the burden of the group's rage at having to work at a task. When people who experienced the Second World War say they were happier then than at any time during their lives, they are referring less to the pleasure of fighting and killing (although in some cases that will be there) than to the experience of an intense group cohesion in the face of an external, 'evil' enemy. Most work units have an internal or external scapegoat that can be mobilized to take the blame when the pressures of work seem too much to bear.

This takes us to organizations. De Board (1978) talks about the strength of projection within organizations and the way in which it can prevent work being done. Menzies-Lyth (1989) shows how in a teaching hospital anxieties – which in a hospital tend to be very primitive, connected to illness and death – are dealt with by the development of a bureaucratic organization, which is counterproductive. It is generally the case, whether talking about organizations or politics, that if something creates an anxiety, there are calls for new forms of organization that, in phantasy, will remove the anxiety. In practice the anxiety is moved somewhere else, usually, in hierarchical organizations, downwards. On the individual level, the phantasy of an escape from anxiety is very powerful.

Whether it is a matter of dependency, fight–flight, pairing or the use of bureaucracy to alleviate anxiety, individuals within the group inhibit their own creative thinking processes and collective work becomes very difficult. The contrast between a well-defended, highly anxious group and a group that can mobilize individuals in a collective creative process is immense, and I will return to this type of issue in the final part of the book, when I discuss the process of psychotherapy.

Conclusion

The work of the modern Kleinians has developed Freud's work on symbolization and an epistemophilic drive, the search for knowledge. The developments have taken place through work with schizo-phrenic patients, who have great difficulty in symbolizing and making links, and this stream of thought has continued to develop through thinking about group and organizational dynamics and aesthetics. I would argue that it is one of the more consistently origi-nal strands of thought in psychoanalysis and one that leads directly to the processes involved in psychotherapy, which will be discussed in Part III.

7

Infancy and Object-Relations

We begin now to move into one of the richest and most highly textured areas of psychoanalytic theory and practice, although I will concentrate more on the practice in later chapters. Object-relations theory is not, in general, systematic and in that sense manifests the suspicion of theory that characterizes British intellectual culture. One of my aims in this chapter will be to try to situate these ideas within the wider theoretical framework I have been trying to elaborate up to this point.

Types of theory

I have talked of different levels of the psyche, and the work of Freud and Klein fits such a model. I have already suggested that as we move into the development of object-relations theory we move closer to the surface and we also find a different type of theorizing. One way of characterizing the difference is to distinguish between a synthetic theorizing and an analytic theorizing. The former goes beyond what is immediately available to observation; this was what Freud did when he went beyond his clinical experience to develop his metapsychology. This rarely happens in object-relations theory, and when it does, it is of a different order to Freud's theorizing. Analytic theorizing, on the other hand, stays much closer to observations and classifications.

I have already used the metaphor of a map to talk about psychoanalytic theory. Freud and Klein supply large-scale maps that can tell us where we are and enable us to think about where we might want to go and how we might try to get there. Each individual needs to pick out his or her own route. Free association is the major, perhaps the only, form of transport. The more systematic object-relations theorists seem to me to draw maps of areas inhabited by a few people, their patients, from whom they generalize, often with less depth of detail. I have also argued that the originality of psychoanalysis as a clinical discipline is that it enables an understanding of specific individuality, and the purpose of psychoanalytic theory is to map out the routes that might enable us (and especially the patient) to find this individuality. The process of theorizing through building up types takes us away from individuality, from the particular to the general, from what is specific to what is common. The best of the object-relations theorists, I would suggest, are not systematic thinkers but those who build detailed maps of particular hamlets and mark out specific features of experience from which we can learn possible dimensions of individuality rather than the more grand contours of human experiences.

The focus of the thinkers I will be discussing here tends to be clinical practice and the psychodynamics of child development. The nuances of the relationship between child and carer and patient and analyst are seen as reflecting each other, and this tends to generate the idea that the analyst is in some way engaged in a process of re-parenting the patient. There might be a limited sense in which this is true, but it is also a very dangerous idea – it leads to the belief that history can be changed in the analytic relationship. But if my mother ignored me or my father beat me up, I will always be a person who was ignored by his mother or beaten up by his father. What might change are the ways open to me of being such a person: what mixtures of bitterness and defeat, strength and hope, hatred and forgiveness can I bring together in my attempt to live the consequences of such a background?

Also implicit in these ideas is the ghostly causal relationship that haunts psychoanalysis – the idea that if somebody is unhappy, or suffering from some form or another of mental illness, then the cause must lie back in this person's childhood, and particularly in his or her parenting. It is true that most people who come for psychotherapy or psychoanalysis have had difficult childhoods to some degree or another. I suspect that it is also true that most people who don't come for psychoanalysis or psychotherapy have had difficult childhoods to some degree or another. There are borders of ill treatment that if crossed are almost certain to produce difficulties, but I have yet to meet somebody who, when it comes down to it, does not feel that he or she experienced some ill treatment as a child. Progress through the oedipal stage, for example, involves several years of being refused and frustrated by people bigger and stronger than oneself. When we talk about infancy in contemporary society, we must be aware of the tendency to idealize the child (see, for example, Miller 1987, and for an intelligent discussion of these issues, see Gittins 1997) and to see (mistakenly) temporal succession as involving a causal relationship.

With one or two exceptions the ideas we will be looking at here are closer to a conscious level of experience, often to a phenomenology of self-experience when it comes to the less systematic thinkers. However, I will begin with the more systematic thinkers – Fairbairn, whom I have already mentioned in connection with Klein, and H. Guntrip and Otto Kernberg. I will then look at attempts to understand the earliest experience of the infant that began to appear after the Second World War before moving on to contemporary figures.

General theories of object-relations

Fairbairn and Guntrip

Josephine Klein (1987) contrasts Fairbairn to Freud, claiming that the former's major step forward was to suggest that we cannot start from the isolated individual and his or her drives but must begin with people in relationship to each other. In this respect I think Freud displayed more intelligence than his critics attribute to him. Freud's drive theory is precisely about people in relationship to each other: the people are members of the family, parents and siblings, exactly the same people with whom object-relations theorists are concerned. And what happens to these drives, their development, depends upon the people with whom we interact. Once again the opposition between the two approaches is a false one. Fairbairn's argument is that for Freud psychic energy is distinct from psychic structure, whereas in fact, as we saw earlier, the drives and their development in relation to the external world lead to the development of psychic structures. For Fairbairn it seems that the structures somehow produce the energy, or both energy and structures are produced by relationships. But of course relationships must depend on energy, and that takes us back to Freud.

As we noted in chapter 5, Fairbairn worked in Scotland, in comparative isolation from his contemporaries. He has always been on the fringe of British psychoanalysis – one of those characters whose move to the centre of the stage is constantly announced but who never seems to get there. On closer examination of his work, I think it is possible to see why this is so. Whereas from Freud onward, including most object-relations theorists, the assumption is that either we are not born with an ego or that we are born only with an elementary ego or self and that we develop from this starting point, Fairbairn's starting point was that we are born with the ego already in place and that splits occur as we develop.

There is a classificatory process at work in Fairbairn's account of this development. He suggests that ego structures develop around three types of object-relation – those that give pleasure (the libidinal ego), those that frustrate or bring displeasure (the anti-libidinal ego) and those that are feelingless (the central ego). I think that it would be very difficult to establish that any experience was feelingless, a state that might be achieved only in unconsciousness or death. The frustrating experiences are dealt with by splitting, by envious attack, denial and repression; Fairbairn has his own versions of the standard psychoanalytic defence mechanisms, but I am not sure that they add much.

The defences, however, lead to personality types. The moving force in all these developments seems to be the environment, the way in which parents or others treat the child, and particularly their frustrating of the child. If I take in these unpleasant experiences and regard them as my own fault, then I develop a depressed personality. Like Klein, Fairbairn sees the depressed personality as more integrated than the schizoid personality, which simply splits the various types of experience from each other. Guntrip (1961), one of Fairbairn's analysands (Guntrip 1971), developed an elaborate typification from his work, listing eight types of object-relationship, which in turn generate fourteen relationship patterns. While fourteen types are much better than the twofold contrasts I will look at shortly, I do not think that they are that much better, and they share the problem that most people can be put into most types.

Some thoughts on morality and civilization

One of the most interesting aspects of Guntrip's classifications is the value-laden terms that he employs to describe his different stages of development: pre-moral and pre-civilized, moral, civilized and mature. To someone from a sociological background, aware of the relativity of these terms, their use in this context carries implications of social control: a matter not of conditioning and policing people's actions, but of conditioning and policing people's personalities.

Having crudely characterized this position, I want to play the polemicist's usual trick of saying that things are not so simple. But I do think that my criticisms are sometimes right, or perhaps always have a degree of truth in them. Psychoanalytic theory and practice seem to me to be unavoidably involved in making judgements about good and bad, usually masking them in terms of health and illness, maturity and immaturity, and in Guntrip's case civilization or lack of civilization. These values have some relationship to wider social values – they may reinforce dominant social values and ideologies or lead to a critical attitude towards them, or perhaps offer an alternative to them. And as I have already pointed out, psychoanalysis can be influenced by these wider values. Whatever happens, we cannot avoid issues of morality and politics (see Rustin 1991).

Freud produced a psychoanalytic history of civilization, but this is not what Guntrip is talking about. He seems to mean 'civilized' in the common-sense way in which people might talk about 'behaving in a civilized manner'. Guntrip's definition of the mature, civilized level of personality organization involves libidinal and moral maturity, engaging in relationships between emotional equals that are spontaneous, co-operative and stable and preserve individuality and difference. Morality is implicit in such a relationship.

This is not a list of bad things, and I guess that the world would be a happier place if we could all achieve some of them some of the time. Some, of course, are not possible, or, if they are possible, are to be distrusted. Everything I have argued about psychoanalysis indicates the complexity of the psyche and suggests that 'spontaneity' can be achieved only through a denial of some part or parts of the personality – those parts that want to go in a different direction. And the complex and divided nature of the psyche indicates that mutuality and co-operation – insofar as they are the result of individual and collective psychodynamics rather than institutional and structural necessity – are only temporary achievements.

Given that most of these ideas developed through the late 1940s into the 1950s, coincident with the development of the welfare state, the sociologist in me suggests that this ideal personality is appropriate to the period of comparatively stable, organized and planned capitalism that followed the Second World War and went with the general optimism that developed as the war receded. It is not that such an analysis of the personality is false; it is one-sided and, I think in the case of Fairbairn, self-contradictory.

Kernberg: the differentiation of experience

Otto Kernberg's name has become known outside psychoanalytic circles through his work on narcissism (see Lasch 1980). Generally, I think he carries the burden of ego psychology: too great an emphasis on internal integration and external adjustment. And like Fairbairn and Guntrip before him, he sees development in terms of the internalization and integration of external material. As we grow up, earlier meanings are integrated into new wholes but do not disappear altogether and can be called upon or regressed to in different circumstances.

Josephine Klein (1987) claims, rightly I think, that one of Kernberg's most important contributions is to insist on the unitary nature of experience. We can find in the academic world different branches of psychology – cognitive psychology, the psychology of perception, studies of the emotions, and so on – but our lived experience involves all of these together. However, they are not necessarily coherent with each other, something that Kernberg seems to neglect. Kernberg is, perhaps, closer to cognitive psychology in that he relies on notions of memory traces to talk about internalization, and it is difficult from this position to think about non- or pre-linguistic memory. In any case what we know about memory indicates that it is very slippery. Just as our internalizations, our memories, change as they accumulate over the years, so they change depending on our present standpoint and purposes. I am not sure that they have the solidity to build into mental structures.

As our experience builds up, Kernberg suggests that it divides into structures related to a sense of self, those related to our sense of other people and objects, and those related to both. There is a beginning of a typology of people who do not separate self and feeling and people who do not separate others and feeling. There is a continuous processing – 'metabolizing' – of experience through splitting, merging and relating. Kernberg suggests that the basic organizing principles of experience are pleasure and pain, associated in turn with libidinal and destructive or aggressive drives. The process of organization is started through the experience of pain, which pushes us into making distinctions between ourselves and the outside world, which is responsible for the pain.

Before continuing with the discussion of Kernberg, there is a more general point to be made here. It is not only in the very early stages of development that pain is an important motivating force. Pain, in the sense of lack of satisfaction, or more generally in the sense of anxiety about both the outside world and the inner world, is a major motivating force in human psychological life on all levels. For Bion, remember, the experience of the bad breast was at the origin of thinking. It is the unpleasant parts of our infantile experience that provoke projection and the beginnings of the experience of ourselves as separate beings; it is the continued experience of internal conflict that is thus set up that pushes us into developing increasingly sophisticated psychological structures to handle our inner life, and it is this same conflictual inner life and the frustrations of our desires and the threats presented by the outside world that push us into the activities of what we like to call culture – rational thought, the many forms of artistic production, and so on.

In the recognition of this I think that Kernberg maintains the original Freudian insight, but it gets lost in the later stages of his description of development as a steady process of abstraction and integration – the implicit notions of conflict get lost, as does the notion of a varied and complex inner life. Something that I think is present in Kernberg's work is the idea that 'health' is a matter of relationships to the outside world rather than relationships in the internal world. Feelings are relational: we feel *about* something or somebody, and if our feelings cannot be so related, then there is something wrong with us; we have detached our feelings from the original object as a defence. The healthy person has a clear sense of self and of others and is not subject to inexplicable waves of feeling. I might once have been frightened by a train in childhood but I have learnt to distinguish between that train and the train I catch every morning to go to work, and I am not flooded by the fear that was detached from the original experience and that might reappear in relation to some unconnected object.

However, I am not keen to use the word 'healthy' in this connection. It is probably better, in the sense that it makes life a little easier, to be able to recognize our dominant feelings in a particular situation, when they are related to that situation. If we go back to the Freudian model, however, the unconscious is always at work, and we are always responding to internal unconscious desires and phantasies.

We might, defensively, split off a feeling from its original object, but we might also, defensively, look for an external object to which we can attach a feeling rather than learn to contain the feeling as part of the flux of our subjective life. If I were to use the word 'health' at all in the context of mental life, it would only be in connection with complexity, in this case a recognition that feelings are always con-tradictory, that they are not always related to the outside world, and the most powerful are there to be felt but not necessarily trusted or acted upon. Where the feelings belong is important, but more impor-tant is discovering how to bear our feelings, and that involves a deeper understanding and not only the ability to recognize where they belong but also the ability to allow ourselves to feel. What we might call the 'relatively autonomous inner life' seems to disappear in the Kernberg account, together with the internal rhythms of emotion. It is important to insist both on what one might call the 'ownership' of one's own emotions and on their frequent irrationality.

The contradictions in these approaches (Fairbairn's, Guntrip's and Kernberg's) lie in the role that Kernberg gives to destructive forces and Fairbairn gives to frustrating experiences. The implications of their arguments are that we develop and grow through such experi-ences. That it is through our suffering and destructiveness and the way that we handle them that we become adults and we become indi-viduals. A different sort of morality emerges from this point of view, which has to do with the ability to tolerate and explore internal con-flict, to recognize one's own destructive urges. This tends to disap-pear as these theories develop into notions of health and stability, so that the morality espoused by Guntrip, for example, seems to me an inhuman reality, a statement pronounced by a punitive super-ego rather than an understanding of the human condition and its conflicts.

These attempts at a more systematic classification of object-relationships, then, tend to move away from an emphasis on inter-nal conflict and towards notions of integration and health, which is characteristic of much contemporary object-relations theory. At the same time they seem to me to lose the richly textured nature of the less ambitious later theorists. I want now to turn to two theorists in this tradition whose work developed in Britain after the Second World War and who were concerned with the very early experience of the infant. I think that it is fair to say that although we still find attempts at classifying character types, there is an increasing concern with the detail of experience.

The emergence of a sense of self

The basis for ideas about early infantile experience of the self and the world comes from three sources: first, psychoanalytic work with adults, in which it is thought that the patient regresses to or reproduces ways of relating, fantasies and experiences of early infancy; second, psychoanalytic work with young children, and especially autistic children; and, third, from the process of infant observation, which is part of most significant psychoanalytic trainings.

I have already discussed arguments about the existence of an ego at birth, whether there is an elementary sense of separation or only a sense of being merged with the mother. I suggested that there seems to be no reason why we should not conceive of the infant as moving between the two positions. The studies from cognitive and developmental psychology indicate that prior to birth all important cognitive equipment is in place and the infant is already learning, but there is also observational and clinical evidence for the experience of merging (Chamberlain 1987). In fact there are experiences in adult life, especially those connected with sexual relationships and what we call 'falling in love', where we seem to return to an experience of something like merging with another person – an experience that can be exciting and frightening at the same time.

In the period after birth, it is perhaps separation that is most frightening: the infant cannot survive without the mother, of whom it has been a part for so long. It seems reasonable to suggest that the dominant part of its first out-of-womb experiences are those of being merged with the mother or her substitute. I am not so sure of this last point, since it seems that there is evidence to suggest the baby can recognize its mother's voice and general feel so a substitute might involve the recognition of difference. In any case we can surmise as well that this is also a necessary experience. The psychological to and fro of merging and separation is a means by which we come to recognize that we *are* different from the mother but none the less related to her. The dangers of not recognizing the difference are illustrated in Marie Cardinale's fictional study of her own analysis (Cardinale 1983): when, as an almost grown girl, she is allowed to go out on the street by herself for the first time, she is forever bumping into lampposts and other people; she no longer has an adult to guide her.

The opposite, the inability to merge or to make contact, is explored by Frances Tustin and her work on autism (Tustin 1972, 1981, 1986).

Another detour is necessary here. I have already warned against drawing psychoanalytic ideas into culturally popular causal explanations. It is also part of our culture to look for heroes, villains and victims, and child-rearing is an area pervaded with guilt and anxiety. Accounts of child-rearing can lead people to claim that the parents are the villains, and Tustin's work was sometimes taken up in this way by those in the helping professions. I think Josephine Klein (1987) is particularly sensible about this, pointing out that any parent can have an autistic child and there is no clear cause – in fact there might be several causes. I would go on to suggest that it is actually the experience of autism and our ability to understand the experience that is at least as important as seeking a cause.

According to Tustin, the earliest experience we have is of a fluid, gaseous existence, which needs to be contained and formed into discrete objects. The main carer, usually the mother, acts as the initial container (an idea developed later by Bion and Winnicott); she provides, and if all is well, the infant takes on, a 'skin'. It is through the way in which we are held that we gain a sense of our physical and therefore our psychological boundaries, the limited realm over which we hold sway. Tustin seems to be talking metaphorically when she suggests that the infant who, for whatever reason, does not develop such a skin develops a 'muscular type of self-containment', what others might call a false self. This is necessary because without boundaries everything feels like an invasion. One 'normal' example of the absence or inadequacy of the holding skin, which I imagine most people who have had prolonged experience of babies might recognize, is when the infant becomes flooded with its own distress. What starts off as normal crying becomes more and more urgent as the child fails to find a container for distress; as Josephine Klein puts it, the child 'becomes frightened that it may become intolerably frightened' (Klein 1987: 88).

If I have no sense of my skin, I can have no sense of my body or my self, and any sort of contact feels like an invasion; I have to keep clear of everybody. We all have autistic dimensions to our personalities. There are times, for example, during a busy day when I move from class to class, lecture to lecture, and there are students and colleagues constantly demanding my attention, when I feel that I have no boundaries, that I am flowing all over the building (I might say when I get home that 'I've been running around all day'). In such states I often lock myself in my office at the first opportunity – the office walls provide me with a very solid skin while I try to recover my own. In such circumstances the telephone becomes a major intrusion. Whenever we adopt an attitude or a belief that we feel protects us from the intrusions that go with a relationship – when we avoid ringing a friend, or decide we can't face a party – we are deploying a mild level of autistic protection of our sense of self.

Tustin talks vividly of the internal experience of the autistic child, the 'volcanoes' and 'waterfalls' of its feelings. In treatment, the firmness of the therapist and of the situation provides a container for these feelings and hopefully enables a skin to develop. It is difficult, however; the sort of child about whom Tustin is talking tends to avoid firmness or hardness (even, she suggests, hard lumps of food) because it is experienced as an infringement of the flow of experience. Yet a paradox of the experience is that the contact with another that seems so threatening is also experienced, as the infant becomes aware of real physical separation, as having been painfully lost. Josephine Klein (1987) makes the interesting suggestion, for which she frankly admits there is no evidence, that perhaps autism is a result of being born with undeveloped sensory apparatus that prohibits or inhibits the taking in of messages. In terms of what has gone before we can think of Tustin as describing the extremes of infantile omnipotence – anything that seems to restrict the flow of my body cannot be tolerated; it is an insult, as Josephine Klein points out, in the sense that a physical attack, or major surgery, is an insult.

Self and others

The centre of object-relations theory has to do with relationships between self and others, and especially when we deal with the parent–infant relationship it seems to me too easy to lose sight of internal relationships. This criticism does not apply to Tustin because she is describing an experience which can perhaps best be described as only internal – the autistic child has no outside.

Michael Balint's work seems to fit in neatly here in that it is concerned with the emergence of self or ego from the interpenetration of self and environment. Balint was a Hungarian analyst who trained under Sandor Ferenczi, one of the clinically more interesting first-generation analysts, and one of the first analysts to think in terms of working with patients at a pre-oedipal level. The orthodox Freudian view of psychoanalysis is that it deals with problems which arise at the oedipal stage, which involves the ability to operate in a threesome, and to separate oneself from the others, learning to accept that they can engage in a relationship from which one is excluded. I might want to know what goes on between my parents behind their bedroom door but I can go off and do something else without banging on the door and screaming that I want to be let in. When one reaches this stage it is possible to take part in conversations that recognize the purpose of language, that is, the communication of meaning. In the psycho-analytic session, something else might happen. Balint (1968) tried to link ways of relating to language to stages in the development of a separate sense of self (see also Stewart 1996).

At this stage of my argument it is important to distinguish between my use of the term 'self' and 'ego'. I use 'ego' to refer to Freud's concept of an internal agency or structure that is in part conscious and in part unconscious and is defined by its relationship to the other internal structures, the id and super-ego. In my earlier discussion of Tustin's work, and now again in relation to Balint, the term 'self' is more appropriate, referring not to a mental structure or agency but to a sense (or lack of it) of oneself as an object for oneself. It might be helpful to think of one's self, or one's sense of self, as a surface, or closer to surface, effect of relationships between the underlying structures. This means that it is closer to consciousness, and there-fore more accessible and perhaps therefore more readily understand-able than the unconscious processes in which Freud was originally interested.

Balint (1968) suggests that pure love describes what the infant experiences *in utero*, and in the period after birth the infant experi-ences an intermixing of itself and its environment that generates a need to be loved – birth itself seems to bring to an end the possibil-ity of primary narcissism and initiates the beginning of an ego or a sense of self that might or might not develop:

> ... the individual is born in an intense state of relatedness to his or her environment, both biologically and libidinally. Prior to birth, both self and environment are harmoniously 'mixed up', in fact they inter-penetrate each other. In this world ... there are as yet no objects, only limitless substances or expanses.
>
> Birth is a trauma that upsets the equilibrium by changing the environment radically and enforces – under a real threat of death – a new form of adaptation. This starts off, or at any rate considerably accelerates, the separation between individual and environment.

> Objects, including the ego, begin to emerge from the mix up of sub-stances and form the breaking up of the harmony of limitless expanses. The objects have, in contrast to the friendlier substance, firm contours and sharp boundaries which henceforth must be recognised and respected. Libido is no longer in a homogenous flux from the id to the environment; under the influence of the emerging objects, concentra-tions and rarefactions appear in its flow. (Balint 1968: 67)

We can see here links with Tustin, but perhaps more importantly with drive theory, the drive theory that tends to get forgotten as object-relations theory develops.

Balint suggests that it is at this point, as the infant has to deal with increasingly solid and recalcitrant objects, that a 'basic fault' can occur involving a withdrawal of libido back to the ego – a secondary narcissism. This involves the infant in a withdrawal from the envi-ronment, which results in a lack of fit between it and those around it. Both Balint and Josephine Klein, in her account of Balint, put this lack of fit down to unsympathetic adults, and whilst this is certainly the case in some more obvious examples, the same old problems of causality arise. I have come across many patients who show or repro-duce this lack of fit in therapy groups. They seem unable to hear the emotional tone of, or understand the meaning of, the words that other members of the group speak to each other, and their contribu-tions will be out of key to the main flow of communication, like a choir member who cannot sing in tune. Words will be heard as attacks or statements of love rather than bearers of meaning. These patients will often describe backgrounds where nobody seems to have cared or sought to understand them. At the same time there are patients who describe backgrounds equally unsympathetic who none the less can find their place in the group's music. Most people move between the two positions.

The same problem emerges with the way in which Balint develops this idea into the depiction of two personality structures: the ocnophilic and the philobat. The basic fault is the inability to move forward to the oedipal position and grasp language as a tool and a means of communication. I think it is a matter of degree here: a mature use of language can convey a range of subtle shades of feeling; those still struggling at the level of the basic fault seem to deal in blunt and simple feelings. In any case, they have difficulty in handling relationships to others. There are, Balint suggests, two options. In a book entitled *Thrills and Regressions* (1959) he offers a famous psychoanalysis of the funfair and the activities it offers. If I am a 'philobat', I look for the excitement of exposing myself to a danger of which I am conscious, but that I hope to tolerate and overcome. In terms of the primitive experiences of object-relations, the philobat lives in a world where discrete and dangerous objects are to be avoided in favour of the friendly expanses, the flow of experience out of which object formation occurs. I am not sure that Balint's psychoanalysis of the funfair really works – one might expect the philobat to avoid dangerous objects – but the general point is intelligible: the philobat keeps a distance between him- or herself and others and operates by sight: things are safe if they can be seen. He or she develops the skills that enable the control of dangerous objects. One could think of the philobat as illustrating a 'liveable autism', finding ways of dealing with solid objects but keeping them at arm's length.

In his psychoanalysis of the funfair, Balint opposes thrills to regressions, aggressive pleasures that involve smashing things, shooting at them, throwing balls at coconuts, darts at targets, and so on. These are what attract the 'ocnophil', whose strategy is to cling to others rather than avoid them. The destructive pleasures are not dangerous but presuppose a harmony between those taking part. If the philobat lives in a world of safe spaces and dangerous objects, the ocnophil lives in a world of dangerous spaces and safe objects, and the fairground allows a regression to what might be called a safe destructiveness. On an everyday level the ocnophil lives in a phantasy world where objects – other people – will protect him or her. I have noticed that any number of my group patients have talked about my role as group therapist being one of protecting people from each other; this is often asserted after an argument between two or more members of the group in which I have not intervened. It is as if the phantasy of my protective function has to be reasserted. Often at the beginning of an experiential group of trainees or professionals there is a demand for a mutual guarantee of confidentiality that can only be provided in an imaginary world. The ocnophil overvalues the other person and is dependent on the object at the expense of developing the skills that would enable him or her to pursue a relatively independent course through life. The thought of separation raises great anxiety.

My comments earlier on the notion of the basic fault were largely about causality, and I think that they can be linked with what I want to say about Balint's typology. Both are too general. Balint recognized that we do not find the two types in a pure form but in various forms of combination. However, I think that in practice the problem is not just the empirical mixing of types but the difficulty in assigning any particular behaviour to one type or the other. Thus I can think of one patient in a group who is consistently and determinedly looking for the 'answer' to his problems. He wants clarity and control; he spends much of his time manipulating objects, making and building things. He is constantly trying to control me in the group, trying to persuade me, for example, to commit myself not to introduce certain types of people into the group. Now on one level this might be seen as philobat behaviour – trying to control objects, master the world; at the same time the same behaviour can be seen as ocnophilic, clinging to those relations and situations where he phantasizes that he is safe. At the same time as he tries to control the group and its members as 'hard' and dangerous objects, he clings to them and becomes very anxious as group breaks approach.

Now the problem here is that illustrated by the old criticism of psychoanalysis that you can say anything about anything – the same accusation that is levelled at explanations based on Freud's concept of the unconscious. There is, I think, an attractive but false opposition between the philobat (safe wide expanses and dangerous objects) and the ocnophil (safe objects and threatening open expanses) that disappears if we drop causal models and typologies and turn to a hermeneutic model. Just as Freud enables us to understand the starting point of metaphors that we continue to elaborate throughout our lives, so Balint provides us with an understanding of the primitive models by which we begin to organize our experience of the world through libidinal impulses, and the situations in which one of these models dominates, or in which we find it useful to revert to it, will vary from individual to individual.

Further, it seems to me that we have here a useful metaphor for the way in which we live the flow of experience. It is a model which is not dissimilar to that developed on a cognitive level by the phenomenological philosopher and sociologist Alfred Schütz (1972). In Schütz's rationalizing account we pluck similarities from the flow of experience and build up what he calls 'typifications', and then typifications of typifications, until we have a manageable universe. The object-relations account adds an experiential/affective dimension to this – the typifications are the hard objects that we encounter in the experiential flow. It seems to me that we discover objects in this flow throughout our lives, objects that can be both sources of danger, because they make us aware of our limitations and vulnerability, or sources of comfort that will protect us from the open sea of experience that threatens to drown us.

Before moving on to more contemporary theorists I want again to talk about levels and types of theory. I criticized Balint's typification of ocnophil and philobat on the ground that the basis of the typification did not allow sufficient differentiation between actions. I suspect that this is true for any attempt to build up psychological typifications. I can understand that they might have a heuristic benefit in that the comparison of opposite types enables a better understanding of the experience that is being described, but it would be wrong to suggest that they have any meaning beyond this. A principal, if not the principal, message of psychoanalysis is that the existence of any one affect, of any one idea or any one psychological process always implies the existence of its opposite. Psychological life is necessarily a matter of opposition and conflict, with maybe momentary feelings of wholeness that should perhaps always be mistrusted.

It is perhaps a paradox of object-relations theorists that they seem to offer very large-scale maps – Fairbairn, Kernberg, Balint – or very small-scale maps – the thinker whom we are now going on to consider.

The self: Winnicott

I want now to turn to the work of D. W. Winnicott, whom I am tempted to call the doyen of object-relations. He is the thinker to whom many turn and hold on to in their search through psychoanalytic theory and practice. I have heard him described as a 'very sunny' man, which certainly comes across in his writings, and there is no doubt that he was a brilliant clinician. His pre-analytic training was as a paediatrician, and there is also no doubt that he had the peculiar (in the best sense) skill of being able to put himself in the place of the very young child and the patient in regression – something attested to by primary and secondary accounts of his practice and his own case studies (see Davis and Wallbridge 1981; Jacobs 1995; Little 1985; Phillips 1998; Winnicott 1980, 1989).

I think as well that the contemporary tendency to idealize children, to see them as doing no wrong except that which comes to them from the outside (see Miller 1987), is responsible not only for some of

Winnicott's popularity but also for some of the ways he is misread or misunderstood. He also tends to get caught up in feminist arguments about motherhood and mothering, and this too influences the way he is read. He can be taken as demanding that women sacrifice themselves to their babies, or as portraying everything that is good, caring and loving about the feminine – particularly, of course, when compared with the masculine.

Winnicott falls very firmly within the tradition that I have been criticizing over recent pages, with a number of saving features, one of which is his lack of systematic theorizing and a pleasing sense of paradox. In the many descriptions of little hamlets that we can find in the psychoanalytic literary map, he is subtle enough to supply as part of his own mappings some more general features whilst implicitly warning that to treat them as universal is to do violence to the patient. We can find in his work a praiseworthy emphasis on individual understanding over against general theory.

On the other hand Winnicott does make things rather too one-sided. He seems to see human development not as a struggle with a restricting outside world and conflicting inner processes. Instead, I think the right metaphor for Winnicott's idea of development is the one with which he was first presented to me many years ago – a bud opening into a flower. In the best circumstances, development is smooth and steady, and the best circumstances are provided by parenting, primarily the mother, protected by the father. It is difficult to know how much of Winnicott's work on mothering is a result of the historical period during which he was writing – the mid-twentieth century, when such a model was the conventional ideal – and how much is necessary to what he was saying in general. It seems to me that it is a bit of both: some fathers can mother as well as or better than some mothers, and what is most important is that the baby has consistent care from consistent people – that is, one or two people most of the time. It is also true that the more we learn from pre-natal psychology, the more clear it is that the relationship with the mother (and to a lesser extent the father if he is around) is well under way by the time the baby is born and that a separation after birth is actually just that: a separation that has to be handled carefully.

Well before empirical psychological evidence became available, Winnicott was writing as if such a relationship was beyond doubt. In the case of pre-natal development, he talks about the 'ordinary devoted mother', who in the final stages of pregnancy and early weeks of the baby's life develops what he calls a 'primary maternal preoccupation' (Winnicott 1988). The language here points to some of the difficulty that contemporary readers have with Winnicott. It might have been the case that when he was writing, the phrase 'ordinary devoted mother' did not have the emotional and political connotations that it has now. Motherhood and child-rearing have become what might be called socially problematic, a process with many intertwined roots, some long predating the era in which Winnicott was writing, but which in combination have changed perceptions radically compared with the mid-twentieth century. First, there was the division of work and family that came with the industrial revolution; then the decreasing rate of family size that always seems to accompany growing wealth; the increasing role of the state in child-rearing; and more recently the rise of feminism. Increasingly birth and mothering and child-rearing have to be taught; they are no longer skills that are passed on from generation to generation in a comparatively unproblematic way.

In such a situation, the state comes to rely on its own agencies – from social workers and kindred professions to the education system and criminal justice system – to govern child-rearing. I think that there is little doubt that in Britain psychoanalysis has been one of those professions (see Rose 1990). Its emphasis on the importance of the environment takes it right to the centre of this task. This means that it is at the centre of a number of debates, and the phrase 'ordinary devoted mother' now carries implications of social control, even social oppression, that it did not carry forty or fifty years ago. Even if mothers are devoted, so the argument might go, that devotion is exploited at their expense.

Primary maternal preoccupation is not something that every mother experiences, but whether it is experienced or not it leaves the mother with equally difficult tasks in her relationship with the child. It refers to a comparatively short period before and after the child's birth when the mother seems to be completely absorbed in her child, as if there is a real psychological identity between them – they are not just one body but one psyche. Often the mother's behaviour will change in uncharacteristic ways: I have a friend who, in the last weeks of her pregnancy, would sit knitting and nursing the cat – activities that I have not known her engage in at any other time in her life. Interest in the outside world wanes – Winnicott suggests that if somebody who wasn't pregnant behaved in this way, we would think that perhaps he or she was becoming mentally ill. The preoccupation can continue after birth: the baby becomes the most important thing in the mother's world, even if the mother is aware that she has conflicts about her mothering and her role in the external world. But it must also change. Winnicott sees development in terms of a movement from complete dependence (and possibly identity) to one of relative dependence. This leads to another way in which Winnicott can be drawn into contemporary political debate – and this might have surprised him – namely that one of the concerns of some contemporary forms of counselling and psychotherapy has become a valuing of *independence*, of being in control of one's own life, whereas a vital and I think basically correct implication of Winnicott's work is that there must always be some degree of dependence on other people.

One of the features of the 'facilitating environment' that enables this move towards relative independence is the 'good enough mother'. This tends to run into the same difficulty as the 'ordinary devoted mother', even though one can almost feel the phrase being coined to avoid adding to the mother's doubts and fears about her own ability – doubts and fears generated by the historical changes I described earlier. Winnicott was always urging mothers to rely on their own gut reactions to their children and assuring them that normally this would be sufficient. Yet even so, the texts of broadcasts he gave in the 1940s (Winnicott 1964) sound rather paternalist and condescending to contemporary ears.

At the root of Winnicott's psychoanalytic theory is a rather limited conception of evolutionary theory. Given the right environment, children will develop into mature adults, in much the same way as, given the right conditions, rose-buds will develop into roses. Such an approach tends to lose not only drive-based conflicts but also the fissures and conflicts that (we shall see later) arise with the acquisition of language. Winnicott's theory also continues the phenomenological concern with self and self-experience that I have noted throughout this chapter.

There are a number of tasks that the infant must achieve from a very early stage, which can be summed up as movements towards integration. Winnicott talks about three states: integration, which one hopes is our normal waking adult state (within reason); disintegration ('he/she went to pieces'); and unintegration, which is a difficult state to describe and a very important developmental achievement. In becoming integrated, the infant must first become rooted in and feel at home in its body. This might sound strange on first hearing – how could it be otherwise? But even well-integrated (in Winnicottian terms) adults will remove themselves from their bodies in an attempt to protect themselves in a traumatic or dangerous situation. People will remember, or even experience, car crashes or violent attacks from above themselves, and I have heard patients who have suffered extremes of brutality talk about the comfort they gained from the psychological ability to imagine that they were flying. Unintegration, as I understand it, is a state of allowing oneself to fall back, without panic, into a sort of pre-integrated state once some integration has been achieved. It is connected with the ability to be alone – and not lonely – and to relax.

Winnicott comments on the way in which the mother, without quite knowing why, will wake the baby up gently, so that it will not be frightened by finding itself in a different position. Time is needed for the infant to find its way back into its body. It seems to me that the adult is often in the same position on waking, only we find our way back rather more quickly. Winnicott talks about holding as one of the ways in which we learn our boundaries; it is not quite the same as Bion's notion of containment, which I think is more explicitly emotional, and less physical. But contact with another person is one of the ways we learn where we begin and end; there are of course other ways as well – such as playing with those funny things waving in front of our eyes that we later learn to call hands and feet. We do not always remain comfortable in our bodies – Winnicott talks of a patient who experienced herself as sitting behind her eyes driving her body as a car-driver might drive a car. I doubt in fact whether our identification with our body is ever complete. Our knowledge of our eventual death makes our body suspect – it is the decay of our body that eventually kills us, and our body makes us vulnerable to violence, fast cars, crashing aircraft, cancer and AIDS. Again the contradictions of our existence, here between our physical and symbolic existence, are ignored (Becker 1973).

Integration involves the development of the ego. Winnicott is unclear exactly where the ego comes from, but, as always with his work, we seem to be turned towards the environment. The mother acts as an 'external ego', the abilities of which are taken in by the infant. Initially the mother has to deal with what Winnicott describes as 'unthinkable anxieties', which in a famous list he names as: going to pieces; falling for ever; having no relationship to the body, having no orientation, and becoming completely isolated through there being no means of orientation (Winnicott 1965: 58). Holding here takes on a physical meaning: the fear of falling, disintegrating and losing contact with the body would be generated by a sense of physical insecurity – of being moved too suddenly, of being dropped or nearly dropped, and so on.

Integration here is not between different psychic structures or agencies but between different experiences in time and space. My sense of existence comes from a grasp of my physical boundaries and the realization that I am the same person when I wake up as when I go to sleep, when I am satisfied after a good meal as when I am hungry, when my nappy is clean as when it is dirty, when my mother is holding me as when my father is holding me, and so on. All this involves a steady process of making contact with the outside world, and for Winnicott, the space between the self and the world is particularly important.

One of Winnicott's best-known ideas is that of the 'transitional object'. Many children will have a special cuddly toy or other object, possibly just a piece of material. For many years a boy of my acquaintance carried around a small duvet named 'cloud'. I have also known a similar object transferred through two different children born some years apart – for the first it was called 'blanky-blanky', for the second 'cuddly'. Such an object is of vital importance for the child; to be separated from it is unbearable, however dirty or smelly it may be – until one day it gets forgotten or lost. It is a transitional object not in the sense that it enables development from one stage to another, but in the sense that it enables movement between the inner and outer world. In Winnicott's words, it is meaningless to ask whether this object comes from the outside world or the inner world – it is essential that it belongs to both. In adults we can talk about a transitional area – the area in which we create new things out of material which belongs to neither world and both worlds at the same time. This book is an example, but so are many everyday things where something new is created: do-it-yourself work in the home, decoration, anything where something different emerges and we do not slavishly follow plans. For some people the creativity lies in the way in which they create worthwhile relationships from a damaged psyche.

In adult life, the acknowledgement of a transitional object or transitional area is often felt to be a sign of weakness. We often hear of students bringing their teddy bears and dolls with them when they come to university, but if this became public knowledge about one specific individual it would be likely to cause great embarrassment. I recently attended a creative writing class where each contribution was preceded by an apology, which in my case was certainly an attempt to protect something that was in the public realm but at the same time very private. The transitional area involves unfashionably vulnerable inner depths and unfashionably vulnerable dependence on external objects.

The baby during its early period out of the womb imagines that it creates the whole of the external world – when it cries at night it has no sense of the mother or father getting out of bed and preparing a feed; it cries and as a result the food comes. There is a sense in which the care must fail the baby in order for it to become aware of the reality and resistance of the outside world, but this must not happen too early. To begin with the baby's omnipotence must, in Winnicott's words, 'be implemented'. The baby must be allowed to find and create the breast by rooting for the nipple, not clamped on it as if it were a car being filled with petrol. The more it is allowed satisfaction on demand (what my parents' generation disapprovingly called 'spoiling'), the stronger the sense of itself and its abilities, and the more it will be able to bear the frustrations of reality.

Winnicott does not portray an entirely rosy picture of motherhood – he points to reasons why a mother will hate her child and the reason why she needs to be able to tolerate that hatred. He goes so far as to suggest that a mother's fear of her own hatred forces her to retreat into masochism, and it is this that gives rise to the myth of female masochism (Winnicott 1958).

So here again something that Freud situates at a level of unconscious agency and mechanism is in object-relations turned into what phenomenologists might call an act of consciousness, even if that act remains obscure to the actor. Winnicott traces the vicissitudes of consciousness rather than the vicissitudes of the instincts. We can see this most clearly if we compare Winnicott's notion of the mirror stage with that of Lacan, at whom we will look in more detail later. For Winnicott the mirror is the mother's face and it offers a reflection of the self that the infant can take on as part of its move to integration. For Lacan it is an imaginary identification that divides us from ourselves (Rudnytsky 1991).

The nearest that Winnicott gets to the divisions that Lacan sees in the human subject is in his notion of the 'false self', but for Winnicott this is more a pathology than part of the human condition. It is a defence, of course, and one that we use in our routine everyday interactions. Josephine Klein (1987) likens it to an automatic pilot. We develop it in its strongest form as a result of a failure of holding or containment in the early environment. The carer is anxious, and this is conveyed to the developing infant in such a way that it learns that it must act to relieve that anxiety, and adjust its behaviour, its being, to what the caretaker wishes. Instead of the carer containing the anxieties of the infant, the infant has to contain the anxieties of the carer and develops a prematurely adult, coping personality that acts as a sort of shell. Consequently the infant develops into adulthood as someone who remains out of touch with his or her underlying feelings and out of touch with – untouched by – the feelings of others. Yet he or she is apparently operating reasonably well in the outside world. He or she is, in words regularly used by one of my patients, a 'people pleaser', yet out of touch with his or her needs.

Winnicott, wisely, does not talk much about the nature of the 'real self', and one suspects that this might be a vulnerable undefended entity. However, enthusiastic counsellors and therapists take up the mission to liberate the real selves of their patients, and this seems to amount to 'implementing' their omnipotence – to feeding narcissism rather than introducing reality. It is as if they try to correct one form of bad parenting by engaging its equally damaging (for adults) opposite form. As long as we remain with the idea that it is possible to achieve a more or less integrated, more or less unitary self without fundamental fissures and conflicts, we will encourage narcissism.

Winnicott is scathing about intellectuals, or at least intellectualism, in a way that reinforces the sort of criticisms I have been making of him: '. . . a person with rich intellectual endowment in terms of grey matter can function brilliantly without much reference to the human being. But it is the human being who, by an accumulation of experiences duly assimilated, may achieve wisdom' (Winnicott 1986: 60). Now there is a truth in this yet a major falsehood that I think has the unfortunate effect of feeding a reluctance to think amongst certain psychotherapists. It is of course true – a truism – that wisdom comes through an accumulation of experience, but without the intellectual ability to sort through and organize experience, we do not accumulate wisdom. I do not think that there could be such a thing as an ignorant, or, perhaps more accurately, an unthinking, sage. I do not think it is at all true that it is possible to function brilliantly without reference to the human; there might be people around who try to do that – and not just in the academic world – but in my experience they do not get very far, or do not produce the work that others might expect of them. In my introduction I talked about the division between the psychoanalytic and the academic worlds, and this is one of the ways in which it regularly appears. Each side easily falls into usually unconscious expressions of envy of the other side.

Conclusion

I want now to try to bring this chapter to a close by drawing together some of the themes into what can only be called a structure of paradoxes that I will try to develop over the concluding chapters. There are of course many other object-relationship theorists; amongst the most interesting I would include Christopher Bollas (1987, 1992, 1995) and Masud Khan (1974, 1983), who add to and modify the Winnicottian model of self and self-experience, and who seem to maintain notions of 'wholeness', encouraged by notions of helping and cure, which are emphasized within the medical profession on the edges of which psychoanalysis exists. This, taken with all the other influences, such as the comparatively simple interpretation of biological evolution, and the general cultural move towards narcissism, hides the emphasis on internal structures and divisions that seems to me to give Freud's work its value.

Now the values of object-relations theory are mixed. Some goals are impossible to achieve: we are by nature divided between different worlds, torn by contradictory drives, divided between different psychic structures. At the same time the theory's concern with creativity is important, but I would suggest that human creativity comes from the very divisions and conflicts that the theory tends to lose sight of as it moves away from drive theory. The discovery of the real self is not easy because it is not there, and it is precisely the suffering entailed by our internal divisions that pushes us into our individuality and our creativity.

8

Psychoanalysis as a Science of Child Development

Introduction

The notion of a causal connection between infantile experience and adult character haunted the discussion of object-relations theory in the previous chapter, and in contemporary society it is a common-place that what happens to us as children has some sort of effect on the sort of adult that we come to be. Parents feel responsible if something 'goes wrong' in their children's development; as adults we blame our parents if we do not feel all is well. Perhaps they did not love us enough, or take enough interest in what we were doing; perhaps as a parent I feel I do not spend enough 'quality time' with my child(ren) or I feel that I get angry with them too often or that in some unspecified way I will damage them. There are shelves of books in libraries and bookshops telling us how we should treat our children.

Yet the connection between infancy, childhood and adulthood is often not really known, and the certainty about the connection is combined with a generalized angst around parenting. There are good social and historical reasons for this that were discussed in the previous chapter. The role of the family is becoming reduced to one of early socialization, after which the state and peer groups play an increasingly important role. At the same time family size is decreasing and there are many people who do not have contact with babies until their own are born – and perhaps not even then. Parenting has become something that must, it appears, be taught, and infants have become a central concern for psychological investigation. David

Chamberlain (1987) points out that the number of scientific papers on infants increased from 500 in 1950 to 2,000 in 1970, and now even that number seems small, and that:

> The literature shows how badly infants have been underestimated. Schedules established by experts indicating when various abilities become operative have required adjustment to times earlier and earlier in the first year of life. A remarkable number of important abilities have been traced back to birth itself, surprising the investigators, ruining theories and violating a venerable rule that complex processes take time to develop. (Chamberlain 1987: 31)

It is clear from the material that Chamberlain considers that many of our abilities are not only present from birth but are there prior to birth, and that the newborn infant learns faster than at any other stage in his or her life. There are already studies in the psychoanalytic tradition that attempt to link *in utero* behaviour with later personality development (Piontelli 1992). Inevitably some of this work has been popularized in such a way that parental anxiety is bound to increase (Verney and Kelly 1981).

In this chapter I will look at two different approaches that take us to the borders of psychoanalysis – the borders that it shares with cognitive and developmental psychology. The depth psychology of Freud and Klein fades into the background and is replaced by empirical studies of infant and child behaviour. In one line of development, found in the work of John Bowlby in Britain, evolutionary theory becomes important; in the American development, in the work of Kohut and Stern, the phenomenology of self-experience dominates. However, the end results in both cases are similar.

Attachment theory

The psychoanalyst who has done most to establish the empirical evidence for a specific link between damaging childhood experience and later life is John Bowlby. He is distinguished from most psychoanalysts by his conception of himself as an empirical scientist and what Holmes (1993) calls his espousal of 'a narrow version of science', which Holmes compares with the European and Jewish intellectual tradition in which the dominant psychoanalytic thinkers are based. As a scientist Bowlby's interest was ethology, which the *Oxford English Dictionary* defines, first, as the 'portrayal of character by mimicry' or simply 'the portrayal of character' and, second, as 'the science of ethics'. In the Addenda there is a third definition – the study of instinctive animal behaviour in relation to environment. The first definition is close to, but does not capture, what Bowlby was actually doing. The second is a long way from his work. The third is closest. He placed himself in a tradition of evolutionary biology that is perhaps rather more questionable today than it was thought to be when he was working with it after the Second World War.

Perhaps Bowlby is celebrated (or demonized) most as the theorist of maternal deprivation, an issue that has been close to the centre of political arguments whether in relation to working mothers and their supposedly bad effect on children after the Second World War, or through issues raised by contemporary feminism. His early work (Bowlby 1952) suggests another sociological reason for the modern concern with parenting: in societies with low levels of unemployment and (supposedly) adequate welfare provision, the emotional care provided by parents is primarily responsible for providing or not providing an adequate family life. Bowlby tended to focus on the lack of maternal care and its relationship to delinquency, using statistical research of his own and others to back up his case. Holmes (1993) suggests that Bowlby makes sweeping statements at this stage of his work and his demonization is as the man who says that women who work damage their children. He talks, for example, about the mother gaining satisfaction by caring for her child for 365 days and nights a year until he or she becomes an adult. I think that one can see the feminists' point.

However, even at this earlier stage Bowlby was making reference to a carer who might not be the mother but who can fulfil the mother's function, and in his later work, and in the work of others who have followed it up, a more open and interesting theory develops. The emphasis is still on the quality of care, but on the importance of a carer rather than the biological mother in particular. Deprivation of care is not seen as leading automatically to delinquency or anything else. Rather it is seen as a predisposing factor that increases the probability that some things might go wrong in later life. There is much evidence to support Bowlby's suggestions, and his work has led to changes in nursing practice in hospitals and in nurseries. But now it is time to set out his theory.

Evolution

Bowlby's work is rooted firmly in evolutionary biology; Darwin was his great hero and Bowlby's last major publication (Bowlby 1990) was a biography of Darwin using his (Bowlby's) psychological ideas. Elsewhere (Craib 1994) I have set out some criticisms of Bowlby's interpretation of evolutionary theory: he overemphasizes the role of the environment and underemphasizes the role of chance in evolution. This gives his theory normative and deterministic dimensions: normative in that it presupposes a 'normal' state and teleological development towards such a state; deterministic in that the success of the development depends upon the environment and we lose an understanding of the *interaction* between child and environment and the contributions of the child's inner life to the process.

Attachment theory can be placed in an evolutionary context in the sense that it deals with behaviours and relationships that, Bowlby suggests, are essential for survival. In his own studies on the effects of separation and loss on children, and in others' studies of animal behaviour, he identified something that he called 'attachment behaviour'. This refers to the child's dependency on the parent, and in particular to what happens if there seems to be some threat to the dependent relationship. Bowlby defines it as 'the resultant of a distinctive and in part pre-programmed set of behaviour patterns which in the ordinary expectable environment develop during the early months and have the effect of keeping the child in more or less close-proximity to his [*sic*] mother figure' (Bowlby 1988: 3). Bowlby suggests too that parenting behaviour is learnt but also has strong biological roots (established through studies of animal behaviour), and these roots are responsible for the strong emotions around parenting. One of the features of attachment behaviour on the part of the child or the adult is the strong feelings that go with it, and this is true for other biologically rooted forms of behaviour: sexual behaviour, exploratory behaviour and eating behaviour. Each type of behaviour serves a distinct biological function, and attachment behaviour serves the survival of the individual and the species through protecting the young until they become independent. The central feature of Bowlby's conception of parenting is 'the provision by both parents of a secure base from which a child or adolescent can make sorties into the outside world and to which he [*sic*] can return, knowing for sure that he will be welcomed when he gets there, nourished physically and emotionally, comforted if distressed, reassured if frightened' (Bowlby 1988: 11). Important here is the proximity or availability of the loved one; one of Bowlby's favourite images is of a parent and child in a park, the child moving away from the parent and then returning, perhaps each time moving a little further away and staying a little longer. In many ways this is a metaphor for life and adult relationships in later life. The process not only goes on when the parent is alive but it also continues in the mind and experience of the child when the parent is dead. Attachment behaviour occurs when this relationship is threatened or interrupted from either side, whether, for example, it is a matter of my adolescent son's anxiety when I become seriously ill or my anxiety when he goes off to his first rock concert.

It often strikes me that it is very difficult to acknowledge attachment feelings, especially in a society that seems to devalue our dependence on other people – have you ever heard the words 'dependency culture' used to refer to something desirable? It is publicly embarrassing and perhaps privately threatening to admit a need for another person; universities are on the surface full of strong and independent young people and we cannot see the hours of homesickness locked away in bedrooms. Yet the strength of our attachment needs can be seen in the way that people can cling to violent or abusive parents or partners. We cling to our attachment figure all the harder the greater the danger of losing him or her.

The developmental paths of attachment

The full detail of Bowlby's theory can be found in the three volumes that comprise the heart of his work (Bowlby 1971, 1975, 1981), and here I am concerned only with its general outlines. Bowlby was influenced not only by psychoanalysis but also by systems theory, and he is much closer to a cognitive approach than are most of the thinkers considered in this book. Basically the idea is that as children we learn from our attachment figures the behaviour that we will expect from those to whom we will become attached throughout our lives – we develop working models of attachment that govern our expectations from close relationships. If our early attachment is problematic, our working model is faulty; we become anxious about the reliability of the attachment figure, and instead of basing our actions on an accurate understanding of the relationship, we expect the carer to be erratic or rejecting and see ourselves as having to accommodate to his or her wishes.

A securely attached child will be more or less distressed at a separation from the main carer but will be able to restore the relationship and receive comfort when the two come together again. There are three principal forms of insecure attachment. The first (avoidant) involves denying or repressing both the implicit rejection of the loved one and the child's own neediness; when the two are reunited the carer will be ignored and the child will try to carry on as usual. The second (adherence) involves clinging behaviour, and the third (ambivalent attachment) involves alternating between clinging and angrily attacking the carer on coming together again. A fourth category, identified by more recent research, has been called 'insecure-disorganized', and involves more severe disruption and produces a wide range of confused activity (Ainsworth et al. 1978).

There is now much research backing up this model and tracing the development of attachment behaviour as the child gets older (Ainsworth et al. 1978; Bretherton 1985; Fonagy et al. 1991; Main, Kaplan and Cassidy 1985; Parkes, Stevenson-Hinde and Marris 1991). There is an intuitive validity to these ideas – that we learn what people are like from the way our parents relate to us, and we expect other people to whom we become close to behave in the same way. If we think back over times when we have parted from people we love, whether the big occasions like leaving the parental home, or small occasions, a partner or friend going away for a few days, most people will recognize pangs of pain in response to which we tell ourselves not to be silly; or perhaps we will remember the pre-leaving row which makes it easier for us to go, or the unexpected row that erupts out of the apparent happiness at a partner's return. For some of us these reactions will be more exaggerated than for others, and it is sometimes possible to think back to the situation that must have created the pattern – evacuation during wartime, parental break-up, infantile or parental illnesses or death. It is in fact no surprise that Bowlby wrote some important papers on children's reactions to death (Bowlby 1960, 1961) and that attachment theory provides a backcloth to one of the most important modern works on mourning (Parkes 1987).

The range of reactions to separation can be seen in most therapy and training experiential groups. Some people will be able to talk fairly easily about a range of feelings around breaks in the therapy, perhaps about missing the therapist and/or the group but also welcoming the extra free time. For some this will shade over into worrying about their ability to survive the break without the support of the group, and some will worry about the ability of the group to get together again after the break – will other people come back to the group? Others will be puzzled by these reactions – the break is just a break and of course everybody will be back, and why should I feel anything about all this? However, some people who voice these latter feelings will miss the last session before the break or the first session(s) after the break. And, occasionally, there will be an attempted suicide or a crisis during the break.

The status of attachment theory

Despite the intuitive sense of attachment theory it is important to make the point that it is not the causal theory that it might appear to be. Early separation from the mother, or an emotionally distant mother (in his later work Bowlby tended to give more emphasis to the emotional presence of the carer), will not automatically lead to problems for the children in later life. They will be more vulnerable to physical or mental illness, will tend to achieve less in their education or work life, and have difficulties in establishing relationships, but these are statistical probabilities. The same is true for more recent but perhaps basically similar studies about the effects of divorcing parents on children (Wallerstein 1985), and steps can be taken to decrease (or, if parents or social institutions are careless about these things, increase) the risk of later difficulties in forming and maintaining relationships and realizing human potentialities. One of the unquestionably beneficial effects of Bowlby's work has been the changes brought about in hospital care where young children are concerned and in nursery care. Until the 1960s or even later in Britain, it was customary to keep children away from a hospitalized parent, particularly a mother, or parents away from a hospitalized child, usually on the grounds that the children (and parents) would be upset. This of course was true – it was an upsetting situation for all concerned, but the attempt to handle it by avoiding and denying appropriate emotions increased the probability of later difficulties. Most hospitals now will allow parents open-ended visiting and overnight accommodation with a child if required. It is interesting that similar arguments are used in divorce disputes about contact with the non-custodial parent, usually the father. The contact *is* upsetting for the child and for the parents, yet the same arguments apply. In nurseries, the change has been from task-oriented nursing, which inhibited relationships, to relationship-oriented care. A number of films made by Robertson in the 1950s show the effects of separations in different situations (for example, Robertson 1952, 1958).

Bowlby: a critique

Bowlby's work is at the scientific end of psychoanalysis, in one of the more restricted senses of the word 'science': seeking empirical, statistical regularities and setting them in the context of an evolutionary theory in which the environment takes the most important role. In my criticism of this I do not want to go too far. It is clear that badly and insensitively handled separations of carer and child in early infancy or even later can lead to difficulties for the child in later life, as can emotional distance on the part of the carer, and a range of more obviously abusive activities from systematic violence through to incest. If we imagine a continuum of harmful activities by which parents can cause suffering and damage to their children, then most would agree on what should be at the most damaging end. Yet even there, people can survive atrocious acts of physical violence and sexual abuse with widely differing degrees of success.

Bowlby's method and his classifications tend to gloss these individual differences and to reinforce that view of psychoanalysis that sees it as a form of medical treatment for behavioural disorders. The studies and the theory emphasize behaviour and emotion rather than meaning, and where meaning is considered the emphasis tends to be on the cognitive (the working models) rather than the unconscious, the individual's creative phantasy life and personal play of meanings. Bowlby's view of psychotherapy seems to be rather less optimistic than others, and tends to emphasize the reality of the therapist–patient relationship as enabling the patient to experience a secure relationship rather than the gaining of insight, although contemporary attachment theorists see a cognitive understanding of the cause of problems as important (Eagle 1997). In this context, Rustin (1991: 146) expresses some scepticism about Bowlby's therapeutic methods.

It is of course a matter of emphasis, and I do not think that any of these ideas I have mentioned are 'bad' or undesirable, and they have their place in most forms of psychoanalytic therapy. Indeed some achievements have to be reached at this level before the processes of interpretation can open up psychic space and enable a degree of creativity. My fear is that the concentration on the child–adult link as if it were primarily causal rather than primarily hermeneutic closes down possibilities rather than opens them up. I think that this is true of any approach that presupposes a 'normal' path of development, especially one driven by biological necessity; psychological paths of development can be much more open and difficult, and the role of unconscious phantasies and connections is always likely to disrupt and transform the more conscious learning processes. Further, the notion of random variation is an important loss in the transfer of an evolutionary model to psychology – for in a rapidly changing environment, which modern Western society has been for at least the last two hundred and fifty years, it might be that the psychological structures that adapt to such a society are – for good or for ill – different from those that enabled adaptation to more traditional societies, and they might even change from generation to generation. Bowlby's work seems to consider only one, unquestioned and unchanging form of social environment that either succeeds or fails. I am not sure that human beings can be understood in this way at all, and I am certain that they cannot be understood in this way alone.

Self psychology

Kohut

Heinz Kohut asserts that the oxygen of psychological life is to be found in an affirming, supportive and validating milieu and that the need for such an atmosphere exists from birth to death.

Siegel, *Heinz Kohut and the Psychology of Self*

We now jump across the Atlantic to another modern psychoanalyst, one who has aroused interest in Britain comparatively recently although he has been publishing since the 1950s. I would suggest that what puts Heinz Kohut in the same camp as Bowlby, despite some very obvious differences, is, first, that he offers a comparatively simple conception of the internal world, with the emphasis on cognition, and, second, his work is connected to empirical psychological research in child development.

There are ways in which Kohut's work (1971, 1977) reflects the traditional optimism of American culture and provides some confirmation for the 'culture of narcissism' thesis. I have already suggested that as it developed in different contexts psychoanalysis took on elements of its surrounding culture and so developed different emphases. If Bowlby represents British scepticism and faith in empirical science, there is something distinctly expansive about Kohut's work. Mario Jacoby (1990) suggests that, in contrast with Freud's analytic and scientific stance, trying to theorize psychological structures and mechanisms, Kohut's attitude towards his patients is empathic and has led him to different theoretical concerns that have to be used in alternation with more traditional forms of theory. This new concern is with the self. In the language of realist philosophy it is a move away from underlying structure to the surface, away from the structural analysis of experience towards a phenomenology of experience, from trying to explain what we feel to describing what we feel. Whereas Freud was concerned precisely with analysis, with breaking down into parts, the concept of the self brings us to the idea of *wholeness*, which, Kohut argues, is more than the sum of its parts, the drives and defences that make up psychic structure. The radical movement that Kohut makes in this argument is to subordinate the drives to the whole of the self, but this subordination occurs after birth, through the way in which the carer relates to the infant. In Kohut's own words, it is an 'experience-near' theory.

Now this is where Kohut's psychoanalytic theory becomes a developmental theory only slightly different to Bowlby's. For Bowlby there is a biological patterning at work and the responsibility for successful development lies primarily with the environment; Kohut does not make any reference to a biological patterning but the environment in the form of the carer is as important if not more so. Kohut begins with a theory very close to the 'mirroring' theory that we can find with different emphases in psychoanalytic thinkers as far apart as Winnicott and Lacan. The baby has no self at birth but develops a self through the way the carer treats it – in what one hopes is a caring, understanding and responsive way.

This basic self – or perhaps more accurately self-concept – Kohut calls the 'selfobject' (in his earlier work the 'self-object'). The carer is experienced by the infant as part of itself. I don't think that there is any dispute about the existence of such an experience, since it continues to some degree through childhood and even into adulthood. It is difficult to see in the way that we treat our own parents, but it is clearer, if not obvious, in the way that our children treat us or others treat their parents. The teenager's expectation that the parent will always be available when required (and not there when not required) is but one sign of the way in which we treat others as if they were part of our selves. If they see me outside of the consulting room, my patients often seem taken aback by the realization that I am not a permanent fixture in that room. I had a similar experience when I first saw my therapist from a distance, walking along a street with a shopping bag. She seemed ordinary, one amongst many, yet in my head she was unique, larger and different and a part of me whose independence I did not have to consider.

For the infant the carer appears as all-powerful, and as he or she absorbs the selfobject – identifies with it – so the infant begins to experience itself as omnipotent. As the child matures into an adult, this grandiose self becomes more realistic in its ambitions and its sense of self. Omnipotence is transformed into mature ideals, although a bipolarity remains. There is a tension between ambition and a knowledge of what might be really possible.

The selfobject gradually becomes a 'true' separate object that can be loved and hated. The identification with the selfobject is an idealization, and in the process of maturation the child creates an internal psychic structure as he or she takes in the caring and judging aspects of the selfobject and makes them his or her own. If that does not occur for some reason, the child, and later the adult, is left searching for an idealized figure – another selfobject to whom to attach him- or herself. For some people drugs might substitute for such an attachment, especially if the disruption occurs in the early pre-oedipal stage – up to eighteen months.

If there is some traumatic interruption to the relationship during the next eighteen months of the pre-oedipal period, Kohut suggests that the infant seeks a sexual solution to calming the disturbed narcissistic self, a way of relating to the world that can be carried on into adult life. If the disturbance occurs during the oedipal stage itself (three to five years), then the super-ego does not develop to its full extent and the person will seek approval from another, or others, through his or her life. The process of psychoanalysis takes the patient back through these developments, beginning with the idealization of the analyst and the development of the grandiose self, and then, it is hoped, through the steady adjustment to reality.

According to Kohut, the distance of Freud's theory from the experience of the patient enabled external cultural ideas to influence his notion of a successful treatment. The classic psychoanalytic view of success, he argues, involves the capacity for productive activity, independence and self-sufficiency, dominant cultural values in the West. All these values involve the overcoming of the narcissistic self, whereas Kohut argues that narcissistic structures need to be maintained throughout an individual's life. This is, I think, simply wrong. The values described by Kohut were certainly strong social values when Freud was working, but Kohut's own values are strong in contemporary society – something revealed directly in the work of Christopher Lasch (1980). I would suggest that the closer we stay to experience, the more likely we are to build a theory on dominant cultural values.

Stern and self-development

I want now to turn to the work of Daniel Stern, a developmental psychologist who describes his position as 'far closer to Kohut's and Bowlby's contention that pre-Oedipal pathology is due to deficits and reality-based events – rather than due to conflicts in the psychodynamic sense' (Stern 1985: 255). Stern, like Bowlby, is concerned with linking psychoanalytic ideas with acceptably scientific evidence, and this inevitably takes him, as it does Bowlby, to external relations of causality or quasi-causality.

Stern's work is part of what I have already referred to as a revolution in the way in which we look at the newborn infant that has taken place over recent decades. Drawing on his own research as well as that of others, he produces findings which tend towards confirming the broad vision of infancy that psychoanalysts began exploring some decades ago, not least that what the infant feels, irrespective of what it knows, can be important. Affect is not simply a product of cognition.

Stern talks about 'four senses of self' in the developing infant, the first of which he calls the 'sense of an emergent self'. He argues that the research indicates that infant experience is more unified than the separate disciplines that investigate it. Like Kernberg, he insists on the unity of experience, 'patterned constellations' of experience organized in relation to self and other. This emergent self develops over the first two months of life; Stern seems to think that a defining feature of human life is this ability to organize experience from the word go, or, as some research (Chamberlain 1987; Verney and Kelly 1981) indicates, before the word go.

From the age of two or three months up to six months, another dimension of self appears, what Stern calls 'the core self'. The first stage of this 'core self' is the sense of 'Self vs Other'. The infant gains a physical sense of its self with the mother and without the mother. He suggests that there are four fundamental aspects of this experience. The first is *self-agency*, the sense that I am author of my own actions and not the author of others' actions. I move my arms around, but I do not move my mother's arms. And I learn that there are consequences to my actions – in Stern's example, if I close my eyes, it goes dark. The second aspect is that of *self-coherence*, a sense of physical unity and boundaries and a centre that remains the same whether I am still or moving. I learn where my body begins and ends, and I do not confuse my body with the body of the person who is holding me. Third, there is a sense of *self-affectivity*, 'experiencing patterned inner qualities of feeling (affects) that belong with other experiences of the self' (Stern 1985: 71). Finally there is a sense of *self-history*, of a continuity of one's own existence that lasts through changes. Stern insists that the core self is an experience – we have a sense of it, not a knowledge of it. It normally operates outside of our awareness.

The second stage of a sense of a core self involves a sense of the self with others. Here Stern is critical of theories that argue that the child cannot differentiate itself from the mother or prime carer until some time after birth; rather, he argues, we have a sense of ourselves as separate from a very early age. He suggests that, rather than seeing the infant as undifferentiated, perhaps we should see it as experiencing itself in relation to the other. This could still allow us to think of the infant as having a profoundly social existence, as Winnicott claimed in his observation that 'there is no such thing as a baby' – only a baby in relation to a carer.

Stern argues that the other is a 'self-regulating other' for the infant, regulating the infant's arousal, the intensity of its feelings and the type of feeling it is experiencing: 'In fact, from two to seven months, an enormous sector of the entire affective spectrum an infant can feel is possible only in the presence of and through the interactive mediation of an other, that is, by being with another person' (Stern 1985: 103). He criticizes Bowlby for being too narrow in his focus on attachment experience alone. The presence of another is important for a much wider range of experience to occur and develop. Paradoxically, it seems that Stern manages to endow the infant with a greater degree of autonomy and dependency at the same time; he recognizes what psychoanalysts refer to as the 'merging' of the infant and carer, but he argues that this is an experience for the infant not of merging, but of a change in the core self during an interaction in which the sense of possessing a core self is not breached:

> Merger experiences at this age [three to seven months] are simply a way of being with someone, but someone who acts as a self-regulating other. Any such lived experience includes: (1) significant alterations in the infant's feeling state that seem to belong to the self even though they were mutually created by self with another, (2) the other person as seen, heard and felt at the moment of the alteration, (3) an intact sense of a core self and core other against which all this occurs, and (4) a variety of contextual and situational events. How can all of these be yoked to form a subjective unit that is neither a fusion nor a we-self nor a cool cognitive association between distinct selves and others? This yoking occurs in the form of an actual episode of life as lived. The lived episode – just as in memory – is the unit that locks the different attributes of experience into relationships one with the other. The relationships are those that prevailed at the actual happening. (Stern 1985: 109–10)

These episodes are the units of memory for the infant, 'generalized episodes of interactive experience that are mentally represented – that is, representations of interactions that have been generalized, or RIGS' (p.110) When remembered, RIGS 'evoke' a comparison with other experiences. This, for Stern, is equivalent to Bowlby's working model of the mother.

I have quoted Stern at length here because I will return to his argument as part of my attempt to show the limitations of his work. Before I do that, however, I want to look at his further elaborations on the sense of a core self, which involve, first, a process of what he calls 'affect attunement', and then the development of a sense of a verbal self. Before he deals with either of these developments he talks about a 'quantum leap' that takes place between the seventh and the ninth month of life when the infant discovers that not only does it have a mind of its own but that others have a mind and that subjective experience can be shared – a discovery that amounts to a theory of 'separate minds'; the infant can now experience the carer's empathic responses and the carer is aware of a different 'feel' to the infant. The infant has gained access to a world of intersubjective awareness. This quantum leap develops, he suggests, not as an innate stage of development but through the carer's ability to interpret the infant's subjective states.

The next development, according to Stern, is the sharing of affective states, 'affective attunement'. I will quote in full the paragraph in which he sets out what he thinks is necessary for such attunement, again for the purposes of later criticism:

> For there to be an intersubjective exchange about affect, then, strict imitation won't do. In fact several processes must take place. First, the parent must be able to read the infant's feeling state from the infant's overt behaviour. Second, the parent must perform some behaviour that is not a strict imitation but nonetheless corresponds in some way to the infant's overt behaviour. Third, the infant must be able to read this corresponding parental response as having to do with the infant's own original feeling experience and not just imitating the infant's behaviour. It is only in the presence of these three conditions that feeling states within one person can be knowable to another and that they can both sense, without using language, that the transaction has occurred. (Stern 1985: 139)

The carer is not necessarily consciously aware of his or her part in the attunement, but Stern seems to be saying that what happens is that in this process of attunement the subjective state itself becomes an object of thought and a distinction is made between the subjective state and the overt behaviour to which it gives rise. Those familiar with G. H. Mead's social psychology (Mead 1934) will recognize the similarity with the latter's social behaviourism.

Affective attunement makes possible the development of a verbal capacity, which, interestingly in respect to what I will be arguing shortly, Stern refers to as a two-edged sword. On the one hand it opens up a wide range of new possibilities in interpersonal relationships, but on the other it also divides interpersonal experience into what is lived and what is represented in speech and the two do not necessarily coincide. This opens up the possibility that speech may alienate one from one's experience.

Here Stern's affinities with Mead become more explicit as he argues that the acquisition of language makes it possible to reflect on the self as an object and involves the ability to play. It also takes us to what many therapists would see as a central aim of psychotherapy, that of enabling the patient or client to put feelings into words, or in Stern's terms, to articulate core-self experiences. Stern recognizes what he calls the 'outer edge of the sword': that it creates new forms of being with another person but it also creates problems with being with another person.

The problems with Stern   The effect of Kohut's approach, which is also clear in Stern's work, is that psychological development is more dependent on the external world, and the quality of care that the infant receives, than it is on any internal dynamic. Given the right external care, the internal world will develop along its proper course. There is no space within the 'self' of self psychology for conflicts that are there from the beginning, and as with Bowlby, the weight – and definition – of successful development depends on the outside world.

I commented earlier on the paradox that for Stern the child was dependent on the carer for the environment that will enable it to develop in a satisfactory manner, yet at the same time it is already from birth psychologically separate from the carer. We can see this as a contradiction: if there is psychological separation, as opposed to some degree of merging, then how does communication become possible at all? Anderson points out a connected contradiction in his work: 'Stern strongly feels that during the domain of core-relatedness (2–6 months), the baby does not experience any emotional penetration by mother's or others' mental states. Yet . . . he also presents a schema [Stern 1985: 120] to demonstrate how mother's fantasies about her baby can influence baby's self-perceptions' (Anderson 1992: 37).

There is the same sort of difficulty with the long quotations above. It seems to me reasonable to suggest that psychological relationships are not as one-dimensional as Stern argues – that there are moments of separation and moments of interpenetration and a movement between the two that is in many ways a lifelong experience. Evidence offered by Verney and Kelly (1981) seems to suggest that the interpenetration begins prior to birth through the chemical reactions attached to the mother's feelings.

Throughout the earlier quotations, Stern's discussion of the infant is in terms of its cognitive abilities, its acts of *knowing*, or its sense of self, of being (or having?) a core self. These two levels, of thinking, or memorizing, and of sensing one's self, are comparatively close to the surface. To say this of course implies that the human psychic structure has a number of levels, that it has a depth. Our sense of self, the level at which Kohut seems to concentrate, is arguably almost entirely conscious – it is my sense of wholeness and integrity that, as Kohut argues, includes all the other levels and psychological phenomena; in a healthy state they are subordinated to the self. The cognitive processes that Stern discusses are deeper, and perhaps we have little conscious access to them, although we clearly experience their results. They seem to be primarily neurological processes rather than psychological processes, which do not start properly until the acquisition of language. Of course the neurological and the psychological are related, but they are not identical, and if Stern is right in assuming that the infant experiences itself as separate from birth, we would expect psychological processes to be there from birth also. Paradoxically, Stern's comments about the double-edged nature of language direct us to the psychoanalyst who is about as far away from his work as we can get: Jacques Lacan.

Conclusion

Psychoanalysis has always possessed developmental theories, and as I argued in my discussion of Freud's developmental theory, they can provide a very broad framework of understanding. However, none of them describe simple cause–effect processes and none of them enable us to understand the specificity of individual experience or meaning. The development of the self and the relationship with the mother or prime carer is clearly important, but the self is deeper and more complex than the self discussed by Bowlby, Kohut or Stern. These interpretations tend to move away from the difficulties that Freud himself faced head on. They turn psychoanalysis into a theory of pathology rather than the beginnings of an understanding of the range of human experience and its problems.

At the same time these theories are not meaningless; not only are they broad frameworks for understanding development, they are also guides to the possible origins of psychic pain and living difficulties. But they are not explanations. Becoming aware that my mother left me alone in hospital when I was a few months old, or that she was constantly critical of my actions from an early age will not solve my problems nor make them easier. These theories tell incomplete stories about ourselves, and the import of my comment that they deal with surface or near-surface processes, with what we consciously experience in the way of our emotions and our feelings about ourselves, is that to fill out our stories, we have to look at underlying psychological structures and processes.

9

Lacan and the Return to Freud

Introduction

If object-relations theory moves us closer to the surface of experience and a phenomenology of the self, and the work of Bowlby takes us towards the theory of evolution and cognitive psychology, then the French development of psychoanalysis takes us back to the depths of depth psychology. The work of Lacan was often hailed as a return to Freud, at a moment in French intellectual history when returns to original thinkers were popular: Louis Althusser (1969) was returning to Marx and Roland Barthes (1967) and others were returning to the work of Saussure. These returns were propelled by developments in the history and philosophy of science, one of the results of which was contemporary critical realism (Benton and Craib 2001). All the above thinkers, together with the anthropologist Claude Lévi-Strauss (1969) and the historian of ideas Michel Foucault, were identifying underlying structures of their objects of study and claiming that the discovery of these underlying structures marked off that area of study as a science. The ramifications of the structuralist movement are only important here insofar as they enable us to understand Lacan's psychoanalysis, which is also coloured by his history as a surrealist and the influence of French Hegelian scholars.

This is a comparatively short chapter in relation to the preceding chapters but it should not be taken as indicating my view of Lacan's importance. It should be remembered that Freud's work has developed over a century, and Kleinian theory, object-relations theory and even attachment theory have been around for between fifty-five and seventy years, whereas the Lacanian school is in one sense the youngest and, to the extent that Lacan does take us back to Freud, in another sense the oldest of the different schools. One significant dimension to Lacan's work is the way his psychoanalysis has been taken up into philosophy, social theory and literary theory, and in this sense his work is responsible fundamentally for the blossoming of psychoanalytic thought in universities, and, less directly, for the existence of this book. I will be looking at one aspect of his wider importance in the following chapter when I compare the ways in which the different schools have been taken up by feminists.

Lacan's appropriation of linguistics

In one of his more famous claims, Lacan (1968) states that the unconscious is 'structured like a language'. What has become known as structural linguistics was developed by Ferdinand de Saussure (1974) in the early part of the twentieth century. The crucial feature of his work was a distinction between 'language' and 'speech'. The latter is what one might expect: the spoken word, our statements, what we say to other people and to ourselves. These utterances are unique and not the subject matter for scientific inquiry. This marked a break with traditional linguistics, which concerned itself with the history of languages as spoken. By 'language' Saussure means an underlying structure or system that makes speech possible.

Language, for Saussure, is a *convention*. There is no *necessary* connection between a word and the thing it refers to – my trousers do not come down from God with the word 'trousers' stamped on them, and I am not compelled by divine decree to call them trousers. It is simply what English speakers agree to call them. The meaning of the word does not come from the particular object that it refers to; rather it comes from its relationship to other words in the linguistic system we call English (or French or whatever). One implication of this is that meaning is not 'in' the word itself but between words, in the relationship that words have to each other. For example, we only understand the meaning of 'up' in relation to 'down' and 'sideways'.

Saussure analyses language as a combination of signs, and a sign is in turn a combination of 'signifier' and 'signified'. The signifier is the material element, the noise in the throat or the marks on a piece of paper; the signified is the concept that the noise or the marks represent. It is important to remember that the signified is a concept, not an object. The marks 'dog' refer to a concept of a particular type of animal, not to the living thing but the idea. Saussure makes a methodological break with the notion of language as representing something in the outside world. It is this that enables him to think of language as a structure, and distinguish it from speech.

Saussure was part of a movement in twentieth-century philosophy that has become known as the 'linguistic turn', and that has spread through philosophy and social theory. Part of the turn has involved our understanding of language being used as a metaphor for a range of cultural phenomena and for the working of society itself; and on an even wider scale language is taken as coextensive with the world. It is argued that the language that we speak defines the reality in which we live. What starts off in Saussure as a methodological strategy goes on, in the light of neo-Kantian philosophy and the work of Wittgenstein, to become a metaphysical assumption about the nature of language and reality. We can see both of these ideas at work in Lacan's psychoanalysis: in the way that workings of language become a metaphor for the workings of the unconscious, and the central role that he gives the symbolic over the real.

Saussure's analysis of language works along two dimensions: the analysis of the *syntagmatic* level involves identifying the rules that govern the combination of signs (sounds) in a linear order (at a higher level this would involve the rules of grammar); the analysis of the *paradigmatic* level involves identifying those signs that can be substituted for each other in the syntagm without the sentence losing its meaning. For Lacan, these two dimensions are equivalent to condensation and displacement in dream work, and the same ideas have been taken in literary criticism as referring respectively to metonymy and metaphor. These transfers always seem to me to be rather loose. The important one is metaphor, which takes us back to the foundations of psychoanalysis. In Lacan's use of these concepts the signifier takes priority over everything else. Unconscious processes involve a constant movement from signifier to signifier – from metaphor to metaphor to metaphor. The fundamental insight here, which is stronger in Lacan than it was in Freud, is that once we enter the realm of language we move away from the biological and physical conditions of human existence into a world of potentially infinite variations of meaning.

As we move further into Lacan's work, it will become apparent that for him psychoanalysis is not a comforting practice or discipline;

he seems to work on the principle that the more difficult his writing, the more he makes people think. Psychoanalysis as a whole may not offer easy answers, but Lacan doesn't even offer easy questions. However, he is a theorist in the Freudian tradition; not in his style, for Freud seems to have managed always to be open and limpid, but in his development of Freudian theory. Lacan moves towards a map of the world, not a hamlet.

We have already seen that there are many important aspects of psychoanalysis that are less concerned with the external 'real' world than with the internal meaning with which we endow it. The linguistic turn in that sense is wide open to adoption and adaptation by psychoanalysis, and Lacan is the theorist who has built these ideas into psychoanalysis in the most systematic way, adding new regions to Freud's thought, although I suspect that he would claim only to be elaborating Freud. Lacan is a real theorist, in the sense that a central concern is the systematic, even if difficult, elaboration of a theory or theories, rather than the elaboration of an intuition.

The psychic realms

In his work, Lacan identifies what I can best call a number of psychic realms: the real, the imaginary and the symbolic. Sarup (1992) calls these 'registers', which for me implies that we can intentionally move through each area in the way that a musician might play an instrument, which is certainly not Lacan's meaning. Evans (1996) calls them 'structures', which makes them too close to Freud's id, ego and super-ego or his conscious, preconscious and unconscious systems. I do not think that they are replacements for Freud's concepts, but nor do they sit easily within Freud's framework; nor for that matter do Freud's concepts fit easily into Lacan's theory. Bowie (1991) talks about these orders as 'shifting gravitational centres' for Lacan's thought, and certainly to look for clarity in Lacan's writings is not very helpful. I prefer 'realms' because it suggests that there might be levels of existence (or non-existence) through which we can move (not at will) and it resonates with my map analogy. One might think of these realms as lower or higher regions where the structures are situated – perhaps with each structure being in one region, with some overlap.

Approaching Lacan's work from the position of British psycho-analysis, it would be tempting to present it as describing a developmental process from the imaginary to the symbolic to the real, but I think that this would do violence to Lacan's ideas and in effect restrict their force; whatever else, it is certain that the real is not the end point of development.

The real

Sarup actually suggests that the real is close to the 'id' in that it is unknowable and a constant source of disruption. As ever, Lacan is ambiguous if not self-contradictory. In places we can find him citing Hegel to the effect that 'the real is the rational', which is an assumption that everything is rationally ordered and therefore intelligible. At other times he suggests that the real is unknowable. The latter version is certainly at the centre of his later work.

My understanding of the 'unknowability' of the real puts it closer to the idea of possession rather than knowledge, referring to the way in which we might possess our objects. In fact we cannot possess them but we take them in and transform them into symbols. We do not have access to the thing in itself, although we do have access to our ideas of things. This way of thinking about it makes sense in the context of Lacan's existentialist and Hegelian background, in which consciousness is conceived as a *lack* of being, not as something in itself. And there is a tenuous link to Bion's discussion of the 'bad breast' as an absence. We are always looking for that sense of substance that will enable us to think or feel that we really *are*, but it cannot be achieved. Sartre (1957) talks about the way in which we try to persuade ourselves that we have achieved it, an inauthentic mode of being he calls *bad faith*. It also makes sense in the context of the structural linguistics that we have just discussed, where meaning is never *in* the sign but in the relationship between signs.

There is another and more dramatic sense of the real as that which is entirely inaccessible – Sartre's *in-itself* or Kant's *thing-in-itself*, that which cannot be symbolized. In one sense this is an absurd idea – we can at least refer to such a reality through the concept 'that which cannot be symbolized' – that is, we can symbolize it. However, in another sense, it seems to me to capture an experience of the world that is common to all of us: the real is perhaps what preceded our birth and will succeed our death. It surrounds our transience. We cannot imagine our life before we were alive, and although we can imagine dying, we cannot imagine death. This I think would be the meaning truer to Lacan's existential background.

We are still left with his comment about 'the real being rational'. Evans refers to another of Lacan's comments, about 'reality' being 'the grimace of the real' (Lacan 1990), and makes the ingenious suggestion that although Lacan is inconsistent in his usage, he is sometimes implying an opposition between the 'real' and 'reality' in which 'the real is placed firmly on the side of the unknowable and unassimilable, while "reality" denotes subjective representations which are the product of symbolic and imaginary representations (Freud's psychical reality)' (Evans 1996: 161). I find this quite a useful distinction, but no more useful than Freud's, which I understand to be a straightforward one between our conceptions of the world and the world itself – respectively psychological reality and external reality. Doubtless there is a difference between them, but this does not mean that we cannot know the world with a greater or lesser degree of adequacy, and for Freud of course the reality principle was of fundamental importance: that against which we test our drives and phantasies. I think here Lacan can be accused of confusing psychology and epistemology, and that is likely only to lead to more confusion. The way in which I see and experience the world is a psychological issue; what I can know about the world with a greater or lesser degree of certainty is an epistemological problem. The two are close together but an approximate distinction between them is of fundamental importance: my occasional fantasy that I can escape through my fourth-floor office window by flying is of a different order to my knowledge of the law of gravity, which tells me that I would be likely to end up dead. The former sense is related to my unconscious, a personal reality governed, or perhaps rather ungoverned, by the laws of the unconscious; the latter is an intersubjective reality governed by the laws of rationality. Lacan carries the intellectual baggage of the linguistic turn and post-structuralism, which makes knowledge judgements difficult or impossible.

The imaginary

The psychological and the epistemological have become confused in the social and human sciences since the Marxist philosopher Louis Althusser (1971) attempted to use a notion very like Lacan's idea of the imaginary in a theory of ideology. I have described and criticized this attempt elsewhere (Craib 1992a). Here I want to discuss the idea simply as a psychological concept.

The imaginary realm develops from an act of identification that originates in what Lacan (1997) calls the 'mirror stage'. The basic idea is that as an infant I experience myself as a host of conflicting urges (Lacan puns on the word *hommelette* – the little man, scrambled eggs), but at some point in my development I see myself reflected, in a mirror or through another person, as a 'whole being' in charge of myself and able to control myself. This image fascinates me; it is the first time that I see myself as a subject. I identify with it.

It is difficult to locate this precisely in Freud's framework, although it is clearly connected to the development of narcissism; for Lacan, however, it represents a development that distinguishes his psychoanalysis in no uncertain terms from the object-relations approaches we have looked at in the previous chapters and from the ego psychology of Anna Freud and American psychoanalysis. It is the origin, the foundation of the ego, and it is a profoundly alienating act – I identify with an external image of myself and I carry this identification around with me for the rest of my life. In the words of Benvenuto and Kennedy, Lacan was 'absolutely and fundamentally opposed to any idea that one should help the analysand to strengthen his [*sic*] ego, to help him adjust to society in any way, or that one should help him tolerate unconscious impulses by building up his ego' (Benvenuto and Kennedy 1986: 60). This opposition would also be to notions of integration or a 'real self'; for Lacan all selves are false.

Lacan holds on to Freud's idea of the human condition as being in the grip of internal and external conflict, but he does not share Freud's view (according to most interpreters) of the ego as a modifying, or reality-testing, agency that most interpreters suggest is the way that Freud sees it. Rather the supposed centre or mediator between super-ego and id is an illusion; though a necessary illusion as without it it is difficult to see how the infant could gain any sense of itself at all. There seems to me to be a paradoxical opposition between Lacan and Winnicott (who also developed a theory of the mirror image): for Lacan the act of identification with the reflected mirror image is a profound alienation; for object-relations theory identification with the other's reflection is or can be a way of discovering some sort of real self; but for both, this sort of identification seems a necessary developmental step.

Again I do not think that Lacan's concept enables us to make the sort of distinctions that we can find in Freud's grouping of concepts, but it acts as a timely counterbalance to notions of a 'real self' or 'true self' and any idea that we are not divided within ourselves. I think of the imaginary as often involving an intense desire to be recognized as something by another person, and indeed Lacan seems to think of the unconscious as an 'Other' ('the discourse of the Other'), the one who looks at us and for whom we should perform. In this sense the unconscious seems to take over the role of the super-ego. On a personal level, perhaps it should be seen as a warning: whenever you want someone to acknowledge your integrity, your dignity, your honesty, your innocence or whatever, you are living in the realm of the imaginary. The concept of the imaginary, and of the unconscious as the 'discourse of the Other', emphasize that it is in the nature of human being to be divided from itself. It seems to me to be a much stronger concept than Klein's notion of unconscious phantasy, with which I have heard some people compare it.

The imaginary order grows out of the identification with the mirror image, and such an identification underlies all adult relationships, and includes our unconscious phantasies and conscious imaginings.

The symbolic

One of the difficulties of Lacan's work is to be found in Evans' account of the symbolic, where he comes to the conclusion that it seems to include everything, thus explaining Lacan's use of the word 'universal' in reference to this realm (Evans 1996). Here again I think there is a confusion of the psychological with the epistemological. The linguistic turn in philosophy, and the French post-structuralism that developed as part of it, reduced everything to language – the symbolic – and therefore the real is never attainable. On the one hand there is the thing-in-itself; on the other there is language. As an ontology, this seems to allow no distinction between forms and levels of reality, and it is of little use to a depth psychology.

If we keep to psychology, however, the notion of the symbolic as it is used by Lacan becomes useful. On one level it is the realm of the ego, and on another it involves a radical deconstruction of what we might think of as the ego. It emphasizes that lack that is human consciousness. The symbolic is the representation of the real that we cannot be or possess; it the nearest we get to possessing the real, but involves the perhaps tenuous recognition that we cannot actually possess it. In this sense the symbolic is, to begin with, the imaginary introjection of the object and our eventual compromise with the symbol. It is a matter of giving up the relentless pursuit of identification.

It is a deconstruction of the ego in the sense that the linguistic theory that Lacan employs to analyse the symbolic denies the possibility of a subject. We do not speak the language; the language speaks us. This seems to me to be true and untrue at the same time. It is true in the sense that language, or a specific discourse, limits what we can say, but with that language we have a choice about what we say and it is possible to use it creatively: the subject might have a more limited scope than it does in the imaginary – certainly more limited than most of us like to think – but we are, as it were, not subjects in complete control, but subjects hemmed in by the materials of our world, our discursive world, our linguistic world, and our external world.

Full and empty speech; the other and the Other

These realms and their shifting relationships in psychic life throw light on a number of other ideas in Lacan's work. Language is always the centre – psychoanalysis is restored to its full meaning as the talking cure. Yet not all talk is of equal value to the analyst or the patient. *Empty speech* is the speech of the ego, of the imaginary – the request for confirmation and support in what I imagine myself to be, and what I want others to see me as being; it is what I say when I know what I am doing, when I am firm and decisive. *Full speech* contains desire, it is meaning-full, and it is that speech for which the psychoanalyst listens. Such a distinction can be found in various forms in modern philosophy. Benvenuto and Kennedy (1986: 85) draw a parallel between Lacan's distinction and Heidegger's distinction between discourse, which is speech which reveals something, and 'idle talk' – a more disparaging concept than Lacan's. I think that there is a rather more tenuous but still interesting parallel with a distinction that Habermas makes, drawing on British linguistic philosophy, between performative and communicative speech acts: the former are intended to persuade the other person to do something, they are instrumental actions; and the latter are intended to achieve a mutual understanding.

Empty speech is addressed to the 'other', the imaginary figure in whom the person is alienated; the source of truth is the Other, with a capital 'O', which speaks through the person often despite that person's will or awareness. The Other is the unconscious, that which speaks through me. The subject, the 'I', is alienated in two directions, torn between the unconscious Other and the imaginary other. But this is not all that is involved in human existence.

Language, desire, pleasure and ecstasy

In his appropriation of structural linguistics, Lacan gives priority to the signifier, and the primary processes can be seen as an endless sliding along signifying chains and an endless production of metaphors and metonyms at all levels. One way of viewing psychosis in this context is as the sliding getting out of hand. What prevents this is that language is anchored at certain points – *points de capiton*, which is the French term for the buttons that pin the covering of a sofa to the upholstery and stop it from sliding all over the place. The oedipal stage is important in this anchoring.

Lacan does not talk so much about the libido as about desire; although this might have its origin in Hegelian notions about the desire for recognition it is also connected with the demand for wholeness, omnipotence, the omnipotence and perfection of the mother. It is a demand that cannot be met or fulfilled although we might attempt to fulfil it through the imaginary; the power of the patient's demand to be told what to do as it is experienced by the analyst is the power of the imaginary. When we enter the symbolic, demand becomes desire, but there is always a lack, an absence. Desire leads to pleasure but the underlying absence is the real, that to which we do not have access, and that is connected to ecstasy – to *jouissance*, the supreme sexual pleasure. In this way the real, death and ecstasy come together, the goal of the life and death instincts.

Conclusion

Lacan, then, takes us back to the original concerns of Freud, but he does so in a way that links psychoanalysis to major themes in modern

European philosophy and refuses to compromise Freud's stark understanding of the human condition; in fact he extends this understanding to take into account an underlying meaninglessness of human existence, which was the message of the existentialist philosophers of the twentieth century. There is no doubt that Lacan's work is a timely reminder of some of Freud's more unpalatable insights, but my own approach to him is moderated by certain problems I have with the philosophical framework. One aspect of this is the confusion of psychological reality and epistemology that I mentioned earlier, and another is what I regard as the metaphysical view of language that he employs, but this book is not the place to go into these issues.

10

Psychoanalysis, Gender and Feminism

Introduction: Psychoanalysis and social theory

When I discussed Freud's oedipal theory I did so in the context of Juliet Mitchell's feminist interpretation of his work. The apparent flourishing of different forms of sexuality in general and the questioning of social roles allocated to men and women have had effects not only on the world we live in but also on the ways in which we understand that world; in particular it has brought psychoanalysis to the foreground in feminist politics and academic and political attempts to understand the position of women in contemporary society. It is no exaggeration to say that much contemporary academic interest in psychoanalysis has stemmed from feminist attempts to appropriate its insights and build them into a general social theory related to a number of different disciplines.

I commented in the introduction that one can find academic works on psychoanalysis that can be read without gaining any sense that psychoanalysis is a therapeutic treatment, or that it involves understanding the complexity of meanings of individual lives. Psychoanalysis can be used simply as a building block in a wider social theory or philosophy – two very different examples of feminist theorists doing this can be found in Benjamin (1990) and Butler (1990, 1993). In this chapter, I will concentrate on feminist developments within the schools I have discussed earlier, usually developments by women who are or have become practising analysts and therapists and whose work is relevant to the general themes of this book. I will be arguing against the idea that psychoanalysis can be used for defining the positions and identities of collectives, including genders. I also want to argue that when this is attempted, psychoanalysis can easily become caught up with different social ideologies. It is always tempting to explain the world in terms of one's own specialism, and sociologists, cultural theorists and psychoanalysts can be as guilty as each other in this respect, but it is something that should be avoided.

In my discussion of Freud and Oedipus I suggested that there are as many ways through oedipal conflicts as there are people to come through them, yet when it comes to men and women there is no doubt that we tend to think about radical differences, in popular culture and in social theory – men are from Mars and women from Venus.

The best explanation I have found for this comes from a paper by Gayle Rubin (1975), who bases her argument on the combination of Lévi-Strauss and Freud that I outlined earlier, and makes the point that men and women are closer to each other than either are to any other animal or object. It is not the case, for example, that men are closer to trout and women to okapi, yet I suspect that even the most egalitarian and liberal amongst us will occasionally experience the opposite sex in such a way. Now it seems that all societies – indeed different subcultures and social classes within the same society – suppose a difference between men and women, but not necessarily the same difference. What seems to be important is that we should *think* and sometimes *feel* that there is a difference between men and women, the nature of the difference being less important than the existence of the difference. The supposed difference is important because it provides a basis for heterosexual attraction – we seek in the opposite sex what we do not find in ourselves.

One way of looking at all this is that the oedipal stage forces the recognition of a significant biological difference onto the psychologically bisexual infant and introduces the idea of difference. This does not *produce* gender stereotypes – the personality characteristics that a society believes are appropriate to men and women. The stereotypes come from history, the nature of the division of labour, the economic and social requirements of a society. These characteristics can then 'cement' the difference realized at the oedipal stage, but they do not remove the internal and external conflicts of our bisexuality at an unconscious level or even necessarily a conscious level; rather they simply add another dimension to the conflicts.

The problem is that this interlocking between psychological and sociological approaches can lead to the impression that one side or the other is dominant when in fact each has its own logic of development. The oedipal metaphor tells us that there is a difference between the sexes; our culture and our society's structure and history tell us what that difference is. So when we start with the oedipal metaphor and try to develop from it the content of the culturally accepted differences, we simply reproduce dominant social ideas of the difference. Rubin's view that there is not much psychological difference between men and women but we often need to think there is seems to me to be the nearest that we can get to the truth.

The rest of this chapter will be concerned with the way in which different schools – Freudian, object-relations, Lacanian and post-Lacanian – approach sexuality and gender, exploring the ways in which they add to the understanding of individuality and become caught up in social ideologies.

Freud and Oedipus: a brief recap

To begin with I will set out a brief account of what Freud has to say about the little girl's journey through the oedipal stage and Mitchell's gloss on what that means for the adult woman. Freud follows the development of the sexual aim, the oral, anal and phallic stages, which he argues are the same for both sexes. The difference appears at the oedipal stage when the little girl has to give up her first love object – her mother – and take initially the father and then later a man of her own as a love object. As with the little boy, the mechanism is castration, but the realization of already having been castrated rather than the fear of castration. The little girl must repress her active aims in order to possess the mother. For Mitchell, the marks of womanhood are masochism (the result of the dominant passive aims), vanity and jealousy (the result of envy of the penis that she does not have and her competition with the mother for the father) and a limited sense of social justice. This last is because she does not have to internalize the rule of the father under threat of castration. The woman then has three options: she can maintain her love for the mother and become homosexual; she can identify with men; or she can accept the absence of the penis and all that it implies and fulfil herself by giving birth to (preferably male) babies.

I will leave further comment on this until I have discussed a more contemporary feminist interpretation of Freud based on object-relations theory.

An object-relations approach to the oedipal stage and gender difference

The work of Nancy Chodorow – an American sociologist who later trained as a psychoanalyst – and of two feminist therapists working in Britain, Louise Eichenbaum and Susie Orbach, offers, on the surface, a convincing alternative account of femininity to that taken up by Mitchell.

I have already indicated that one of the differences between object-relations theory and more orthodox Freudian theory is that the latter tends to focus on internal conflict and allows rather more autonomy to the psychological whereas object-relations theory works a little closer to the surface of the psyche and tends towards seeing the external world, in particular the way the baby is treated, as being as important as, or more important than, the internal processes. This makes object-relations theory more amenable to sociological analysis and this is why Chodorow is initially so enthusiastic about it.

Freud did not have a lot to say about the development of object-relations. From an early auto-eroticism, when satisfaction is gained from the infant's own body, there is a move to a primary narcissism, when the infant takes itself as a love object. Laplanche and Pontalis (1988) suggest that this moment is when the sexual instincts come together for the first time and the ego emerges. I am by no means convinced of this but I do not want to argue through the details of Freud's account. What is important for present purposes is that at this point the infant comes to take itself as a love object, and then, through a process of identification, it can take another as a love object. Perhaps the best way of approaching these issues is to assume that drives, ego and object-relations are all there from the start but vary in their relative strengths and relationships to each other. It is worth noting here that most sociological accounts of the growth of the self reverse this relationship – the unity and sense of the self come from others first, whereas the psychoanalytic position is that the self is the first object prior to relationships outside the self. In any case the object-relations approach leads to a concentration on the detail of the relationship between parent and child and a shift towards the sociological approach.

Chodorow is much less generous to Freud than is Mitchell, producing a series of quotations in which Freud does appear to be saying that a woman is inferior because she does not have a penis. This does not matter so much to Mitchell because the scientific status of the theory can overcome the prejudice of the theorist. Chodorow, however, accuses Freud of allowing his work to be dominated by his own patriarchal values and those of his society; these values include the assumption that only women can mother, and this assumption is important for the sort of politics that Chodorow would like to derive from her theory.

For Chodorow, it is the difference between the little boy and the little girl's relationship primarily to the mother and secondarily to the father that is important. She is barely concerned with drives and what happens to them, although she does make the interesting suggestion that penis envy represents the little girl's desire to maintain her first love object. Her (the little girl's) phantasy is that if she had a penis she would be able to retain her mother's love. This too, I think, must be added to the complex of relationships at the oedipal stage.

Chodorow takes up the object-relations theory concern with the way in which the infant moves towards a relative psychological independence from the mother. We can conceive an 'ideal type' of this relationship as beginning in the mother's womb, where the infant is in fact part of the mother's body. The first move is to birth, and we can talk of a 'mother–baby unit'. Winnicott (1964: 88) comments that there is no such thing as a baby, only a baby in relationship with a carer. As the infant grows, the powers of the carer are internalized until he or she becomes self-reliant. In psychological terms, for the growing child, the mother is now inside the child and the child can move through the world more and more independently of the mother. Whatever we like to think, especially during our adolescent years, the relationship is never broken on a psychological level; we still carry our parents within us.

Chodorow argues that there is an important difference, at least in the modern Western family, in the way in which the little boy and the little girl move through this process. Both deviate from the ideal type but in opposite, and in my view equally 'damaging', ways. I put 'damaging' in inverted commas because I do not really want to create an impression that an 'undamaged' development is possible. Perhaps it would be better to say that each develops in a way that produces a particular set of psychological problems that Chodorow sees as associated with the wider social relationships between men and women.

The most attractive part of Chodorow's work is that she specifically confines herself to talking about patterns of development in Western societies, and the most significant feature as far as child-rearing is concerned is the absence of the father. She is not talking just about single-parent families where there is no father present, but the absence of the father that stems originally from the division of home and work in the industrial revolution, which removed fathers from playing any major part in child-rearing. In this context, the mother's relationship to her baby boy takes on some psychological aspects of her relationship to the absent father – the relationship, Chodorow suggests, is sexualized at an early stage. The boy becomes psychologically 'other' to the mother and is pushed into what we could call a premature psychological separation. Gender identity and sexuality come to be closely bound up with his sense of himself as an individual. Chodorow talks about the development of strong ego-boundaries in a rather misleading way (Craib 1989). I think 'rigid' or 'inflexible' might be better – she is referring to an inability to identify and feel empathy with others, a difficulty in feeling strong emotions and attachments. This emphasizes one side – the 'top side' – of what might be called the dominant male stereotype: men are strong, rational, unemotional beings who are fitted to work in the outside world. However, little boys do not learn this from their fathers as whole people – there is not sufficient contact with the father. Little boys often have to be explicitly taught masculinity ('boys don't play with dolls/cry', etc.) but for little girls learning femininity seems to be a matter of course.

In their work on the same theme Eichenbaum and Orbach (1985) emphasize the 'underside' of this stereotype. According to the stereotype, men are 'independent'; in fact, they argue, this is a myth and men avoid the recognition of their dependency by projecting it on to women and seeing them as the dependent sex. In the economic sense, as a result of the division of labour developed through the nineteenth century, women are often put in an economically dependent situation, but it does not necessarily follow that they are emotionally dependent.

Returning to Chodorow's argument, the mother identifies with the little girl, and sees her as part of herself. This delays the little girl's separation – she has the opposite problem to the little boy. Whereas his process of individuation is moved along too fast, the little girl's process is slowed down. Eichenbaum and Orbach fill out this process. Generally, they argue, women are expected to subordinate their needs to the satisfaction of the needs of others. Faced by a girl baby, the mother has the difficult problem of finding herself faced by a needy female who reminds her of her own denied needs. She has both to satisfy her baby's needs and at the same time teach the child to repress its own needs. The conflict and ambivalence produces a sort of cycle in the mother/daughter relationship which can continue throughout life. There will be periods when the daughter will feel extremely close to the mother, almost unable to tell herself apart from her, and periods when she will feel completely alienated, as if there is a brick wall between them. The adult woman thus comes to complement the adult man, with a less firm sense of herself and her own needs, always tending towards the experience of empathy and treating the needs of others as her own, satisfying herself through satisfying others – a different form of self-alienation to that of men. For Chodorow this explains male dominance – it is a matter of women mothering, being the prime carers of infants.

The politics that she derives from this is much more 'reasonable' than Mitchell's. The latter talks about an acute contradiction in the position of the nuclear family in late capitalism. It has lost its most important socialization and economic roles, and now has only the role of early socialization; it has become socially isolated – a small number of people in a small space, the effects of geographical and social mobility cutting it off from extended kin networks. It is becoming more important as a source of human contact for its members at the same time as it is becoming less important in the wider society. The result is that the people with whom we are most intimate are the very people with whom we are not supposed to have sexual relations. Mitchell seems to be suggesting that the family that reproduces the men and women that she describes is on the way out. However, this seems to be a very long process of evolution at the level of underlying social structures, and it is difficult to see what we could do to hasten it along.

If Mitchell is writing about deeper processes that we perhaps cannot do much about, then Chodorow's politics are, as befits an object-relations theorist, closer to the surface. She argues for the steady inclusion of men in the child-rearing process, and it is comparatively easy to translate this into social policy. However, I have argued elsewhere (Craib 1987) that if this were achieved it would not necessarily lead on to the results for which she hopes, a greater equality between men and women. Social roles are not the same as personality structures. This leads on to my next point.

Stereotypes and psychodynamics

I am not convinced by all of Chodorow's arguments. She goes to some lengths, for example, to argue that mothering is not somehow 'naturally' the function of the birth mother, which is fair enough – of course other women and men can also mother an infant. Life would be very difficult if this were not the case. But there is a sense in which such arguments lose the drama and agonies of the differences between the sexes, the consequences of human biology making men and women dependent on each other for the reproduction of the species. They also hide the traumas of the birth separation.

This, however, is not the centre of my problem with this sort of approach. It illustrates the ease which psychodynamic horses can be hitched to sociological carriages that have comparatively little to do with them. What is interesting here is that Freud's psychoanalytic theory can be used to 'explain' gender stereotypes that were common when Freud himself was working – women were socially irresponsible, vain, narcissistic, irrational (Mitchell) – whilst a more contemporary version of psychoanalysis can be used to 'explain' a more contemporary stereotype – women are caring, concerned with emotion and relationships in a way that men are not (Chodorow). Such stereotypes are also produced by sociological research, but with rather more justification since they are sociological phenomena (Craib 1995; Duncombe and Marsden 1993).

In this connection I want to introduce groups, group analysis and group psychotherapy, where my own clinical experience lies. There are several ways in which group psychoanalysis can be seen as a privileged exercise, not least because each patient is seen within an often rapidly changing series of interactions with other people. I have argued elsewhere (Craib 1995) that in such a situation, one can watch these stereotypes form and dissolve. Women who appear vain and narcissistic in some situations will appear realistic and practical in others, whereas women who appear caring and concerned in some situations will appear cruel and unthinking in others. Similarly men who appear practical and rational in some situations will reveal unexpected emotional depths in others. And men who appear distant and emotionally isolated in some situations will in others be in tears over another person's story. I am suggesting that psychological bisexuality leads to 'bi-gender' characteristics, which will be displayed in some situations and not in others – sometimes social pressures and social stereotypes will dominate an individual and sometimes his or her own voice will come through.

Post-structuralist conceptions of gender identity

One of the more remarkable developments in psychoanalysis over the last thirty years has been the development of a French feminist psychoanalytic theory or, better, theories, built on the work of Lacan. It is remarkable because Lacan is in many ways the most orthodox of Freudians, seeing the infant's progress through the oedipal stage as his or her entry into civilization, and that in turn means accepting the *Nom/n* of the father. These feminist theorists often seem foreign to those who have grown out of the British object-relations tradition. Their style is literary and philosophical, reflecting the background of the authors, and their concerns are often social, literary and philosophical as much as clinical, although the clinical is clearly there. I cannot hope to do them justice in this context, but I hope I can provide a general mapping of the field and enough references for readers to follow up points in which they are interested.

Lacan and the phallus

Lacan's account of the oedipal stage and sexuality brings into play his linguistic metaphor: he talks of the phallus as the most important signifier, standing not for the penis but for the father's *place* – the *Non* (no) or *Nom* (name) of the father who bars the child from realizing its incestuous desire. The phallus marks the entry into the symbolic, and for both sexes it stands for the unobtainable – it is an imaginary object. Castration is less a matter of fearing the loss of the testicles and penis than of the impossibility of gaining the object of our most profound desires. Everybody is, in this sense, castrated and the role of the phallus is not attached to a natural or real father but is a normative role; Lacan talks of a 'paternal metaphor'. This opens the way for the feminist interpretations of Lacan: sexual identity for both men and women is imaginary, but femininity is defined 'against' the phallus and therefore in its terms. For men and women entry into the symbolic is dependent upon the phallus: it is the dominant signifier and the realm of the signifier is where everything takes place. Men and women only exist in language and everybody must be on one side or the other – at least on the level of consciousness, although unconscious awareness of complexity remains. In this light it is on the face of it difficult to see what feminists might find in Lacan's work. The notion that all sexual identities are constructs might be attractive but it is not particularly feminist, and Lacan seems to leave no route for arguing that we can discover a 'real' femininity, any more than we can discover a 'real' masculinity, that is not defined in terms of the phallus. Some feminists have reacted to these ideas by arguing that a feminist politics should be concerned with the undermining of sexual identities (Butler), and this does stem from Lacan's position. With the possible exception of Julia Kristeva, of whom more shortly, I think Lacan's feminist interpreters tend to lose sight of his profound subversiveness in relation to any definite or clear conception of gender identity.

There are a number of paradoxes in the way in which feminists have taken up Lacan's ideas. One direction is to seek something that is specifically feminine, hidden by the phallus, and to do so they tend to go back to the body (where the differences between men and women are most evident) and to the pre-oedipal stage in a way in which Lacan would not approve. One direction is to argue that there is a specific feminine language and way of thinking based on bodily differences. A woman's language is not a new idea – in her classic *A Room of One's Own* (1945) Virginia Woolf talks about the 'feminine sentence', which has not yet been written. In a discussion of Freud's unsuccessful treatment of 'Dora' (Freud 1977c) Tiril Moi (1985) suggests that Freud, largely unconsciously, is working with two epistemologies, each a metaphor for the genitalia of the two sexes. The masculine epistemology, which is his own standard, the knowledge he aims to achieve, but in this case fails, is a complete knowledge, linear from beginning to end – a knowledge that would capture Dora. The feminine epistemology is perhaps represented by Dora's recalcitrance. She broke off the analysis before it had finished, leaving Freud only with a 'fragment'. In Moi's words:

... knowledge and theory must be conceptualized as a whole, rounded, finished – just like the penis ... Dora threatens. Her knowledge cannot be conceptualized as a whole; it is dispersed and has been assembled piecemeal from feminine sources. Dora's epistemological model becomes the female genitals, which in Freud's vision emerge as unfinished, diffuse and fragmentary; they cannot add up to a complete whole and must therefore be perceived as castrated genitals. (Moi 1985: 196)

Hélène Cixous (Cixous and Clément 1986) argues that male discourse would be challenged by writing and from the female body itself.

This is not unlike the work of Luce Irigaray (1985a, 1985b, 1991, 1992, 1993; Whitford 1996), who was expelled from Lacan's psychoanalytic institute. (Lacan was at least as sectarian as Freud.) She represents a radical feminism in both philosophy and psychoanalysis. She suggests that women have been completely excluded from Western philosophy and culture and argues that patriarchal men are unconsciously merged with the mother and therefore women have been allocated everything that men deny about themselves; in particular their dependence on women. The male lack (castration) is seen by men as belonging to women. Irigaray argues that against this rigid and defended male sexuality it is possible to posit an open fluid female sexuality, centring on the *jouissance* of the whole body rather than on a genital orgasm and the release of tension. The origins of this lie in the pre-oedipal mother–daughter relationship. This experience is hidden (or suppressed) by the phallus, excluding the female and women from the symbolic. Female sexuality cannot be expressed in a patriarchal discourse.

In fact, as Anthony Elliott (1992) points out, despite the apparently radical nature of her argument, and the difficulties of her language, Irigaray offers an image of women not that different from Nancy Chodorow's in the sense that femininity has to do with openness of relationships and closeness to the mother, but paradoxically she adds what, in her own terms, can be seen as a very male closure to the debate. For Irigaray, the body, and particularly the genitalia, seems to govern everything. Lacan's imaginary is entirely a male imaginary; a female imaginary would be based on female genitalia. There is no reason, she suggests, why the female genitalia should not be the significant mark of difference.

This seems to me to end up with a sort of biological determinism; the ways in which we experience the world are governed through bodily fantasies, and the problem in Irigaray's work is that the experience of one sex is excluded by the other. Again Freud's notion of early bisexuality, which remains in its various sublimations, seems to be lost and Irigaray reflects the absolutism that she is criticizing. I am not saying that she is wrong, for example, about the projections that men make on women, but these will vary from time to time, person to person and situation to situation. Nor do I think she is wrong about the importance of bodily phantasy. It seems quite reasonable to me to suggest that the way in which we imagine and perceive the world will depend to some degree on the way we experience our bodies, especially organs as sensitive as our genitalia, and this will be different for men and women.

But the genitalia are not the only bodily organs through which we experience the world, and our common human biology gives men and women an identity with each other as well as a difference from each other. Irigaray, perhaps despite herself, seems to present it as an either/or matter. Even if we take Irigaray as talking about culture rather than psychology, it would be difficult to establish that women have been excluded; in cultures, as much as in individual psyches, there is a struggle.

Julia Kristeva

Julia Kristeva (1980, 1986; Lechte 1990) is by far the most interesting of the post-Lacanians to think about women and sexuality and the one who links the social and the psychological together in the most interesting way. She does not derive stereotypes from the processes described by psychoanalysis but rather elaborates on those processes and the way in which they are distorted or fixed by external social processes. She suggests that the notion of a feminine identity is just like the notion of a masculine identity: 'absurd and obscurantist' (Kristeva 1981). In the imaginary the child (of whatever sex) phantasizes that the mother is also all-powerful until they move into the position of wanting what the mother wants – that is, the father. In other words we all experience the mother as phallic and we cannot use her as a way of escaping from the phallic.

Kristeva reconceptualizes the realms of the imaginary and the symbolic in a way that seems to manage to avoid the necessity of the dominant phallus, or rather sees it as the result of demands from the external world. The imaginary is reformulated as the 'semiotic' – a pre-oedipal experience of drives in the oral and anal stages, a complex and largely inchoate experience of self (Lacan's *hommelette*) that is organized into a 'non-expressive' totality by the mother. Semiology is the science of signs and the semiotic is so called by Kristeva because it is achieved through the mother, who is situated in the family and the wider society and therefore carries the sign system of that society. But whereas many people would see this as a profound social determinism, it is clear that it is not so for Kristeva – the semiotic is associated with the intimate somatic rhythms of the body and of language as it is experienced before speech; my own interpretation is that it is the poetic basis of our existence in the world, and the ordering of the experience in the 'chora', as Kristeva calls it, is prior to the acquisition of identity, let alone a masculine or feminine identity. This seems to me more profound than Lacan's imaginary realm, much closer to a fundamental level of 'authentic' rather than alienated experience, although we have to move out of it to some degree to make civilized life possible.

The thetic is the equivalent of the symbolic, but what is important here is that for Kristeva the two realms may continue to influence each other. It is here that the phallus appears as a forced division between the two realms required not so much by the nature of the psyche as by the requirement of a particular form of hierarchical capitalist and patriarchal society. Kristeva holds up the possibility of a more fluid and multi-dimensional subjectivity than does Lacan and in this way aligns herself with a radical politics that is not feminist in the sense that it proposes some specifically feminine quality. In fact she suggests that women are like blacks and Jews in late capitalist society: they are scapegoated, the focus of a disgust originally felt for waste fluids of the infant's and mother's body. They are the 'abject'.

This seems to me a more sensible way of thinking about these issues. On the whole I am not sure that Lacan offers a theoretical framework that is subtle enough to be able to take account of the multiplicity of ways in which human beings use speech or of the multitude of cross-identifications that real people make and experience in the course of their lives. What is valuable in his work and in Kristeva's is the thrust to undermine a sense of certainty and clarity in psychic life, and I have in effect maintained that an emphasis on continuing psychological bisexuality is one way of doing this. It also has the advantage of reflecting what I regard as an unavoidable clinical reality, not to mention an everyday reality, that involves us all. In psychoanalytic terms part of this reality is that we are all, at some level, aware of the impossibility of gaining the phallus, and we all try to gain it; in this sense men suffer from penis (or phallus) envy and castration as much as do women.

One of the interesting effects of trying to move from psychodynamic processes to cultural processes is that we create the impression of a society where everything fits together and it is difficult to see where change can come from. One of the paradoxes of Chodorow's argument is that from her feminist position she produces a sociological analysis that is very close to Talcott Parsons' structural functionalism, a notoriously conservative sociological theory dominant in the United States during the 1940s and 1950s. It is interesting that since she trained as a psychoanalyst she has been much more ready to acknowledge a range of individual differences (Chodorow 1995). However, Kristeva takes us much further along this road, firstly by concentrating on pre-oedipal experience prior to the acquisition of social stereotypes, and secondly by her rejection of simple notions of gender identity, male or female. In this way she comes closest to the heart of the heart of the post-Lacanian feminist project.

Part III

The Nature of Therapy

In the following two chapters I want to convey some idea of what psychotherapy (or psychoanalysis) is about in practice, but I do not want to do it in the normal way of case reporting and clinical vignettes. These make assumptions about effectiveness and meaning that I do not want to take on board. A colleague of mine once described the typical psychoanalytic paper as involving the description of a patient with particularly difficult problems, followed by a description of the patience and brilliance of the analyst, followed by a happy ending. He was over-cynical but a little too close for comfort. There are not that many accounts of failures.

Instead I will attempt not so much to describe therapy as to delineate the space in which it takes place, as I think here we come to the end of theory, or at least we will have done so when I have discussed the theory of therapy. I will use examples, but not stories, vignettes or the other forms of reporting; I am more interested in getting closer to the 'feel' of the session. Much of that feel will be specific to my own work and I will begin with some very general personal observations based on my own experience.

In these chapters we approach the creativity of life and the importance of understanding individual meanings.

11

Understanding Therapy (1)
Introduction

Some personal meditations on the nature and purpose of therapy

We now move beyond theory, or perhaps more accurately to an area that is framed by theory but in which things happen that cannot be grasped by theory. The work of psychoanalysis, the analysis or therapy that it offers, can be a very strange process to those who have not experienced it, and I believe that the best therapists are those who can understand that the therapy begins where the theory finishes.

These first points are really for people who have no experience of psychoanalytic therapy from either end of the couch. I want to spend some time outlining what I think therapy is *not* about in the light of some of my earlier arguments, and presenting my own particular prejudices about psychoanalysis with individuals and with groups. It is *not* about the application of theory, although it is often, but not always, about the *use* of theory. *Nor* is it a matter of an analyst telling a patient what is going on and certainly not what to do. An analyst who simply read off comments and interpretations from a sort of theoretical primer would not get very far, and, more important, neither would his or her patients. I was intrigued by the publication some years ago of a handbook of interventions in my own field of group analytic therapy (Kennard, Roberts and Winter 1993). It consisted of different group therapists giving their responses to hypothetical situations, and its most useful aspect as far as I was concerned was the range of responses that it solicited. There is no magic formula, and no set of instructions for patient or therapist.

I think that psychotherapy is best seen as a mutual search for understanding in which the therapist strives not to let his or her own learning or process of self-analysis get in the way of that of the patient. If you recall my account of Winnicott's view of the importance of letting the baby root for and discover the breast by itself, then perhaps psychotherapy is not dissimilar: the patient must root around in a search for meaning and the therapist, having been a patient, must be patient, knowing most of all when to keep quiet, and often being mistaken. To resort to theory in this context is forced feeding, and what is more, often forced feeding with unhealthy food.

Next, psychotherapy is a matter of enabling a person to *think* and to feel, not to *know*. Knowledge about oneself is, or easily becomes, a defence against the self-questioning that can lead to understanding. I can say to myself, or to others, 'I am just like that' and not do anything more, not respond to criticism, not try to change, not feel I might have to apologize; I avoid anything that might make me uncomfortable. On the other hand, if I say, 'It is too painful for me to change and I don't know how to do it', or if I say, 'I value being what I am more than I would value any alternative', then I am perhaps closer to the truth and I am thinking about the difficulty. Generally, I think of one aspect of 'success' in therapy as the patient learning that his or her knowledge is limited and he or she is the site of numerous conflicts, none of which is soluble. As at the end of a good university degree course, we should leave thinking not about how much we know but about how little we know.

I do not think that psychotherapy is a matter of what most lay-people might think it to be, namely a '*cure*', and it would follow that neither is it a 'treatment'. The medical model is of limited value. However, I have throughout this book used the term 'patient', which belongs to the medical model and implies, for many people, the helpless lay-person face to face with a sophisticated professional. I have employed this term because it points to our dependence on each other and on those who in certain areas have greater expertise than we do ourselves. I use it for essentially political reasons and perhaps because it actually is 'politically incorrect' (see Pilgrim 1992 and my reply, Craib 1992b). We live in a society that overvalues independence and tends to undermine the idea of a benign professional authority. Both tendencies are, I think, the effects of the revived market ideology of late capitalism, which tends to reduce everybody to abstract equals, and my use of the word 'patient' is a gesture against that way of looking at the world. The alternative – 'client' – reinforces the market ideology.

Further, as noted above, I do not think that it is helpful to think of psychoanalysis as a *cure*. This is a term that does not contest the market emphasis of late capitalism but fits neatly into it. As the market has eaten into the British health care system, so increasingly it seems that psychotherapy has to fight on grounds of a narrowly conceived effectiveness, where brevity of treatment and measurable effects are important. Yet what I have been urging here as the central value of psychoanalysis is a long and painful process of self-understanding that is never-ending in its consequences. It is doubtful whether this could be called a cure in any meaningful sense. If I had to choose, I might prefer the word 'healing', but this is only applicable to some of the wounds that we suffer during a lifetime and the major wound is life itself, and that can only be healed by death.

If psychoanalytic therapy works, it does bring about change, but it is not always the change that is expected or desired by the patient at the beginning. I might come to get rid of certain desires or feelings that I feel I shouldn't experience; if things go well I might find that such a feeling is part of life. I am not cured in such a case; rather I discover that I was not ill. Sometimes the change is in being able to tolerate unpleasant feelings, rather than fighting them. I had thought the feelings were my illness, but the 'cure' is to let myself have these feelings more fully.

Psychoanalytic therapy, like the human psyche itself, is full of contradiction and paradox. One way in which the medical model does not apply is that psychotherapy cannot be prescribed. It is always important to make this clear, especially if somebody is referred by those in authority over him or her. I have noticed through my connections with a university counselling service that such a service can be used as a supposedly humane alternative to discipline or punishment, and one often hears vaguely defined 'treatments' urged as part of the way in which we should deal with convicted criminals. Whilst it seems to me that any civilized penal system must give reform at least as much role as punishment, I am less clear that reform should include psychotherapy. And certainly the fact that somebody is undergoing psychotherapy should not be an influence on any decisions to be made about that person except in very special circumstances that I will explore shortly.

I think what is most important for both patient and therapist is a desire to understand oneself, and a desire to change oneself, and I think that these can be present however 'ill' a person might seem, but they are not always present even in the comparatively 'normal' or 'healthy' person. Psychotherapy is a good thing for everybody only in the abstract, and there are some people – perhaps many people – for whom it is not suitable and perhaps many more people who would not, anyway, be interested in it.

I like very much Neville Symington's statement (Symington 1986) that he does not feel he has any right to recommend psychotherapy to his potential patients. They must make the decision themselves. In my own assessment interviews I try to make a number of points clear. First, psychotherapy is not a miracle cure – it is likely to take a number of years and there is absolutely no guarantee of success. Second, you get no more out of it than you put in to it. There is a sense in which the onus rests on the patient at least to open him- or herself to reflection, although of course it is a co-operative enterprise. However, a therapist is not an administrator of psychological medicine. It is up to the patient to find his or her own answers, or, more usually, to cope with the absence of answers. Generally in my experience most people can accept this intellectually, but the emotional understanding takes much longer.

Finally I warn patients that things are likely to get worse before they get better. The reason for this is that psychotherapy involves travelling through regions of experience that we are likely to have spent a long time and a lot of energy avoiding. There are aspects of our past which we try to 'put behind us', aspects of ourselves, our actions, our thoughts and our desires of which we are thoroughly ashamed, but which we need to think about and look at. There will be moments when, just as in the treatment of cancer, the cure will seem worse than the disease. I also make it clear that it is the decision of the patient whether to enter therapy, and that although leaving will be a matter for discussion, the decision about when to leave is also the patient's own.

The one exception I would make to my personal rule that psychotherapy should not be used as an excuse or extenuating circumstance for a patient's behaviour, or rather that the psychotherapist should not allow his or her work to be so used, comes from the fact that at its most intense – when things seem to the patient to be becoming distinctly worse – the process can absorb a great deal of energy and make it more difficult to deal with outside everyday life. Even here I would not say to any authority figure (I am thinking primarily about the university context) that this is definitely happening, simply that I am seeing this person and that the therapy could affect his or her ability to work. I think that to do otherwise would leave the therapist open to manipulation, or simply being fooled, both of which may happen but neither of which is to be encouraged as being beneficial to the process.

Group psychotherapy and individual psychotherapy

Since I have moved on to talking about my work as a therapist, I should also point out that I work with groups and rarely with individual patients. There are differences, not least in the under-development of group analytic theory compared with more conventional theory, although of course psychoanalytic treatment in groups draws on every aspect of the theories I have outlined earlier. My main reason for introducing this issue here is because I have been insisting on psychoanalysis as a process that allows the individual to explore his or her own individuality, and some people have an immediate reaction to group therapy that it would deny that individuality. A second reason is that a number of my examples in what follows are taken from groups. A third, and for me the main, reason is that over the years I have become a partisan of group analysis. I have been rather surprised at this: when I first sought psychotherapy as a patient, I had no idea of the existence of group psychotherapy and I would have been terrified at the idea; I can see that terror in the face of some patients when group work is suggested and in the reaction of various colleagues when the issue of group psychotherapy comes up in discussion.

I want to suggest that group therapy enables people to understand their own uniqueness, their own individuality, more readily than does individual therapy, and the reason for this, and the reason for our fear of groups, has to do with the development of contemporary society. The philosopher Charles Taylor (1989, 1991) suggests that of the many ways in which we have come to understand the self, the instrumental is arguably now dominant. We do not see ourselves as linked by any profound emotional ties to others. It has become increasingly common to see people as engaged in relationships for their own satisfaction, for what can be gained from the relationship. Anthony Giddens, a sociologist who sadly sees this as a step forward in individual freedom, describes the process in terms of the transformation of traditional forms of society. Where sexual relationships were once cemented by strong social (and legal) norms and economic necessity, now this is no longer the case: relationships have to stand on their own four feet. The only reason for staying in a relationship is the satisfaction that it offers. Of course in such a situation children present a difficulty – Giddens refers to them as an 'inertial drag' on the relationship, and talks about a process of 'effort bargaining' between partners. He calls such a relationship a 'pure relationship' because its continuation is entirely dependent on itself (Giddens 1991).

The notion of effort bargaining illustrates my point: it implies a negotiation between two separate individuals about what each puts into the relationship and what each takes out. The pure relationship is a market relationship between two individuals in their search for maximum emotional profit. Hochschild (1994) presents a pointed critique of the way this idea has become prominent in modern feminism, for example in the work of Robin Norwood (1986). In the context of my argument here, what is lost in this way of looking at the world is – to put it simply – any idea of love, any idea that it is possible for a human being to think that another human being is more important than him- or herself. There is no link between people other than the economic, even when it comes to emotional exchanges. Such a conception of human beings has clear links to a historical period in which market capitalism, or perhaps more accurately the ideology of market capitalism, has come again to dominate social thinking.

There is a danger that psychoanalysis and psychoanalytic therapy can get drawn into this way of looking at the world simply by the pressure exercised by dominant ideologies and the fact that psychoanalysis has to sell itself to survive in such an atmosphere (Craib 1994). I would suggest that individual psychoanalysis is more at risk than group analysis. It was born in the massive metropolitan centres of Europe out of a breakdown in traditional forms of society and there is a sense in which it aims to enable the individual to live, love and work with the comparatively limited relationships of the nuclear family in a large, fast-moving, anonymous society.

I think that there are actually conflicting tendencies, at least in modern psychoanalytic theory, in relation to this social process. Whereas it is undermined by Lacanian theory, which constantly challenges the notion of a unitary and coherent self, both object-relations theory in Britain and self psychology in the United States tend to encourage it. There is if you like an 'elective affinity' between the requirement of the market for a self-sufficient instrumental actor, and a person who experiences him- or herself as an integrated self in relation to other people. This does not mean that either or both of these psychoanalytic theories are simply ideologies of late capitalism – object-relations theory's concern with our dependence is one clear counter-tendency – but the dominant culture will pick out and emphasize those strands of psychoanalytic theory that are closest to its way of looking at the world.

The process I am talking about leads to something that Marx called the 'individualized individual', to people who are separated from each other in crucial ways and blind to their mutual dependencies. Orthodox psychoanalysis encourages people to be aware of their dependence on their family of origin, and the present family relationships (of whatever sort), but it seems to me to have little to teach about the wider world, our relationships to strangers. The focus is inward rather than inward *and* outward.

There is a difference between this social structural process of individualization and what is known, say, in Jungian psychology and in critical social theory as individuation (Habermas 1990). Individuation is a more complex and profound notion, a matter of my understanding my own uniqueness and individuality through my relationships with and dependence upon others. It involves recognizing that there are essential ways in which I am dependent on all other people, that I share a common humanity with others and that I can only know myself through recognizing and finding my own place within *and* against them. I am myself in the constant to-ing and fro-ing of identifications and projections not just with my immediate family but with many others too. The concentration of 'the family' into small nuclear groups (whether step-families, single-parent families, homosexual families, or whatever) and the growing importance of childhood experience in specialist institutions run by professionals limit our ability to find ourselves in interaction with a range of different real people whom we experience in the fullness of our humanity. Foulkes, one of the founders of group analysis in Britain, is reported to have said that he could not imagine him separating himself out as an individual except against the background of six or seven people, the size of his family of origin.

This is the crucial way in which group therapy differs from individual psychotherapy. All the more or less normal features of individual therapy can be seen to be occurring in groups, but in a more complex form. Transference, which I will discuss in the following chapter, is a multi-dimensional process that involves a range of objects that are not available in individual psychotherapy. The group itself is an important object but one that is experienced as a set of concrete relationships between real people rather than an abstract object outside of the consulting room, or a remembered family from the past. And of course the group is a stronger container than the individual therapist: if it is working well, it can hold negative experiences that could be beyond individual therapists. One of the main reasons for the distrust of psychoanalytic therapeutic groups in the helping professions is, I believe, the fear that they will unleash everything that is bad about human nature, but the strength of the group can enable it to handle this.

The fact that the group is stronger than the therapist means that the power of the therapist is lessened – he or she is less likely to be taken in as a super-ego with all of his or her prejudices or kinks; rather the complexity and counterbalancing contradictions of the group are taken in – a group analysis can lead to a much deeper understanding of the complexity of subjectivity and therefore of one's own individuality and the complexity of one's relationships to others. Individuation is a matter of relationship to others, not of separation from others, and of relationships between parts of oneself.

Theory and clinical reports

One of the factors that has led me into this discussion is the way in which clinical accounts and theory are related in the psychoanalytic literature. The problem is that there is no clear conception either of what theory *is* or of how it is related to clinical practice. The model for many clinical accounts is, I suspect, the old one of 'scientific reports', where the therapeutic process is written up as a sort of experiment that can confirm or falsify or modify, or perhaps even generate, theoretical propositions. Even where this is clearly not the model, there seems to me to be a tendency to present what might very well be individual meanings as generalizations – nobody is quite sure of the status of suggestions that arise from individual cases. Either the individual case is seen as illustrating some theoretical development or idea, or its theoretical relevance does not seem to be an issue.

I think that it is important to separate the process of theoretical argument and debate and the therapeutic process, even though this was the model handed down to us by Freud. In relation to theory, the main purpose of individual accounts is as examples of what is being argued theoretically. To take an example, I find Christopher Bollas's idea of the 'normotic personality' (the personality able to relate only to external things) an exciting idea, both in its reference to personality types and in its reference to part of everybody's personality. The essay in which he develops this idea uses a number of examples that add to its clarity (Bollas 1995). But the theoretical work of placing the idea in relation to different levels of theory and to changes in the outside world is not undertaken. All too often this last stage in particular is left to non-psychoanalysts.

In relation to practice, however, it seems to me that descriptions of individual cases have a different function. They might be a way of parading the abilities of the psychoanalyst, but if they are sufficiently honest, they speak significantly to other practitioners, communicating the implicit rules of working, dealing with problems, crises, and so on. It is here that the case-book approach is useful, not because it adds to our knowledge in theoretical terms but because it is a passing on of experience, a contribution to a skill that is learnt originally through the psychotherapist him- or herself experiencing psychotherapy on the receiving end as a patient, and then through supervision.

I think that it is important to distinguish between these two ways of writing up case studies as their confusion can create confusion in the reader. I think as well that case studies that fall into the second category, as the passing on of experience, do not work well if the therapist only appears in a good light. There will always be a degree of necessary falsification in writing up case studies. A simple account of a session does not tell us much, and for an outsider it is likely to be boring, perhaps even a series of *non sequiturs*. My experience of group therapy on those rare occasions when I feel I might be working well is of being in the middle of a fast-flowing stream out of which shapes and figures can emerge and disappear. My earlier discussion of Bion's suggestion that the therapist be without memory or desire was highly critical, but I think that he was trying to get at this peculiar state of receptive contemplation in which therapists can find themselves, of absorption in emotional and verbal contemplation that is directed not towards a specific practical end, but towards understanding, and often then understanding only for the fleeting moments of clarity that can emerge and disappear. Accounts that do not convey such sensations and that do not employ the therapist's own 'errors' or blunderings should be mistrusted. The experience of therapy for the therapist is always multi-dimensional and contradictory, as much a matter of aesthetic interpersonal judgement as of scientific precision or accuracy.

In the midst of this experience there is also a discipline and a direction in which the therapist will try as far as it is consciously possible to put the interests of the patient before his or her own, and will devote emotional and intellectual energies towards understanding. As I mentioned earlier, the experience of psychoanalysis is framed by theory, and I will be looking at this in the next chapter.

12

Understanding Therapy (2)
Transference and Counter-Transference

Memories and catharsis

Freud's original understanding of what caused mental distress and what enabled its relief would be very familiar today to anybody who has followed debates about 'recovered' memories and 'false memory syndrome' in connection with child sexual abuse. He thought that the cause of neurosis was a traumatic but repressed memory and the aim of therapy was to bring the memory to consciousness and allow a discharge of the feelings attached to it. As he developed his theory and as he allowed his practice to develop, he left this idea behind, as he left behind the suggestive techniques, such as hypnosis, that he had adopted at the beginning. It is ironic that the return to these techniques and ideas by modern therapists are used by Freud's critics as a reason to attack him (Crews 1997) and that Freud's abandoning of these techniques is also used as a reason to attack him (Masson 1992). From a contemporary standpoint, it seems to me that both recovered memory and catharsis are dubious therapeutic tools. Both contribute to enabling a patient to feel good: catharsis brings with it a sense of release and comfort, and recovered memories often bring a sense of having explained something, whatever their 'reality'. What is questionable, however, is whether the aim of therapy is to enable the patient to, or even 'make' the patient, feel good.

It is clear from a recent account of the aims of psychoanalysis (Sandler and Dreher 1996) that from Freud onwards there has been a tension between psychoanalysis as a therapy and psychoanalysis as a means of research (often conceived of as scientific) into the human psyche. Luckily it has often been arguable that the two go together – that by learning the workings of one's own psyche, particularly its unconscious dimensions, one finds it easier, but not necessarily easy, to deal with life. That is in fact the implication of my arguments in this book – the process of understanding individual complexities of meaning is the prime aim of psychoanalysis, and that one is a better person, and can live with less difficulty, through launching oneself on this process.

It is also apparent that each school will have its own way of describing its aims. For the orthodox Freudian it would be encapsulated in Freud's dictum 'where id was, there ego shall be', a matter of making the unconscious conscious. For Kleinians it would be a matter of enabling the patient to move into the depressive position, and to modify the schizoid and manic defences. For a Lacanian it would be a matter of enabling entry into and the acceptance of the symbolic. For an object-relations theorist it would perhaps be a matter of achieving an integrated self in relationship with others, or a weakening of the false self. Sometimes these theoretical descriptions might in fact mean the same thing in practice, whilst at other times they might mean something very different. Sandler and Dreher are suitably modest in their suggestions: they argue for the importance of differentiating between outcome goals and process goals, and they discuss the complexities that deny the possibility of simple answers to questions about goals of either type. This is an important point: there are no simple answers or goals, and any analyst or therapist who promises a simple answer should not be trusted.

For the moment I will simply state my own definition of the aim of psychoanalysis (as enabling a less difficult life through attaining an emotional and intellectual understanding), but I will be arguing later that it has many radical implications. I want now to turn to the question of what goes on in the process of psychoanalysis and psychotherapy. I ought to say at this stage that in what follows I will be using these terms interchangeably. Many psychoanalysts maintain that it is a vital distinction – psychoanalysis involves five sessions a week for many years whereas psychotherapy requires one, two or three sessions a week for maybe fewer years. Arguments about this type of issue are in part arguments about professionalization and protectionism and I do not want to explore them here. The important point is that psychoanalysis and psychoanalytic psychotherapy both make use of an understanding of the unconscious and make use of notions of transference and counter-transference.

Transference

The notion of transference was developed by Freud in the process of understanding his own work, but it is a process that is arguably an essential part of our everyday relationships. Without transference, no relationship is possible. I will come back to this later. For psychoanalysts transference *is* the psychoanalytic relationship. According to Laplanche and Pontalis, it is 'a process of actualization of unconscious wishes. . . . In the transference, infantile prototypes re-emerge and are experienced with a strong sensation of immediacy' (Laplanche and Pontalis 1988: 455).

Transference was first thought of as an obstruction, the patient falling in love with the therapist, which then threatened a transgression of ethical boundaries. Then, when the limitations of hypnosis became apparent, it was thought that it was an ally in overcoming resistance; then it came to be seen as itself a resistance, turning the therapeutic relationship into an emotional one, rather than one geared to knowing; then it was seen as re-enactment and catharsis – perhaps the centre of the orthodox Freudian view (Hinshelwood 1991). With Klein the transference came to be seen in a more complex way, and as an acting out of present unconscious phantasies. For the moment I will concentrate on the Freudian view, which takes us back to catharsis and memory.

The notion of transference involves any number of complexities: most psychoanalysts see it as the ground on which change is achieved, but it can also be the ground that destroys the effectiveness of the analysis. The model for the process of transference comes from dream analysis; the original object of desire is replaced by a new figure or object with which it is in some way, possibly quite contingently, connected. The new object in this case is the analyst or therapist and the displacement is both more and less obscure than the displacement of dream work. It is less obscure in the sense that the analyst is a person, not a giraffe or a terrapin. It is more obscure in that the therapist is a real person and my feelings for him or her will have all the strength of a 'real' here and now situation. I will, at least for some of the time, be *sure* that I love my therapist or that he or she loves me, hates me, is persecuting me, is leading me in the wrong direction for his or her own pleasure, is keeping me dependent because he/she needs my money or whatever. If I believe one of these things strongly enough, then I can abandon the therapy or stay on, not in the hope of changing but in the hope that my therapist will one day return my undying love.

In many ways transference is independent of the analyst or therapist – a woman analyst may be experienced as a father and a male analyst experienced as a woman; the same analyst may move from one to the other in the course of the treatment. The notion of transference is connected to the idea of the analyst as a 'blank screen' on which the patient inscribes his or her phantasies. The more the patient knows about the reality of the analyst, his or her situation and personality, the less room there is for transference, the less room for the patient's desires and phantasies to come into play and become open to understanding. It is also linked to the rule of 'abstinence'. This is in part a rule that the analyst imposes on the patient – the patient should not, during the course of the analysis, seek satisfactions that are substitute symptoms. For example, there might be a stage during the analysis when I seek to avoid some particularly difficult issue by embarking upon a mad love affair (I have known this happen on a number of occasions). This might happen with the unconscious realization that I will not receive the love from my therapist that I am unconsciously seeking. Desperate not to surrender or modify this desire, which has been a major force in my life since my earliest years, I try to find, or fool myself that I have found, satisfaction elsewhere. The therapist's duty in such circumstances is to modify his or her neutral position and advise the patient of what is more often than not likely to be a disastrous relationship.

The term 'acting out' is used to describe this sort of reaction – a feeling becomes so strong that the patient cannot contain it and explore the unconscious ideas to which it is connected, but rather he or she has to act on it to release tension. The action, however, usually takes place outside of the analytic session. Sometimes it takes the form of 'acting in': I once heard a colleague report that a patient had pelted him with alabaster eggs from a bowl on a table next to the couch. More often it takes milder forms – consuming food, or smoking during a session, jumping up and walking around the room. 'Acting in' is perhaps more common in groups, where members might find themselves strongly attracted to each other or repelled by each other; or on a more mundane level members lend each other books or other items or they continue the session as they leave. All these things are added complications and provide material that, if the process is going well, can be fed back into the analysis for understanding.

The rule of abstinence is also important for the analyst, because it imposes an obligation not to satisfy the patient's desires but rather to interpret and reflect them back for analysis and understanding. On a personal level I find this the most difficult and painful part of the therapeutic task. The demand for comfort and support, for in fact a real parenting intervention, can be next to overwhelming, and I have to remind myself constantly that to satisfy this demand, first of all, is impossible – one cannot provide what was not given several decades ago – and, second, would be counterproductive, since the eventual aim of the therapy is a self-understanding and a relative independence. The frustration of desires provokes thought; the satisfaction of desires avoids thought.

The therapist cannot be a pure blank screen; all sorts of messages are 'given off' (Goffman 1969), often subliminally, and there is an unavoidable process of unconscious communication, which I shall discuss shortly. In the context of a therapy group, what seems important is that the details of the therapist and his or her life be sufficiently limited, or unknown, to enable the group to 'play' with their idea of the therapist. I have listened to groups speculate on whether or not I have children, what my home life is like if I refuse to answer my wife's questions, what my past experience has been, and so on. Some of this is revealing and useful in the sense that different group members might perceive me, say, as a persecutory or as a helpful figure, and this difference will lead them towards investigating their own projections, both in and out of the group. What does it mean that another person in the group sees the therapist in such a different way? Or is there any connection between the way this person experiences the therapist and the way he or she experienced a parental figure? In my own experience, the play between transferences in a group is not diluted because there are more people involved – as is often suggested by individual analysts – but clearer and more emphatic since it is visible to several people, not just the therapist.

At other times transference is useful as a form of play in the group – a collective process of constructing amusing stories that involves an opening up of psychic space, the realization that an internal figure can be used in different ways. This sort of playing can vary widely in its content: one group early on in my career told me that not only was my handwriting bad, but (amidst laughter) that it could be taken as the handwriting of a seriously deranged person – an expression of fears and hopes at the same time. At other times I have been likened to a statue covered with birdshit – which the group interpreted themselves as the way in which they tried to put their own shitty feelings into me. If they had known me as a 'real' person it would have been much more difficult for them to explore the group process in that way. This was even more true on another occasion when a group member insisted that I was a 'piece of dogshit'. But it is also a matter of treading a narrow line: remaining completely impassive could have been identified with a powerful internal persecutory figure that would punish such playing.

Transference, of course, involves projection, and it is the fundamental way in which all human relationships, from before birth onwards, are formed. We imagine what our parents are thinking and feeling, and later in life what our partners and friends are thinking and feeling and what our children will be, or are, thinking and feeling; we are all born into our parents' phantasies. There is a sense in which a human relationship, any human relationship, involves an exchange of parts; it is not a matter of monads bumping into and bouncing off each other, and it follows that any relationship will involve some degree of transference. The austere nature of the psychoanalytic situation enables the transference to come to the fore and, often, to become the focus of the interaction.

There is always a problem about knowing whether what we are dealing with is a matter of the transference or reality. This is both a theoretical and a practical problem. If a patient tells me that his or her mother has died, and assuming that I have no reason to doubt the information, then although the way in which the information is conveyed, the tone of voice, body language, and so on, might very well be part of the transference, the information itself will be real, or true, and of the sort that perhaps takes priority for a while. There are often arguments about what should or should not be dealt with as reality rather than as grist for the mill of transference interpretations: for a good example see Andrew Samuels' discussion of the way in which psychoanalysts of different types deal with their patients' political material (Samuels 1993). The answer to the theoretical problem is that anything that the patient says is likely to have transference aspects and to contain some non-transferential reality, but it is a matter of judgement as to what aspect should be dealt with in the treatment. In some circumstances, a reaction to the transference rather than the reality can damage the therapeutic relationship; in others a reaction to the reality rather than the transference can be a lost opportunity.

There is a wider theoretical problem about how far we can have knowledge of the external world that is not distorted or coloured by what is going on in the internal world. Many of my psychotherapist colleagues seem to surrender the possibility of achieving knowledge on the grounds of a transference-based relativism, but it seems to me that this is a confusion between perception, emotion and cognition. My perception of the world around me is always relative to the place where I am standing and my feelings. My cognition goes beyond perception. I look at my desk, and it appears solid, so solid that I can place heavy objects on it and they will not fall through it. If I touch it, it feels hard, not malleable. This is the world of perception, what I can see, feel, hear, taste and smell. My limited knowledge of physics, however, tells me that the desk is composed of a number of very small pieces of matter vibrating against each other at a uniform rate. This is the world of knowledge. My history, my internal psychodynamic processes, will invest the desk as I perceive it with certain qualities – it will seem threatening if I am over-burdened with work and would rather be enjoying myself; it may suggest comfort and pleasure if I am ready to get down to work and excited by what I am doing. On each occasion it will look different. Whichever may be the case, the laws and theories of physics remain the same and the knowledge they give me about my desk is objective in the true sense of the word: it is knowledge that does not change whatever my perception of it, or internal feelings about it or even my projections on to it, and it is knowledge about an object that does not change whatever my feelings about it. The end product of this argument is not very exciting: it is that responses to a patient's material that has a clear and perhaps pressing reality content is a matter of judgement on the part of the therapist. In my own work I have increasingly found myself thinking that transference aspects can be dealt with better after the power of the immediate reality has subsided.

Another debate is around the function of the transference and the relative value of memory and lived-out repetition (Laplanche and Pontalis 1988). In fact it seems to me that an argument that is carried out in these terms alone is likely to be misleading, although some forms of therapy, and perhaps some psychoanalysts, might think that one or both are effective by themselves. I think that I have said enough about memory to indicate why that by itself is inadequate. I think that the idea of a *repressed* memory might itself be doubtful, although I do think that forgetting is often convenient and, perhaps in a broader sense, useful in helping us survive. But forgetting and remembering together are processes of internal construction that enable us to continue operating within a present situation. A repressed memory does not, in my opinion, *cause* a particular set of problems. If that were the case Freud would not have had to go far beyond hypnosis. The same would be true if it were a matter of lived-out repetition – it is not just a reliving of a situation that brings about a therapeutic change.

I once worked in a group with a patient whom I shall call A who had experience of a different type of therapy that concentrated on recovered memories and emotional release. She saw herself as working, first, towards a release of emotional energy that had been stored up since childhood, and, second, towards remembering whatever it was that lay at the root of this blockage. Now the release of energy is always circular even if it is attached to memories, and however close those memories might or might not be to real events. I came to suspect after a while that this woman's building up and releasing of tension had less to do with memories of ill treatment she received as a child (although I have no doubt that she was ill treated) than with her ability to cope with present internal conflicts. The memories provide a convenient hook on which to hang the emotional energy generated by current conflicts. The belief that the current conflicts are caused by the early events, whether it be the therapist's belief or the patient's belief, denies the patient's agency, and it is difficult to see how therapy can proceed in such a situation. Memories may be employed to 'explain' current conflicts, about which nothing can then be done (my patient's difficulty), or they may be understood as metaphors for contemporary internal conflict and can lead the therapeutic process forward (Haaken 1996).

Therapy, then, is about agency; indirectly about external agency – what the patient does and wants to do in the outside world – but directly about internal agency – what the patient is doing internally, the way external experiences and objects are internalized and processed, and about the patient's awareness and understanding of what goes on in his or her internal space. Memories, release of emotion, and so on, might very well be part of the process but are not its end result. Laplanche and Pontalis touch on the wider problem here when they refer to debates around 'the nature of *what is transferred*: are we concerned with behaviour patterns, with types of object relation, with positive or negative feelings, with affects, with libidinal cathexis, with phantasies, with a whole imago or with a specific trait of an imago – even with "agencies" in the sense this term has in the final theory of the psychical apparatus?' (Laplanche and Pontalis 1988: 456). My suggested answer here is that psychoanalytic therapy involves, or can be seen in terms of, all of these things, all of these transferences, but in different degrees at different times and for different individuals. The one thing that embraces them all is the movement towards a higher degree of self-understanding.

My example of the patient A, whose acting out in the group I came to see as an expression of the emotions associated with current internal conflicts, brings us closer to Kleinian conceptions of transference. Hinshelwood (1991) attributes this development to Klein's working with children sometimes as young as two, when enactments in the therapeutic situation could not be seen as reproducing some long-forgotten relationship. It made most sense to see it as a staging of unconscious phantasies, and this insight was developed into adult analysis. The transference is the acting out of phantasies rooted in the here-and-now relationship between the patient and the analyst. I see this not as an alternative conception of transference but as another level of meaning, but a level that can add to the re-enactment interpretation and avoid the causal implications, the loss of agency, that can occur with the latter.

Later Kleinians (for example, Joseph 1978, 1985) have talked about the many ways in which patients can, in the transference, use the analyst as part of their defence. I often feel that a patient's fantasy that I am a caring person is perhaps a defence against acknowledging persecutory anxieties. If the therapist is a fixed object in the patient's imagination, as opposed to an object that can be played with and take on many different forms, then he or she is more likely to be being used as a defence. Klein also talked about a split transference, which I would understand in terms of the paranoid-schizoid position. There is positive and negative transference, and sometimes a sort of fragmented transference that is a very basic defence against anxieties aroused by the transference. Here the therapist's job is to interpret the manifestations of the transference in such a way that the fragments are brought together and he or she becomes a figure experienced from the depressive position, neither idealized nor demonized as a persecutory figure, but seen as possessing a similar ambivalent reality to that of the patient.

If we stay with Freud and Klein, we can think of the transference as primarily an emotional relationship. At first glance it would appear that the notion would be seen by Lacan as belonging to the realm of the imaginary: the construction of an object through desire unmediated by the symbolic. In fact he adds another dimension to the notion, seeing it also as a symbolic process involving an exchange. Lacan suggests that if one person talks to another in a way that is meaningful to both, in a 'full' rather than an empty way, then there is an exchange that changes both people. The transference belongs in both the symbolic and the imaginary realms.

There are two reasons in Lacan's psychoanalytic theory that suggest that there is no possibility of 'resolving' the transference, and I think that at this point he adds something very important to our understanding of psychoanalytic treatment. The first has to do with what I would describe as the metaphysical assumptions of his theory of language and the rather limited definition of reality that results from his distinctions between the real, the imaginary and the symbolic. This makes any argument about what is real and what is transference material irrelevant since we do not have access to the real. In fact the argument remains relevant if we combine Lacan's insight about the imaginary and symbolic dimensions of transference with a more conventional ontology in which language is a means of making contact not only with other people but also with a shared external and independent world. Although we cannot make absolute judgements about reality, we can make relative judgements about the transference and the real content of the patient's talking, as I suggested earlier.

The second reason is more powerful and interesting: if the transference is in part symbolic, an exchange, then that aspect cannot be resolved: we cannot grow out of the symbolic – we can return to the imaginary or die. When I leave therapy I will carry with me the changes that have occurred through a 'full' exchange with the analyst – he or she will be part of my internal symbolic universe. A resolved transference has the same sort of wishful thinking attached to it as the notion of a perfectly analysed individual, or the integrated individual, or somebody who has been cured, or of somebody who is capable of curing. All these belong to the imaginary.

Counter-transference

So far I have talked about the emotional and cognitive processes in the patient, largely assuming that the analyst actually *is* the blank screen on which the patient projects his or her desires and fantasies. Of course the analyst too is a human being who brings to the analytic situation not only his or her expertise and understanding but also his or her own history, desires and phantasies, unconscious processes and projections. A large part of psychoanalytic training is a matter of the analyst going through the same process through which his or her future patients will go, to gain a reasonable understanding of his or her inner life and to develop an ability to identify when his or her own projections and unconscious processes might be entering the game. It is perhaps going through this process as part of a training rather than as part of an enterprise of self-understanding that leads to the fantasy of the perfectly analysed analyst and the associated punitive super-ego.

Psychoanalysis or psychotherapy is a process of communication between at least two people, and both parties may well be unconscious of dimensions of that communication for some if not all of the time. One of the ways in which psychoanalysts have tried to capture the analyst's contribution is through the notion of *counter-transference*. Sometimes the word is used to denote very specific feelings that the analyst believes are a response to the patient's unconscious, and sometimes it is used to refer to the whole range of feelings experienced by the analyst in the course of the session and which, for that reason, have something to do with the therapy.

Counter-transference in Freudian psychoanalysis

Laplanche and Pontalis (1988) suggest what they call a 'schematic' distinction between three ways in which psychoanalysts approach the counter-transference. First it should be eliminated as far as is possible from the treatment so that the central focus of the analysis is built around the patient's material. It is this position that tends to carry the notion of the perfectly analysed therapist acting as a blank screen. The patient's material of course should be given priority, but this does not mean that the therapist does not bring his or her active unconscious to the situation and that this is not picked up at some level by the patient. In other words I think that there is an implicit denial here that the analytic situation involves a *relationship* between two people, and this inhibits an exploration into aspects of what is going on that might be uncomfortable for the analyst.

I think that it is fair to say that this is the most orthodox Freudian position and perhaps fits in with a great man's self-perception as a physician and a scientist. Freud did not have much to say about counter-transference. He talked, for example, about how patients could not travel further through the analytic process than the therapist had travelled, but he does not follow up such comments. It is sometimes comparatively easy to identify some of the difficulties he ran into in this respect in his own practice. Steven Marcus, a social historian perhaps not bound by the aura of respect that sometimes seems to put Freud above criticism in psychoanalytic circles, points to this difficulty in relation to Freud's study of Dora. 'Dora' was the name Freud (1977c) gave to one of his patients – a young woman caught up in a sexual mesh involving her father, her father's friend and his wife. The analysis did not go well and Dora terminated the process after eighteen months. Freud was just beginning to understand the nature of transference and Marcus quotes Freud's account of termination as part of the transference: Freud had reminded Dora of her father's friend (a Herr K), who had made unwelcome sexual advances towards her. For Freud it was Dora's transference that was the crucial factor in the ending of the analysis. Marcus, however, suggests that:

> We are, however, in a position to say something more than this. For there is a reciprocating process in the analyst known as the counter-transference, and in the case of Dora this went wrong too. Although Freud describes Dora at the beginning of the account as being 'in the first bloom of youth – a girl of intelligent and engaging looks', almost nothing attractive about her comes forth in the course of the writing. As it unwinds, and it becomes increasingly evident that Dora is not responding adequately to Freud, it also becomes clear that Freud is not responding favorably to this response, and that he does not in fact like Dora very much. (Marcus 1985: 89)

It should be evident that this is a major danger for therapists, and perhaps the best practitioners have the courage to refer elsewhere clients to whom they take an immediate dislike. It is more difficult when the dislike occurs in the course of the analysis, and even more difficult if it remains unconscious. But this example shows the danger of *unconscious* counter-transference. It is wrong to think that counter-transference is simply a threat to the analysis – it is so primarily if it is unconscious; and conscious or unconscious, it cannot be avoided.

The second option, according to Laplanche and Pontalis, is to be guided in a controlled way in one's interpretations by one's awareness of the counter-transference. This, they suggest, comes from a comment by Freud that we all possess in our own unconscious an instrument for receiving messages from the unconscious of others. They refer to Freud's notion of 'suspended attention', which I will introduce now because it is the basis for some interesting ideas that have developed in the Kleinian tradition.

Freud encouraged analysts to listen to their patients with a free-floating attention, an equivalent to the free association that the patient is encouraged to allow him- or herself to engage in. This involves not giving any particular utterance priority – for example, the analyst does not listen out for and jump on some comment about the patient's sex life, or his/her relationship to a parent, as representing the meat of what is being said. The analyst should enter the session not as a theoretical expert but as a listener, allowing an interpretation to form, as it were, from the gut rather than from the head. This attitude is difficult to describe and it is reminiscent of Bion's injunction to approach the session without memory or desire, of which I was critical at an earlier stage of my argument. I want to come back to his comment later. For the moment I will leave 'a free-floating attention' as the best way of describing the attitude.

Now I want to make a difficult but important distinction here. Of the contemporary theorists discussed in this chapter, the one who comes closest to this second attitude – an informed use of the counter-transference – is Lacan. Lacan, however, would be very critical of the way in which I have formulated the issue as involving a relationship between analyst and patient. Lacan argues that the prime function of psychoanalysis is to take the patient through the oedipal stage, and this is done by frustrating the patient's demands for a relationship – the analyst learns from his or her unconscious participation in the relationship, but contributes only through interpretations. This is subtly and significantly different from the third option, which developed initially through Kleinian theory and more recently through object-relations theory, and which involves a more active use of the counter-transference in developing interpretations.

Counter-transference in Kleinian psychoanalysis

The starting point for Kleinian notions of counter-transference is a paper by Paula Heimann (1960), who argued that the aim of a training analysis is to produce not a mechanic but somebody who is capable of sustaining feelings rather than acting them out. In this paper and another, Heimann (1950, 1960) argued that counter-transference is not a matter of the analyst's own feelings interrupting the analysis but a specific emotional response to a specific patient that indicates something important about the patient's state of mind.

This was developed in the Kleinian tradition, although not necessarily with the agreement of Klein herself, through to Bion's notion of containment. The key mechanism is that of projective identification. The specific communication from the patient is placed in the analyst because the patient him- or herself cannot bear it and the analyst contains it, feeding it back (we hope) in a manageable, verbal form to the patient. Hinshelwood (1991) insists on the way in which the notion of projective identification enables an intrapsychic or internal account of the interpersonal analytic situation – projective identification is an internal process within each of the involved psyches, analyst and patient, as well as an interpersonal account. There is a tendency with Kleinian analysis in particular to see things intrapsychically, in terms only of the internal world of the patient, rather than as part of a relationship. This comment is only *just* fair as a criticism – I am talking about a tendency rather than a firm position. I believe that it comes from what might be called the normal psychoanalytic tendency to focus on the internal world of one patient, coupled with Klein's specific concern with internal struggles between the life and death instincts. Hinshelwood makes it clear too that this way of looking at counter-transference *also* transforms the analytic situation into an interpersonal encounter.

Hinshelwood's account of counter-transference and projective identification rests upon a distinction that I mentioned earlier – and of which I am suspicious – between normal and pathological projective identification. It is a dangerous distinction because it seems to be judged by intensity – a dynamic criterion that will vary according to internal and external processes and situations, whereas the normal/pathological distinction implies a state, an equivalent of the health/illness distinction. Despite this, Bion's account of the *experi-*

ence of counter-transference, which Hinshelwood also quotes, is useful. He describes it as having

> a quite distinct quality. . . . The analyst feels that he [*sic*] is being manipulated so as to be playing a part, no matter how difficult to recognize, in someone else's phantasy – or he would do if it were not for what in recollection I can only call a temporary loss of insight, a sense of experiencing strong feelings and at the same time a belief that their existence is quite adequately justified by the objective situation . . . .
> (Bion 1961: 149)

The intensity of projective identification here, which I guess would count as pathological, can be compared with Money-Kyrle's account of 'normal' counter-transference, which involves a cycle of introjection and projection (Money-Kyrle 1956). However, one interesting feature of this comparison is that Bion is talking about the experience of counter-transference in groups, and groups can be considered as a context where there is a sense in which pathology can become normal, or, perhaps to put it better, the normality of pathology becomes clearer; or, even better, the difficulties of employing these terms and the extent to which they are context-dependent become clearer.

Counter-transference, reverie and meditation

I want now to return to another aspect of Bion's work, relevant to the notion of projective identification and counter-transference and containment, that goes back to my earlier comments about the psychoanalyst's attitude. When discussing Bion's injunction to the analyst to approach the session without memory or desire, I said that this was impossible, which of course it is if the analysis is to be a thinking enterprise, and if it is a talking enterprise it must be a thinking enterprise. But there are other attitudes to the world that can coexist with and perhaps take precedence over thinking, and that provide a basis for the emotional containment that the analyst must eventually attempt to translate into words.

I sometimes think that in groups some of my most useful comments are those that, when I make them, seem to be misunderstood by group members, and I sometimes think that, likewise, the most useful interpretation of Bion's injunction is not the one closest to his meaning. I would suggest that there is a philosophical confusion in Bion's work that points in two opposite directions at the same time. The model of the movement from emotion to perception to cognition seems to me strictly empiricist, in line with the dominant conception of clinical work held by psychoanalysts of earlier generations. In this context Bion's injunction to approach a session without memory or desire is equivalent to a simplistic scientific empiricist notion of objectivity – of looking for and relying on facts and supposed inductions from and correlations between facts. It is this project that I think is impossible, and, as I have said on several occasions, it reduces objectivity to a subjective attitude.

There is another interpretation that I believe is probably the wrong one, but that can be connected to other parts of his work – those that approach problems of an ultimate reality, an 'O', a Godhead, the source of Truth, and the notion of 'negative capability' – drawing from a letter by Keats, and referring to a state of existing with uncertainty, mystery and doubt, with no 'irritable reaching after fact and reason' (see Bion 1970). This is closer to a mystical state, not unlike that encouraged in *The Cloud of Unknowing*, a central work of English Christian mysticism. The Symingtons (1996) suggest that this is not a state of mind that one should get oneself into before a session but a way of life. In fact I do not think that it is either of these things, but something in between. A life, even for a hermit, involves actions and decisions, and they involve putting doubt and uncertainty into the background. But neither is the 'O' a meditative state we can put ourselves into before an analytic session. My own experience in groups is that it is a state that the group allows me to achieve when it allows me to bear witness to its suffering, and I find myself pulled in two directions when I try to make sense of it.

One is a religious direction in which a right or wrong interpretation, or success or failure in achieving an interpretation, is irrelevant; it feels as if I and the group have achieved contact with some common human understanding that transcends our individuality. My usual response these days to questions about my religious belief is to say that I am a Christian atheist, and if I call anything God it is this transcendent shared understanding. But such a state is not frequent and it cannot last, and individuality emerges again as it must and should.

The second direction in which this idea takes us is towards the notion of maternal containment or holding or reverie. I am following the usual practice of calling it *maternal* reverie, although there is some evidence that fathers have various ways of engaging in such reverie as well (Dixon 1997). In the closeness of parent and baby, the eye contact, and the physical and emotional proximity of reverie, the mother is, at some level, understanding and holding the baby's feelings and returning them through her own understanding. Access to this level of understanding and the ability to articulate what is understood is an important part of psychotherapy and it leads on to a discussion of ideas of transference and therapeutic treatment to be found amongst object-relations theorists.

Counter-transference in object-relations theory

Although Heimann (1950) is often credited with originating the British analysts' concern with counter-transference, there is a root which goes further back to the first-generation Hungarian psychoanalyst Sandor Ferenczi, a colleague and for a while a friend of Freud's, who argued that there were cases in which the orthodox psychoanalytic stance did not work and some interactive involvement was needed on the part of the therapist, including a more honest revelation of his or her own feelings. Freud himself was ambivalent, if not hostile, towards Ferenczi's experiments in this area, just as Melanie Klein was to remain suspicious of Heimann's ideas, but Ferenczi's pupil Michael Balint provided one of the main routes via which notions of counter-transference spread.

In a paper published with his first wife (Balint and Balint 1939) we find the very reasonable suggestion that a counter-transference is normal – an emotion in one person tends to bring forth an emotion in another, and the psychoanalyst cannot be inhuman. They also make the very reasonable observation that no two analysts work in exactly the same way and each analysis produces its own peculiar atmosphere, different from the others. The atmosphere is created by the interplay of transference and counter-transference, and most patients are able to adjust to whatever individual differences in technique there might be. This shifts the focus of analysis onto the conscious and unconscious interaction of the patient and analyst, and brings us further towards seeing it as a human relationship, albeit a special form of human relationship. It was on this sort of basis that Heimann reinterpreted counter-transference as something to be used rather than mastered.

One way of thinking about what has happened as the idea of counter-transference has become more important in Kleinian and object-relations theory is to think of more and more of the analyst's feelings about and emotional responses to the patient being taken into account as part of the analysis. For example, there is a classic paper by Winnicott (1958: 196–203) where he discusses the role of hatred in the counter-transference, particularly in work with psychotic patients, where love and hatred are often immediately conjoined. Hatred is a self-protective emotion that can have an important part to play in life, and must be freely felt by the analyst if the patient is going to be able to experience his or her own hatred; if the analyst can feel and contain and put that hatred into words (not necessarily for the patient), the patient has a chance of containing his or her hatred. This can be very important – one of the most useful things said to me by my supervisor during training was that if I could allow my patients to hate me I would be free to help them. Conversely the avoidance by the therapist of his or her hatred helps nobody. In this way the analyst's own emotional life in relation to the patient becomes a vital part of the treatment.

Another related line of development from Heimann's ideas is represented in the work of Casement (1985, 1990) in Britain and Langs (1976, 1978) in the United States. Here the counter-transference is seen not only as a communication from the patient but also as a corrective communication, a way of telling the analyst something that he or she has not understood or has misunderstood. Casement advocates the development of an internal supervisor through a process of reflective identification with the patient – perhaps, sometimes necessarily, between sessions, in an attempt to understand the reasoning behind a patient's comments or reaction. He differentiates an internal supervisor, an internal figure developed through the analyst's own reflective process, from an internal*ized* supervisor, which is something taken in, on occasions uncritically, from the outside. An example of the latter would be if I responded to a patient by repeating to him or her a comment my supervisor had made about this person, perhaps even using the same words, or when I say something that would please my supervisor rather than help the patient.

One of the functions of the internal supervisor is to listen to messages experienced in the counter-transference in a particular way and to see them as possible indications of what the therapist may be missing, or unable to understand because the patient does not have the words to say it directly – if a patient attacks my abilities, my performance, my training and my overall adequacy as a therapist, it could be that in relation to this patient I have been an inadequate therapist, and I have not understood some pain he or she suffered at the hands of his or her parent; or it may be that the only way that he or she can convey that understanding is to behave like the parent, and make me feel like the patient used to feel. Most often it is likely to be a combination of both.

This approach envisages psychotherapy as a more explicitly interactive process than does the classical position, and this is recognized by many object-relations analysts. I think many would see it as a learning process on both sides, even if the analyst's or therapist's learning is not made explicit (although some of this may be possible at the end of the therapy). It also leads on to the question of what the analyst or therapist learns, or gains, from the process. It is after all one of the more extraordinary ways in which people make a living, and I have never met a psychoanalytic therapist who is only concerned with making money, although I would certainly not claim that such an animal does not exist.

The best description I have come across of the satisfaction of the therapist is to be found in an essay by John Klauber:

> Patient and analyst need one another ... the analyst needs ... the patient in order to crystallize and communicate his own thoughts, including some of his inmost thoughts on intimate human problems which only grow organically in the context of this relationship. They cannot be shared and experienced in the same immediate way with a colleague or even with a husband or wife. It is also in his relationship with his patients that the analyst refreshes his own analysis. It is from this mutual participation in analytic understanding that the patient derives the substantial part of his cure and the analyst his deepest confidence and satisfaction. (Klauber 1981: 46)

Conclusion

What are we to make of these various positions on the place of the analyst and his or her feelings in the course of the therapy? Psychotherapy is not a one-sided process, an administering of textbook interpretations, though I would venture to suggest that no therapist is innocent of doing this on occasions. Nor is the therapist a blank screen, although it might on occasions be useful to the patient and to the therapist to appear to be one. The therapist is in fact all the time engaging in a self-analysis in relation to the patient, and my own experience has been one of adopting all the above positions, of thinking of and using the counter-transference in all the ways I have discussed. It depends on what is happening in the group, in the specific patient and in me.

I suspect that the therapist might have to develop through the various uses of counter-transference as he or she becomes more experienced and confident in his or her work and ability. I have become aware in myself and in other therapists of a process through which we go after completing training that I think of as outgrowing our training. Once learning has been set in motion it can continue without a teacher; a therapy can set in motion a change which continues well after the therapy ends, and a training, rigorous but also open, sets in motion a process of learning that can slow down or speed up, but, if we are lucky, does not come to an end. *If* we are lucky, we become more modest and more subtle therapists at the same time. It is not unlike learning to play a musical instrument, which, through experience, opens up possibilities of interpretation and improvisation. If the operation is successful, perhaps much the same can be said of the patient – he or she can live a life of new variations on an old theme.

13

Conclusion

I want now to try to bring together the critical and the positive themes of this book. In chapter 12 I moved from talking about psycho-therapy as an emotional and thinking process to talking about it as an imaginative process; throughout the book I have talked about the different theories of psychoanalysis as offering an understanding of different levels of the psyche: the deeper underlying structures of the unconscious and the drives; the higher levels of the earlier object-relations theories, beginning with Klein; the phenomenologies of the self of the more contemporary object-relations theorists and of Kohut; and finally the cognitive psychologies of Bowlby and Stern. Throughout I have argued against separating the understanding of the levels of the psyche that are closer to the surface from those that are deeper; the failure to keep the levels in relation to each other has been one of my major lines of criticism of the later theories. In this context the development of Lacanian theory has been a welcome reminder of the deeper levels, but the purity of Lacan's approach does not allow us to deal with the surface levels with the richness that comes with the object-relations theorists.

The first part of this conclusion will be an attempt to organize the different levels of analysis into a coherent framework that comes from modern European philosophy rather than psychoanalysis, and the second part consists of some personal observations on the nature of psychoanalysis.

Levels of analysis and types of science

The framework that seems most readily compatible for my purpose is provided by Jürgen Habermas, the German philosopher and social theorist, whom I have mentioned a number of times in passing in the course of the text, and by recent developments in British philosophy of science. Habermas (1972) suggests that human beings possess what he calls 'cognitive interests': interests in gaining knowledge for particular purposes. These interests lead to the development of different types of sciences and they are based on what he sees as the two distinctive features of human beings: they work to transform their environment, and in the process transform themselves; and they are communicating beings, they possess language.

The first 'interest' comes from work: it is the technical interest, our interest in knowing how the world around us works so that we can change it in order to lead better lives. This interest gives rise to what Habermas calls the 'empirico-analytic sciences'. Basically these include the natural sciences and some of the social sciences, or some dimensions of the social sciences. The standard conception of the empirico-analytic sciences is that they are based on empirical observation, testing and measurement in search of regularities that are given something approaching a law-like status. Of the psychoanalytic approaches examined in this book, the work of Bowlby and the studies following up attachment theory come closest to this sort of scientific activity, and this is what Holmes (1993) refers to as Bowlby's 'restrictive' conception of science. Bion's grid also presents this model of psychoanalysis, but in a more complex and interesting way, and much of Bion's theory overflows the grid.

Over recent decades, an alternative conception of the natural science has emerged under the label of critical realism (Bhaskar 1978, 1979), arguing that what the empirico-analytic sciences are really doing goes well beyond observation, measurement and testing. They are theoretical as well as empirical disciplines that are concerned with establishing knowledge of underlying levels of reality and causal mechanisms that are not empirically visible. What is visible and open to empirical observation is the effects of these structures and mechanisms. In the terms of this book there have already been persuasive attempts to interpret Freud in this light (Collier 1981; Will 1980), and I think that we could add Klein (and, almost certainly against his posthumous will, Lacan). At this level, then, we can regard the depth theories of psychoanalysis as scientific in a realist sense.

The second cognitive interest stems from the human possession of language; Habermas calls it the practical interest – the interest we have in communicating with and understanding each other, which gives rise to the hermeneutic sciences – the sciences of understanding. This would include many areas of social science and philosophy. Throughout this book I have insisted on the priority of psychoanalysis as providing a hermeneutics, based on the analysis of underlying structures of the psyche but using the knowledge of those as a basis for interpreting the meaning of human action and speech. We cannot read off these meanings from our knowledge of the underlying structures in some straightforward way. That simply gives us a crude psychoanalysis – for example, we end up saying that somebody who smokes is stuck at the oral stage or somebody who dresses in black is depressed. This last example was the experience of a fashionably dressed student of mine on her first visit to a psychotherapist; she did not return. This sort of reading-off is not possible because of the internal and unconscious processes of condensation and displacement that are constantly in play. So although we can see psychoanalysis as providing a hermeneutic, that in itself is not sufficient. This brings us to Habermas's third cognitive interest: the emancipatory interest. This arises from the practical interest. Communication can become distorted for a variety of reasons: inequalities of power and wealth; systematic discrimination against different social groups; lack of acquaintance with necessary information, and so on. This interest gives rise to the critical sciences, of which Habermas offers psychoanalysis as an example. He suggests that it works at all three levels, enabling the analysand to become informed about the effects of his or her body, to understand him- or herself more fully, and also to gain purchase over his or her difficulties in communicating. Moreover, the process itself is one which removes the inequalities between the participants. Analyst and analysand start off unequal to each other but the process of analysis enables the analysand to take in and understand what the analyst knows; it is precisely a process of emotional and intellectual learning. This account is parallel to the version of the developmental process offered by many psychoanalysts: it is the movement through the oedipal stage, with the conflicts and acceptance of paternal authority that that involves, to the point where the patient reaches a suitable level of maturity and integration, just as the child develops into an adult and takes his or her place in the world of adults. In this process, each of the different understandings and uses of counter-transference can find its relevant place.

Some final observations

My criticism of Habermas and of the traditional psychoanalytic way of understanding this process is that it is too linear, and in Habermas's case, too cognitive. It is a *process* but it is a multi-dimensional process, working at intellectual, emotional, deeper structural and wider conscious levels all at the same time. If it is going well, it is closer to the process of free association, displacement, condensation and symbolization rather than a steady 'maturing', although that might provide a very broad framework. The maturing is perhaps best thought of as a movement from the simple to the complex, an increasing depth of self-understanding on the part of the individuals concerned, and of the relationship between them. I would suggest that notions of cure, maturity, integration, tend towards limiting such an opening up on all levels. It is through such ideas that psychoanalysis gets caught up in wider social practices that are also restrictive.

The most intelligent criticisms of psychotherapy (for example, especially Szasz 1964) tend towards seeing it as part of what is sometimes called the 'therapeutic society'. Although there are different versions of these arguments, they involve the proposition that psychoanalysis and psychotherapy have become involved in a process of social control, a matter of, in Nikolas Rose's words, 'governing the soul' (Rose 1990). One might argue that in contemporary society, social order is maintained not only by a uniformed police force but also by a plain-clothes psychological police force involved in a process of managing not crime, but emotional and mental disorder and unhappiness. A less systemic and perhaps less paranoid way of looking at the same situation is Szasz's suggestion that modern Western society has developed an attitude to life that defines the normal processes of living, which are always and for many reasons problematic, as indicating an illness of some sort. People tend to treat 'normal human misery' as a problem or a symptom about which something should be done. Once a professional mental health service develops, backed up by a huge, profit-making pharmaceutical industry, there is a tendency to define more and more ordinary life processes as problems that need treatment – as I have indicated before, perhaps mourning is the clearest example (Craib 1994).

There are ways in which psychoanalysis can open itself up to this sort of criticism, or, more importantly, can allow itself to be absorbed into institutional systems that turn it into an activity that does not open up an ability to feel, think and imagine, but that aims directly or indirectly to close down such abilities. The critical aspect of my critical introduction is aimed at these tendencies.

If we turn psychoanalysis into a developmental psychology with implicit causal connections linking the emotional and parental environment to pathological outcomes, we run the risk of losing a sense of agency and psychological depth and creativity. This is reflected in psychotherapy in patients who believe that they have found the cause of their problems in the way that their parents treated them but don't know what to do next. It becomes difficult to see how one takes and develops one's childhood experience into ways of behaving that are not inevitable. Using psychoanalysis in this way loses the complexity of internal processes and any notion of emancipation. The attempt to insist on psychoanalysis as a natural science or to model it on the natural sciences produces a similar result.

Psychoanalysis certainly treats human beings as rooted in their bodies, and this rightly opens the door to biology, especially evolutionary biology, neurology, medicine. It also directs us towards developmental psychology, and this includes the universal human development through various forms of growth and then decline and decay to death. But it also involves the recognition that we are divided beings, physical and 'natural' beings but also users of symbols that give a meaning to our bodies, a meaning that is caught up in our symbolic systems and transformed according to rules that are very different from the laws of nature that govern our bodies. These rules and systems of rules mean that we can never produce causal explanations of human behaviour, even though human behaviour grows out of causal processes – that space between our physical and symbolic existence that Sartre called a 'nothingness' is what makes understanding human life so interesting and difficult.

This is also what makes it difficult to legislate for relationships – whether they be sexual partnerships, work relationships or parent–child relationships. If we take the latter, for example, we can lay down very general rules – we know that if we beat and bugger our children we will make life difficult for them; we also know that if we gratify their every desire we will make life difficult for them, but these are rules of humane common sense. Sadly there are perhaps social strata (from ghettoes to the schools of the wealthy) where, for very different reasons, humane common sense is in short supply. Expert knowledge can offer a guide to this very basic level of relationships but can easily become an attempt to exclude the troublesome emotions that are part of any human relationships: love itself, hatred, envy, jealousy, anger – all of these are essential ingredients and disrupters of relationships and, thankfully, cannot be subjugated to rules.

If we take up my account of the therapeutic process as involving rational, emotional and imaginative dimensions, we can begin to think of a human life as a work of art that might never properly be realized or that might be meaningless to most other people or satisfying to some smaller or larger degree to the one who lives it. That life will always involve 'pathologies' of some sort, and they might be strong enough to limit its possibilities or they might conceivably be strong enough to open up its possibilities. The role of psychoanalysis in this is not to cure but to enable a better understanding of the materials out of which the work is to be constructed and some understanding of the abilities and lack of abilities that are there to be deployed.

Throughout this book, I have tried to emphasize internal complexity, different levels of structures and internal conflicts and contradictions, as well as existential contradictions and difficulties with the outside world. There is something important in this that we find in theorists as far apart as Kernberg, Bion and Lacan: that loss, frustration, pain and conflict are necessary for growth and development. What I want to suggest here is that we become who we are, develop our individuality, our uniqueness, our own work or art, through our conflicts within and without ourselves, through the way in which we suffer. We do not grow through having our needs satisfied; we grow, develop and change through having them frustrated, denied or redirected, and it is the experience of the frustrations that highlights the joys on those occasions when we overcome them. Another way of describing the process of psychotherapy is that it enables us to suffer.

This is not a goal that is likely to impress many health service managers, doctors or perhaps even lay-people, although one might hope that the latter might have a better intuitive grasp of what is at stake. If our suffering is part of the human condition, a condition troubling to those who want people to behave only in routine and organized ways, notions of cure or of clear, or definable, or even measurable, goals strengthen those aspects of psychoanalysis that can lead to it becoming a means of social control and organization; it becomes, in Habermas's terms, a form of instrumental rather than communicative reason. We enforce what are to me undesirable tendencies in the wider culture through the denial of individual complexity. The type of 'goal' that I am suggesting here is simply one of enabling a better self-understanding that might enable a psychologically 'easier' life. The implication of all this is that what psychoanalysis has to offer is something that challenges and undermines the beliefs and institutions of the wider, instrumentally based culture. It does this not so much through the content of its knowledge and the achievement of effective 'cures' as through the internal experiential processes that it sets in motion and the possible relationships that it opens up. One of the tasks for psychotherapists is to be aware of the meaning of their work, and of their goals, in relation to the wider society. It is not so much the goals of psychotherapy that we should be concerned with as the process itself, which is important and effective for its own sake.

Bibliography

Abraham, K. (1927) *Selected Papers on Psychoanalysis*. London: Hogarth Press.

Ainsworth, M., Blehar, M., Waters, E. and Wall, S. (1978) *Patterns of Attachment Assessed: In the Strange Situation and at Home*. Hillsdale, NJ: Erlbaum.

Althusser, L. (1969) *For Marx*. London: Allen Lane/Penguin.

Althusser, L. (1971) *Lenin and Philosophy*. London: New Left Books.

Anderson, M. K. (1992) 'Should We Be Stern With Daniel Stern? A Personal Appraisal of Daniel Stern's Book *The Interpersonal World of the Infant*', *British Journal of Psychotherapy* 9: 33–9.

Badcock, C. (1988) *Essential Freud*. Oxford: Basil Blackwell.

Balint, M. (1959) *Thrills and Regressions*. London: Hogarth Press.

Balint, M. (1968) *The Basic Fault*. London: Tavistock.

Balint, M. and Balint, A. (1939) 'On Transference and Counter-Transference', *International Journal of Psychoanalysis* 20: 223–30.

Balswick, J. O. (1982) 'Male Inexpressiveness: Psychological and Sociological Aspects', in K. Solomon and N. P. Levy (eds) *Men in Transition: Theory and Therapy*. New York: Plenum Press.

Barker, P. (1991) *Regeneration*. Harmondsworth: Penguin.

Barker, P. (1993) *The Eye in the Door*. Harmondsworth: Penguin.

Barker, P. (1995) *The Ghost Road*. Harmondsworth: Penguin.

Barthes, R. (1967) *Elements of Semiology*. London: Jonathan Cape.

Barthes, R. (1970) *Mythologies*. London: Jonathan Cape.

Beauvoir, S. de (1960) *The Second Sex*. London: Jonathan Cape.

Becker, E. (1973) *The Denial of Death*. New York: Free Press.

Benjamin, J. (1990) *The Bonds of Love*. London: Virago.

Benton, T. and Craib, I. (2001) *Philosophy of Social Science: Philosophical Problems in Social Theory*. London: Macmillan.

Benvenuto, B. and Kennedy, R. (1986) *The Works of Jacques Lacan: An Introduction*. London: Free Association Books.

Bettelheim, B. (1983) *Freud and Man's Soul*. London: Chatto & Windus/Hogarth Press.

Bhaskar, R. (1978) *A Realist Theory of Science*. Brighton: Harvester.

Bhaskar, R. (1979) *The Possibility of Naturalism*. Brighton: Harvester.

Bick, E. (1968) 'The Experience of the Skin in Early Object Relations', *International Journal of Psychoanalysis* 39: 484–6.

Bion, W. (1961) *Experiences in Groups*. London: Tavistock.

Bion, W. (1962) *Learning from Experience*. London: William Heinemann.

Bion, W. (1963) *Elements of Psycho-Analysis*. London: William Heinemann.

Bion, W. (1965) *Transformations*. London: William Heinemann.

Bion, W. (1967) *Second Thoughts*. London: William Heinemann.

Bion, W. (1970) *Attention and Interpretation*. London: Tavistock.

Blos, P. (1993) 'Son and Father', in D. Breen (ed.) *The Gender Conundrum*. London: Routledge.

Board, R. de (1978) *The Psychoanalysis of Organizations*. London: Tavistock.

Bollas, C. (1987) *The Shadow of the Object: Psychoanalysis of the Unthought Known*. London: Free Association Books.

Bollas, C. (1992) *Being a Character: Psychoanalysis and Self Experience*. London: Routledge.

Bollas, C. (1995) *Cracking Up: Unconscious Work in Self Experience*. London: Routledge.

Bourke, J. (1999) *An Intimate History of Killing: Face-to-Face Killing in Twentieth-Century Warfare*. New York: Basic Books.

Bowie, M. (1991) *Lacan*. Cambridge, MA: Harvard University Press.

Bowlby, J. (1952) *Child Care and the Growth of Love*. Harmondsworth: Penguin.

Bowlby, J. (1960) 'Grief and Mourning in Infancy and Childhood', *The Psychoanalytic Study of the Child* 15: 9–52.

Bowlby, J. (1961) 'Processes of Mourning', *International Journal of Psychoanalysis* 42: 317–40.

Bowlby, J. (1971) *Attachment and Loss*, Vol. 1: *Attachment*. Harmondsworth: Penguin.

Bowlby, J. (1975) *Attachment and Loss*, Vol. 2: *Separation, Anxiety and Anger*. Harmondsworth: Penguin.

Bowlby, J. (1981) *Attachment and Loss*, Vol. 3: *Loss, Sadness and Depression*. Harmondsworth: Penguin.

Bowlby, J. (1988) *A Secure Base*. Harmondsworth: Penguin.

Bowlby, J. (1990) *Darwin: A New Biography*. London: Hutchinson.

Bretherton, I. (1985) 'Attachment Theory: Retrospect and Prospect', in I. Bretherton and E. Waters (eds) 'Growing Points of Attachment Theory and Research', *Monographs of the Society for Research in Child Development* 50: 3–35.

Browning, C. R. (1999) *Ordinary Men: Reserve Police Battalion 101 and the Final Solution in Poland*. New York: Harper Perennial.

Bruhle, M. J. (1998) *Feminism and Its Discontents*. Cambridge, MA: Harvard University Press.

Butler, J. (1990) *Gender Trouble: Feminism and the Subversion of Identity*. London: Routledge.

Butler, J. (1993) *Bodies That Matter*. London: Routledge.

Cardinale, M. (1983) *The Words to Say It*. Cambridge, MA: Van Vector and Goodheart.

Casement, P. (1985) *On Learning from the Patient*. London: Routledge.

Casement, P. (1990) *Further Learning from the Patient*. London: Routledge.

Castoriadis, C. (1991) 'Cornelius Castoriadis Interviewed', *Free Associations* 24: 483–506.

Chamberlain, D. B. (1987) 'The Cognitive Newborn: A Scientific Update', *The British Journal of Psychotherapy* 4: 30–71.

Chodorow, N. (1978) *The Reproduction of Mothering: Psychoanalysis and the Reproduction of Gender*. Berkeley: University of California Press.

Chodorow, N. (1985) 'Beyond Drive Theory: Object Relations and the Limits of Radical Individualism', *Theory and Society* 14: 271–320.

Chodorow, N. (1995) 'Gender as a Personal and Cultural Construction', *Signs* 20: 516–44.

Cioffi, F. (1970) 'Freud and the Idea of a Pseudo-Science', in R. Borger and F. Cioffi (eds) *Explanation in the Behavioural Sciences*. Cambridge: Cambridge University Press.

Cixous, H. and Clément, C. (1986) *The Newly Born Woman*. Minneapolis: University of Minnesota Press.

Collier, A. (1981) 'Scientific Realism and the Human World', *Radical Philosophy* 29: 8–18.

Craib, I. (1987) 'Masculinity and Male Dominance', *Sociological Review* 35: 721–43.

Craib, I. (1989) *Psychoanalysis and Social Theory: The Limits of Sociology*. Hemel Hempstead: Harvester Wheatsheaf.

Craib, I. (1992a) *Modern Social Theory*. Hemel Hempstead: Harvester Wheatsheaf.

Craib, I. (1992b) 'Response', in W. Dryden and C. Feltham (eds) *Psychotherapy and its Discontents*. Buckingham: Open University Press.

Craib, I. (1994) *The Importance of Disappointment*. London: Routledge.

Craib, I. (1995) 'Some Comments on the Sociology of the Emotions', *Sociology* 29: 151–8.

Craib, I. (1998) 'Sigmund Freud', in R. Stones (ed.) *Key Sociological Thinkers*. London: Macmillan.

Crews, F. C. (1997) *The Memory Wars: Freud's Legacy in Dispute*. London: Granta Books.

Davis, M. and Wallbridge, D. (1981) *Boundary and Space: An Introduction to the Work of D. W. Winnicott*. London: Karnac.

Dixon, R. (1997) 'A Reinterpretation of the Couvade'. Unpublished Ph.D. thesis, Department of History, University of Essex.

Duncombe, J. and Marsden, D. (1993) 'Love and Intimacy: The Gender Division of Emotion and "Emotion Work"', *Sociology* 27: 221–42.

Dworkin, A. (1981) *Pornography: Men Possessing Women*. London: Women's Press.

Eagle, M. (1997) 'Attachment and Psychoanalysis', *British Journal of Medical Psychology* 70: 217–29.

Eichenbaum, L. and Orbach, S. (1985) *Understanding Women*. Harmondsworth: Pelican.

Elliott, A. (1992) *Psychoanalysis and Social Theory in Transition*. Oxford: Basil Blackwell.

Elshtein, J. B. (1984) 'Symmetry and Soporifics: A Critique of Accounts of Gender Development', in B. Richards (ed.) *Capitalism and Infancy*. London: Free Association Books.

Erikson, E. (1977) *Childhood and Society*. London: Triad/Paladin.

Evans, D. (1996) *An Introductory Dictionary of Lacanian Psycho-analysis*. London: Routledge.

Fairbairn, W. R. D. (1952) *Psycho-Analytic Studies of the Personality*. London: Routledge.

Feyerabend, P. (1975) *Against Method*. London: New Left Books.

Firestone, S. (1970) *The Dialectic of Sex: The Case for Feminist Revolution*. New York: Bantam.

Fonagy, P., Steele, M., Steele, H., Moran, G. and Higgins, A. (1991) 'The Capacity for Understanding Mental States: The Reflective Self in Parent and Child and Its Significance for Security of Attachment', *Infant Mental Health Journal* 12: 201–18.

Foucault, M. (1972) *The Archaeology of Knowledge*. London: Tavistock.

Freud, A. (1936) *The Ego and the Mechanisms of Defence*. London: Hogarth Press.

Freud, S. (1973a) 'Anxiety and Instinctual Life', in The Pelican Freud Library Vol. 2: *New Introductory Lectures in Psychoanalysis*. Harmondsworth: Pelican.

Freud, S. (1973b) 'The Dissection of Psychical Reality', in The Pelican Freud Library Vol. 2: *New Introductory Lectures in Psychoanalysis*. Harmondsworth: Pelican.

Freud, S. (1976a) *The Interpretation of Dreams*. The Pelican Freud Library Vol. 4. Harmondsworth: Pelican.

Freud, S. (1976b) *Jokes and Their Relation to the Unconscious*. The Pelican Freud Library Vol. 6. Harmondsworth: Pelican.

Freud, S. (1977a) 'Character and Anal Eroticism', in The Pelican Freud Library Vol. 7: *On Sexuality*. Harmondsworth: Pelican.

Freud, S. (1977b) 'The Dissolution of the Oedipus Complex', in The Pelican Freud Library Vol. 7: *On Sexuality*. Harmondsworth: Pelican.

Freud, S. (1977c) 'Dora: Fragment of an Analysis of a Case of Hysteria', in The Pelican Freud Library Vol. 8: *Case Histories 1: 'Dora' and 'Little Hans'*. Harmondsworth: Pelican.

Freud, S. (1977d) 'Female Sexuality Complex', in The Pelican Freud Library Vol. 7: *On Sexuality*. Harmondsworth: Pelican.

Freud, S. (1977e) 'The Infantile Genital Organization', in The Pelican Freud Library Vol. 7: *On Sexuality*. Harmondsworth: Pelican.

Freud, S. (1977f) 'On Transformations of Instinct as Exemplified in Anal Eroticism', in The Pelican Freud Library Vol. 7: *On Sexuality*. Harmondsworth: Pelican.

Freud, S. (1977g) 'Some Psychical Consequences of the Anatomical Distinction between the Sexes', in The Pelican Freud Library Vol. 7: *On Sexuality*. Harmondsworth: Pelican.

Freud, S. (1977h) 'Three Essays on the Theory of Sexuality', in The Pelican Freud Library Vol. 7: *On Sexuality*. Harmondsworth: Pelican.

Freud, S. (1984a) 'A Note on the Unconscious', in The Pelican Freud Library Vol. 11: *On Metapsychology: The Theory of Psycho-*

analysis. Harmondsworth: Pelican.

Freud, S. (1984b) 'Beyond the Pleasure Principle', in The Pelican Freud Library Vol. 11: *On Metapsychology: The Theory of Psychoanalysis*. Harmondsworth: Pelican.

Freud, S. (1984c) 'The Ego and the Id', in The Pelican Freud Library Vol. 11: *On Metapsychology: The Theory of Psychoanalysis*. Harmondsworth: Pelican.

Freud, S. (1984d) 'Instincts and Their Vicissitudes', in The Penguin Freud Library Vol. 11: *On Metapsychology: The Theory of Psychoanalysis*. Harmondsworth: Pelican.

Freud, S. (1984e) 'Mourning and Melancholia', in The Pelican Freud Library Vol. 11: *On Metapsychology: The Theory of Psychoanalysis*. Harmondsworth: Pelican.

Freud, S. (1984f) 'On Narcissism', in The Pelican Freud Library Vol. 11: *On Metapsychology: The Theory of Psychoanalysis*. Harmondsworth: Pelican.

Freud, S. (1984g) 'Repression', in The Pelican Freud Library Vol. 11: *On Metapsychology: The Theory of Psychoanalysis*. Harmondsworth: Pelican.

Freud, S. (1984h) 'The Unconscious', in The Pelican Freud Library Vol. 11: *On Metapsychology: The Theory of Psychoanalysis*. Harmondsworth: Pelican.

Freud, S. (1985a) 'Civilization and its Discontents', in The Pelican Freud Library Vol. 12: *Civilization, Society and Religion*. Harmondsworth: Pelican.

Freud, S. (1985b) 'Group Psychology and the Analysis of the Ego', in The Pelican Freud Library Vol. 12: *Civilization, Society and Religion*. Harmondsworth: Pelican.

Freud, S. (1985c) 'Obsessive Actions and Religious Practices', in The Pelican Freud Library Vol. 13: *The Origins of Religion*. Harmondsworth: Pelican.

Freud, S. (1985d) *The Psychopathology of Everyday Life*. The Pelican Freud Library Vol. 5. Harmondsworth: Pelican.

Freud, S. (1986) 'The Question of Lay Analysis', in The Pelican Freud Library Vol. 15: *Historical and Expository Works on Psychoanalysis*. Harmondsworth: Pelican.

Freud, S. (1990) 'Leonardo Da Vinci and a Memory of his Childhood', in The Pelican Freud Library Vol. 14: *Art and Literature*. Harmondsworth: Pelican.

Friedan, B. (1997) *The Feminine Mystique*. Harmondsworth: Penguin.

Gay, P. (1988) *Freud: A Life for Our Time*. London: Dent.

Gellner, E. (1985) *The Psychoanalytic Movement*. London: Paladin.

Giddens, A. (1991) *Modernity and Self-Identity: Self and Society in the Late Modern Age*. Cambridge: Polity.

Gilbert, M. (1996) *The Boys: Triumph over Adversity*. London: Phoenix.

Gittins, D. (1997) *The Child in Question*. London: Macmillan.

Goffman, E. (1969) *The Presentation of Self in Everyday Life*. Harmondsworth: Penguin.

Goldmann, L. (1970) *The Hidden God*. London: Routledge and Kegan Paul.

Greenberg, J. R. and Mitchell, S. A. (1983) *Object Relations in Psychoanalytic Theory*. Cambridge, MA: Harvard University Press.

Greer, G. (1971) *The Female Eunuch*. London: Paladin.

Grunbaum, A. (1984) *The Foundations of Psychoanalysis: A Philosophical Critique*. Berkeley: University of California Press.

Guntrip, H. (1961) *Personality Structure and Human Interaction*. London: Hogarth Press.

Guntrip, H. (1971) 'My Experience of Analysis with Fairbairn and Winnicott', *International Review of Psychoanalysis* 2(2).

Haaken, J. (1996) 'The Recovery of Memory, Fantasy and Desire: Feminist Approaches to Sexual Abuse', *Signs* 21: 1069–93.

Habermas, J. (1972) *Knowledge and Human Interests*. London: Heinemann.

Habermas, J. (1990) *The Philosophical Discourse of Modernity: Twelve Lectures*. Cambridge: Polity.

Hartmann, H. (1939) *Ego Psychology and the Problem of Adaptation*. London: Hogarth Press.

Heimann, P. (1950) 'On Counter-Transference', *International Journal of Psychoanalysis* 31: 81–4.

Heimann, P. (1960) 'Counter-Transference', *British Journal of Medical Psychology* 33: 9–15.

Hill, S. (1997) *Violet*. Newcastle Upon Tyne: Bloodaxe Books.

Hinshelwood, R. (1991) *A Dictionary of Kleinian Thought*. London: Free Association Books.

Hochschild, A. R. (1994) 'The Commercial Spirit of Intimate Life and the Abduction of Feminism: Signs from Women's Advice Books', *Theory, Culture and Society* 11(1): 1–24.

Holmes, J. (1993) *John Bowlby and Attachment Theory*. London: Routledge.

Hopkins, J. (1996) 'Psychoanalysis and Scientific Reasoning', *British Journal of Psychotherapy* 13: 86–105.

Horney, K. (1993) *Female Sexuality* (ed. H. Kelman). New York: Norton.

Irigaray, L. (1985a) *Speculum of the Other Woman*. Ithaca, NY: Cornell University Press.

Irigaray, L. (1985b) *This Sex Which Is Not One*. Ithaca, NY: Cornell University Press.

Irigaray, L. (1991) *The Irigaray Reader* (ed. M. Whitford). Oxford: Basil Blackwell.

Irigaray, L. (1992) *Elemental Passions*. London: Athlone Press.

Irigaray, L. (1993) *An Ethics of Sexual Difference*. London: Athlone Press.

Isaacs, S. (1952) 'The Nature and Function of Phantasy', in M. Klein, P. Heimann, S. Isaacs and J. Rivière, *Developments in Psychoanalysis*. London: Hogarth Press.

Jacobs, M. (1995) *D. W. Winnicott*. London: Sage.

Jacoby, M. (1990) *Individuation and Narcissism: The Psychology of Self in Jung and Kohut*. London: Routledge.

Janov, A. (1973) *The Feeling Child*. New York: Simon and Schuster.

Jones, E. (1948) *Papers on Psycho-Analysis*. London: Ballière, Tindall & Cox.

Jones, E. (1961) *The Life and Work of Sigmund Freud*. London: Pelican.

Joseph, B. (1978) 'Different Types of Anxiety and Their Handling in the Analytic Situation', *International Journal of Psychoanalysis* 50: 223–8.

Joseph, B. (1985) 'Transference – The Total Situation', *International Journal of Psychoanalysis* 66: 447–54.

Kennard, D., Roberts, J. and Winter, D. A. (1993) *A Workbook for Group Analytic Introductions*. London: Routledge.

Khan, M. (1974) *The Privacy of the Self: Papers on Psychoanalytic Theory and Technique*. London: Hogarth Press.

Khan, M. (1983) *Hidden Selves: Between Theory and Practice in Psychoanalysis*. London: Hogarth Press.

King, P. and Steiner, R. (eds) (1992) *The Freud–Klein Controversies 1941–45*. London: Tavistock/Routledge.

Kernberg, O. (1976) *Object Relations Theory and Clinical Psychoanalysis*. New York: Jason Aronson.

Kernberg, O. (1980) *Internal World and External Reality*. New York: Jason Aronson.

Klauber, J. (1981) *Difficulties in the Analytic Encounter*. London: Free Association Books.

Klein, J. (1987) *Our Need for Others and Its Roots in Infancy*. London: Tavistock/Hogarth Press.

Klein, M. (1930) 'The Importance of Symbol Formation in the Analysis of the Ego', *International Journal of Psychoanalysis* 11: 24–39.

Klein, M. (1975a) 'The Development of the Child', in Collected Works Vol. I: *Love, Guilt and Reparation*. London: Hogarth Press.

Klein, M. (1975b) 'Envy and Gratitude', in Collected Works Vol. III: *Envy and Gratitude*. London: Hogarth Press.

Klein, M. (1975c) 'On the Development of Mental Functioning', in Collected Works Vol. III: *Envy and Gratitude*. London: Hogarth Press.

Klein, M. (1986) 'Mourning and Its Relation to Manic Depressive States', in J. Mitchell (ed.) *The Selected Melanie Klein*. Harmondsworth: Penguin.

Klein, M., Heimann, P., Isaacs, S. and Rivière, J. (1952) *Developments in Psychoanalysis*. London: Hogarth.

Kline, P. (1977) 'Cross-Cultural Studies and Freudian Theory', in N. Warren (ed.) *Studies in Cross-Cultural Studies*. London: Academic Press.

Kohon, G. (ed.) (1986) *The British School of Psychoanalysis: The Independent Tradition*. London: Free Association Books.

Kohut, H. (1971) *The Analysis of the Self*. New York: International Universities Press.

Kohut, H. (1977) *The Restoration of the Self*. New York: International Universities Press.

Kristeva, J. (1980) *Desire and Language*. Oxford: Basil Blackwell.

Kristeva, J. (1981) 'Women Can Never Be Defined', in E. Marks and I. de Coutivron (eds) *New French Feminisms*. Brighton: Harvester.

Kristeva, J. (1986) *The Kristeva Reader* (ed. T. Moi). Oxford: Basil Blackwell.

Kuhn, T. (1970) *The Structure of Scientific Revolutions*. Chicago: University of Chicago Press.

Lacan, J. (1968) *Speech and Language in Psychoanalysis*. Baltimore: Johns Hopkins University Press.

Lacan, J. (1990) *Television: A Challenge to the Psychoanalytic Establishment*. New York: Norton.

Lacan, J. (1996) 'The Meaning of the Phallus', in R. Minsky (ed.) *Psychoanalysis and Gender: An Introductory Reader*. London: Routledge.

Lacan, J. (1997) *Écrits*. London: Routledge.

Langs, R. J. (1976) *The Therapeutic Interaction*. New York: Jason Aronson.

Langs, R. J. (1978) *The Listening Process*. New York: Jason Aronson.

Laplanche, J. and Pontalis, J.-B. (1988) *The Language of Psycho-analysis*. London: Karnac Books.

Lasch, C. (1980) *The Culture of Narcissism: American Life in an Age of Diminishing Expectations*. London: Sphere Books.

Lechte, J. (1990) *Julia Kristeva*. London: Routledge.

Lévi-Strauss, C. (1969) *The Elementary Structures of Kinship*. Boston: Beacon Press.

Little, M. I. (1985) 'Winnicott Working in Areas Where Psychotic Anxieties Predominate: A Personal Record', *Free Associations* 3: 9–42.

Main, M., Kaplan, K. and Cassidy, J. (1985) 'Security in Infancy, Childhood and Adulthood: A Move to the Level of Representation', in I. Bretherton and E. Waters (eds) 'Growing Points of Attachment Theory and Research', *Monographs of the Society for Research in Child Development* 50: 3–35.

Marcus, S. (1985) 'Freud and Dora: Story, History, Case History', in C. Berheimer and C. Kahano (eds) *In Dora's Case: Freud–Hysteria–Feminism*. London: Virago.

Marcuse, H. (1969) *Eros and Civilization*. London: Sphere Books.

Masson, J. (1992) *The Assault on Truth: Freud and Child Sexual Abuse*. London: Fontana.

Matte-Blanco, I. (1959) 'Expression in Symbolic Logic of the Characteristics of the System Unconscious', *International Journal of Psychoanalysis* 40: 1–5.

Matte-Blanco, I. (1975) *The Unconscious as Infinite Sets: An Essay in Bi-Logic*. London: Duckworth.

Matte-Blanco, I. (1976) 'Basic Logico-Mathematical Structure in Schizophrenia', in D. Richter (ed.) *Schizophrenia Today*. London: Pergamon.

Matte-Blanco, I. (1988) *Thinking, Feeling and Being*. London: Routledge.

Mead, G. H. (1934) *Mind, Self and Society*. Chicago: University of Chicago Press.

Megary, T. (1995) *Society in Prehistory: The Origins of Human Culture*. Houndsmills: Macmillan.

Meltzer, D. and Williams, M. H. (1988) *The Appreciation of Beauty*. Perthshire: Clunie.

Menzies-Lyth, I. (1989) 'The Functioning of Social Systems as a Defence Against Anxiety', in Selected Essays Vol. 1: *Containing Anxiety in Institutions*. London: Free Association Books.

Miller, A. (1987) *The Drama of Being a Child*. London: Virago.

Millet, K. (1970) *Sexual Politics*. New York: Doubleday.

Milner, M. (1950) *On Not Being Able to Paint*. London: Heinemann.

Milner, M. (1955) 'The Role of Illusion in Symbol Formation', in M. Klein, P. Heimann and R. E. Money-Kyrle (eds) *New Directions in Psycho-Analysis*. London: Tavistock.

Milner, M. (1958) 'Psycho-Analysis and Art', in J. Sutherland (ed.) *Psycho-Analysis and Contemporary Thought*. London: Hogarth Press.

Milner, M. (1969) *The Hands of the Living God*. London: Hogarth Press.

Minsky, R. (ed.) (1996) *Psychoanalysis and Gender: An Introductory Reader*. London: Routledge.

Mitchell, J. (1974) *Psychoanalysis and Feminism*. Harmondsworth: Pelican.

Mitchell, J. (ed.) (1986) *The Selected Melanie Klein*. Harmondsworth: Penguin.

Mitchell, J. and Rose, J. (eds) (1982) *Jacques Lacan and the École Freudienne: Feminine Sexuality*. London: Macmillan.

Moi, T. (1985) 'Representation of Patriarchy: Sexuality and Epistemology in Freud's Dora', in C. Berheimer and C. Kahano (eds) *In Dora's Case: Freud–Hysteria–Feminism*. London: Virago.

Money-Kyrle, R. E. (1956) 'Normal Counter-Transference and Some of Its Deviations, *International Journal of Psychoanalysis* 37: 360–6.

Norwood, R. (1986) *Women Who Love Too Much*. London: Arrow Books.

Parkes, C. M. (1987) *Bereavement: Studies of Grief in Adult Life*. Harmondsworth: Penguin.

Parkes, C. M., Stevenson-Hinde, J. and Marris, P. (eds) (1991) *Attachment Across the Life Cycle*. London: Routledge.

Perls, F. (1971) *Gestalt Therapy Verbatim* (ed. J. O. Stevens). New York: Bantam Books.

Phillips, A. (1988) *Winnicott*. London: Fontana.

Pilgrim, D. (1992) 'Psychotherapy and Political Evasions' (and the following debate) in W. Dryden and C. Feltham (eds) *Psychotherapy and its Discontents*. Buckingham: Open University Press.

Piontelli, A. (1992) *From Fetus to Child: An Observational and Psychoanalytic Study*. London: Tavistock/Routledge.

Popper, K. (1969) *Conjectures and Refutations*. 3rd edn. London: Routledge and Kegan Paul.

Rayner, E. (1990) *The Independent Mind in British Psychoanalysis*. London: Free Association Books.

Roazen, P. (1971) *Freud and His Followers*. London: Allen Lane.

Robertson, J. (1952) *A Two-Year-Old Goes to Hospital* (Film). Ipswich: Concord Films Council.

Robertson, J. (1958) *Going to Hospital with Mother* (Film). Ipswich: Concord Films Council.

Rose, N. (1990) *Governing the Soul: The Shaping of the Private Self*. London: Routledge.

Rubin, G. (1975) 'The Traffic in Women: Notes on the "Political Economy" of Sex', in R. Reiter (ed.) *Toward an Anthropology of Women*. New York: Monthly Review Press.

Rudnytsky, P. L. (1991) *The Psychoanalytic Vocation: Rank, Winnicott and the Legacy of Freud*. London: Yale University Press.

Rustin, M. (1991) *The Good Society and the Inner World: Psychoanalysis, Politics and Culture*. London: Verso.

Samuels, A. (1993) *The Political Psyche*. London: Routledge.

Sandler, J. and Dreher, U. D. (1996) *What Do Psychoanalysts Want? The Problem of Aims in Psychoanalytic Therapy*. London: Routledge.

Sartre, J.-P. (1957) *Being and Nothingness*. London: Methuen.

Sarup, M. (1992) *Jacques Lacan*. Hemel Hempstead: Harvester Wheatsheaf.

Saussure, F. de (1974) *Course in General Linguistics*. London: Fontana/Collins.

Schütz, A. (1972) *The Phenomenology of the Social World*. London: Heinemann.

Segal, H. (1964) *An Introduction to the Work of Melanie Klein*. London: Heinemann.

Segal, H. (1979) *Melanie Klein*. London: Fontana/Collins.

Segal, H. (1981) *The Work of Hanna Segal*. New York: Jason Aronson.

Segal, H. (1983) 'Some Clinical Implications of Melanie Klein's Work', *International Journal of Psychoanalysis* 64: 269–76.

Sereny, G. (1996) *Albert Speer: His Battle With Truth*. London: Picador.

Siegel, A. M. (1996) *Heinz Kohut and the Psychology of the Self*.

London: Routledge.

Stanton, M. (1990) *Sandor Ferenczi: Reconsidering Active Intervention*. New York: Jason Aronson.

Stern, D. (1985) *The Interpersonal World of the Infant: A View from Psychoanalysis and Developmental Psychology*. New York: Basic Books.

Stewart, H. (1996) *Michael Balint: Object Relations Pure and Applied*. London: Routledge.

Sutherland, S. (ed.) (1995) *The Macmillan Dictionary of Psychology*. Basingstoke: Macmillan.

Symington, J. and Symington, N. (1996) *The Clinical Thinking of Wilfred Bion*. London: Routledge.

Symington, N. (1986) *The Analytic Experience: Lectures from the Tavistock*. London: Free Association Books.

Szasz, T. (1964) *The Myth of Mental Illness*. New York: Harper and Row.

Taylor, C. (1989) *Sources of the Self*. Cambridge, MA: Harvard University Press.

Taylor, C. (1991) *The Ethics of Authenticity*. Cambridge, MA: Harvard University Press.

Turkle, S. (1992) *Psychoanalytic Politics: Freud's French Revolution*. New York: Basic Books.

Tustin, F. (1972) *Autism and Childhood Psychoses*. London: Hogarth Press.

Tustin, F. (1981) *Autistic States in Children*. London: Routledge and Kegan Paul.

Tustin, F. (1986) *Autistic Barriers in Neurotic Patients*. London: Karnac.

Verney, T. and Kelly, J. (1981) *The Secret Life of the Unborn Child*. New York: Summit Books.

Wallerstein, J. S. (1985) 'Children of Divorce: Preliminary Report of a Ten Year Follow-Up of Older Children and Adolescents', *Journal of the American Academy of Child Psychiatry* 24: 545–53.

Weber, M. (1949) *The Methodology of the Social Sciences*. Glencoe, IL: Free Press.

Whitford, M. (1991) *Philosophy in the Feminine*. London: Routledge.

Will, D. (1980) 'Psychoanalysis as a Human Science', *British Journal of Medical Psychology* 53: 201–12.

Williams, M. H. (1999) 'Psychoanalysis: An Art or a Science? A Review of the Implications of the Theory of Bion and Meltzer', *British Journal of Psychotherapy* 16(2): 27–35.

Winnicott, D. W. (1958) *Collected Papers: Through Paediatrics to Psycho-Analysis*. London: Tavistock.

Winnicott, D. W. (1964) *The Child, the Family, and the Outside World*. Harmondsworth: Penguin.

Winnicott, D. W. (1965) *The Maturational Processes and the Facilitating Environment: Studies in the Theory of Emotional Development*. London: Hogarth.

Winnicott, D. W. (1980) *The Piggle: An Account of the Psychoanalytic Treatment of a Little Girl*. London: Penguin.

Winnicott, D. W. (1986) *Home Is Where We Start From: Essays by a Psychoanalyst*. Harmondsworth: Penguin.

Winnicott, D. W. (1988) *Babies and Their Mothers*. London: Free Association Books.

Winnicott, D. W. (1989) *Holding and Interpretation: Fragment of an Analysis*. London: Karnac.

Wollheim, R. (1971) *Freud*. London: Fontana.

Wollheim, R. and Hopkins, J. (eds) (1982) *Philosophical Essays on Freud*. Cambridge: Cambridge University Press.

Woolf, V. (1945) *A Room of One's Own*. Harmondsworth: Penguin.

Index

Lightning Source UK Ltd.
Milton Keynes UK
12 September 2009

143629UK00001B/55/P